This second edition is dedicated to family law scholars and researchers everywhere

Preface to the First Edition

When I was invited by the Faculty of Law of the University of Otago to visit New Zealand in 2005 as the New Zealand Law Foundation Distinguished Visiting Fellow, I had already written a paper on the theme of friendship which forms chapter 2 of this volume. That paper arose as a result of an interview I conducted in a research project with my colleague Mavis Maclean at the Oxford Centre for Family Law and Policy (OXFLAP), in which it emerged that the household contained an additional person as a result of quite remarkable circumstances. These are explained in that chapter. An early version of that paper appears in a memorial volume to my friend and colleague, Professor Dr Petar Sarcevic, and is published with the permission of Selliers European Law Publishers. I then decided to explore family law as refracted through other 'themes', and, as the invitation required lectures and seminars to be given at the main New Zealand law schools, I thought I would try these ideas out on my New Zealand hosts. In the end I was able to discuss the papers on 'Friendship', 'Truth', and another which later became 'Power', in New Zealand, while I presented a short version of 'Respect' as a keynote address at the 12th World Conference of the International Society of Family Law, at Salt Lake City, on the way there. The responses encouraged me to think of combining these papers into a small book, which I have now done with two additional papers, one on 'Responsibility' and the other on 'Rights'. The former was presented to a Conference on Responsibility in Family Law held at the University of Sussex in September 2005.

I must record my immense gratitude to The New Zealand Law Foundation, to whom this volume is dedicated, not only for its generosity, but also for providing the occasion to prompt me to undertake this project. In particular, I must thank Mark Henaghan and his colleagues at the University of Otago for all they did to make the visit so useful and enjoyable.

While engaged on this process, it seemed to me that I was pursuing a wider purpose, which was to suggest how the legal regulation of people's personal lives might be defended. This involved making political, or ideological, assumptions against which justifications for such regulation could be set. The assumptions I have made will look like those of liberalism, but I have been careful not to make any claims about the nature of liberalism. Instead, I have preferred to use an expression which carries less theoretical baggage: the 'open' society. I argue that the historical manifestation of formal and informal regulation of family practices has been through the exercise of power. This inevitably owes much to feminist scholarship, whose analysis of family law in terms of power relations between the genders is now taken for granted. However, my exposition puts as much, if not more, emphasis on the exercise of power between the present generation of adults and the next as on gender relations. Indeed, the attempt by previous generations to control their successors is a major preoccupation of the text. Furthermore, the exercise of power is shown to have adopted two main forms: instrumentalism and welfarism. In counterpoise to this account, the book concludes with the argument that modern notions of rights have created the possibility of redistributing the exercise of power achieved under welfarism. The argument requires the exposition of a theoretical understanding of rights, including children's rights, cultural or group rights, and human rights, and an evaluation of their role in an open society. Within this framework, the text explores the interrelationship between the legal regulation of people's personal lives and the values of friendship, truth, respect, and responsibility. In doing this, a variety of controversial issues are examined in the light of those values: these include the legal regulation of gay and unmarried heterosexual relationships; freedom of procreation; state supervision over the exercise of parenthood; the role of fault in divorce law; the way parenthood is allocated; the rights and responsibilities of parents to control their children; the place of religion in the family; the rights of separated partners regarding property and of separated parents regarding their children; and the freedom of children to determine their own destinies.

The result provides, I think, a new way of looking at much of family law (or, as I now prefer to call it, personal law). The area of legal activity covered is wide. In order not to weigh down the text with too much detail, I have made extensive reference to the literature, including the occasions when I have discussed the detail at greater length. This has, I hope, allowed a sharper focus on the issues raised by the themes and values. If it is, as I think, instructive to view one area of law in the context of these themes and values, it is also instructive to reflect on the concepts they represent in the light of the part they play in this area of life. But again, I did not want the book to become a detailed theoretical analysis of all aspects of these concepts. I have provided such analysis as seemed necessary in order to engage with them, and to consider how their practical applications in this context could influence the ways we think about them. To that limited extent this is not just a book about personal law, but is also a comment on legal theory.

I hope that the book will demonstrate that personal law, possibly more than any other area of law, affects the most profound aspect of people's lives and of what it means to live in human communities. In writing it I have had to confront and try to take a position on these issues, which I hope amounts to a coherent whole. There are many things over which others are bound to disagree with me. But if I have set out a framework for thinking about them, and even as a means for evaluating laws and policies, I will have achieved my objective.

John Eekelaar

Oxford
May 2006

Preface to the Second Edition

I am grateful to Oxford University Press for agreeing to publish a second edition of this book. A good deal has happened in family law over the past ten years, and the previous edition had become outdated. I felt that it would be profitable to re-examine the issues it discussed in the light of developments in law and scholarship over this period. In updating, I have taken the opportunity to tighten up the overall structure of the book, which reflected its origin in a series of lectures, by strengthening arguments when appropriate, removing some repetitious passages, and re-ordering the sequence of chapters (which had already been expanded by the inclusion of a new chapter on 'Community' in the 2007 paperback edition) so that the overall thrust of the basic approach appears more clearly.

John Eekelaar

Oxford
March 2017

Contents

Table of Cases

UNITED KINGDOM

EUROPEAN COURT OF HUMAN RIGHTS

NEW ZEALAND

Table of Cases

1

Power

FAMILY PRACTICES AND THE DIFFUSION OF POWER

Power, norms, and communities

The nature of power is complex. It has been explained variously as a feature of social structures, or of the way social relations are interpreted, or of the way ideology, economic resources, and military and political power are organized.[1] My present concern is the way power has been and is manifested in what are commonly understood as family practices and family law. I recall Michael Mann's observations that 'societies are constituted of multiple overlapping and intersecting sociospatial networks of power' and that the 'monopolization of norms is one route to power'.[2] The following passage from an introductory text on kinship and marriage published in 1967 provides an illustration. The author is discussing matrilineal descent systems:

> The nearest example outside the Nayar of this form of grouping is found amongst the Menangkabau of Malaya who are similarly matrilineal. The well-known Ashanti of Ghana approached this method, but their case is complicated and seems to be an amalgam of several solutions. The Ashanti have been made famous in anthropology for what has been called the 'visiting husband' solution. This is virtually the same as the Nayar method. Any evening in an Ashanti town, we are told, one will

---

[1] For example, A Giddens, *The Constitution of Society* (Polity Press, 1984); M Mann, *The Sources of Social Power*, vol 1 (Cambridge University Press, 1986); M Foucault, *Discipline and Punish: The Birth of the Prison* (Penguin Books, 1991).
[2] Mann, n 1, 22.

see children running between the houses carrying dishes and bowls of food. They are taking it from the mother's house to the father's house. The father will be at home with his mother, and his sisters and their children. Already we can see some differences from the Nayar situation. The children here have an accepted father and their mother has at least to cook for him. The Ashanti live in towns, and so the houses will be quite near and this arrangement is feasible. Already then the husband–wife bond appears to be stronger than in Malabar. There has been more 'intrusion' by the husband: he can make more demands. What is more, in many cases amongst the Ashanti he is able to bring his wife home to live with him. But here is the rub: his children are not his—they belong to his wife's lineage—so that at some point they must return to the lineage house where the mother's brothers live. This problem makes the nuclear family of the Ashanti a tenuous thing: and it is often short-lived, with the wife going home to mother.[3]

This passage is typical of many which appear in the anthropological literature. It identifies certain social, or ethnic, groups by their kinship practices. The phrase 'amongst the [...]' (used twice in this extract) recurs constantly in this literature. It implies that, to be one of [...], a person must follow the stated practice ('the mother *has at least to* cook for him'; 'the husband ... can make more *demands*'; 'at some point (the children) *must* return to the lineage house where the mother's brothers live'). The practices are felt as obligations which must be accepted by individuals in order to be accepted as members of the group. They are therefore also examples of the manifestation of the exercise of power within the society: in this case, of fathers over mothers, husbands over wives, and adults over children.

While power may be exercised through formal institutions, it may also be subtly diffused throughout society, creating the impression of a stable, timeless community, with clear obligations. Such communities are largely assumed in these anthropological accounts. They talk of behaviours 'amongst the [...]', not, usually, of a *range* of behaviours amongst them, or of behaviours pertaining only to some of them. Some versions of family history of western societies are presented in similar terms. Peter Laslett, whose work significantly altered previous perceptions about the nature of family life in Britain in earlier times, tends to present a relatively uniform view of society over time, based

---

[3] R Fox, *Kinship and Marriage* (Penguin Books, 1967) 101–2.

on broad demographic data.[4] Even Michael Anderson, who observed that, at least as far as western Europe is concerned, 'there is, except at the most trivial level, no Western family type',[5] wrote of English family behaviour after the mid-twentieth century as if it were a comparatively homogenous phenomenon, writing:

> A young person aged say, 14, looking forward in the 1960s, could, with a reasonable probability of being right, have predicted within a very few years the timing of his or her future life course—leaving school, entering employment, leaving home, marrying and setting up home, early patterns of child-bearing and rearing. None of this would have been possible in the nineteenth century.[6]

Tamara Hareven, however, questioned the assumption of homogeneity, commenting that 'the main dissatisfaction with the studies of change over time that have emerged in the 1970s has been their linearity and their generalizations for an entire society based on the experience of one class, usually the middle class'.[7] Janet Finch, writing in the late 1980s about change in the nature of familial obligations over time, was aware of this problem, for although she often generalized about the British population as a whole, she was alert to possible class differences,[8] and, when comparing the past with the present, cautioned that 'we are not comparing like with like' because of (among other things) changes in the composition of the population as a whole:

> In addition to all the differences which I have itemized in terms of age structure, family formation and lengths of generations, we should note also that the British population in the past was less racially and ethnically diverse, being almost exclusively white.[9]

---

[4] P Laslett, *The World We Have Lost: Further Explored* (Methuen, 1983) especially ch 4. Among the 'misbeliefs' Laslett exposed were that children married young, and that most of our ancestors lived in households consisting of extended families. Many households were indeed large, but this was mainly because of the presence of servants.

[5] M Anderson, *Approaches to the History of the Western Family* (Macmillan, 1980) 14.

[6] M Anderson, 'What is new about the modern family?' (1983) OPCS Occasional Paper, *The Family*, 31, reprinted in M Drake (ed), *Time, Family and Community: Perspectives on Family and Community History* (Blackwell, 1994) 80, 81–2.

[7] TK Hareven, 'Recent Research on the History of the Family' in M Drake (ed), *Time, Family and Community: Perspectives on Family and Community History* (Blackwell, 1994) 38.

[8] J Finch, *Family Obligations and Social Change* (Polity Press, 1989) 82.

[9] Ibid 84–5.

In the 1989 Lewis Henry Morgan Lectures, Marilyn Strathern, who explained variations in family patterns in terms of individuality, was still willing to generalize: for the English, she wrote, 'we might usefully take the individual as a modern fact of kinship'.[10] But who are the English? On this account they are identified as those for whom that generalization holds true. Strathern recognized this circularity.

> The English were thus self-defined in an overlapping way as at once a people and a set of cultural characteristics. I exploit the ambiguity in my own account, and refer to the English as though they were identifiably both.[11]

But helpful as these definitions of cultural groups are, they do not necessarily hold for entire populations inhabiting certain geographical areas, not even if they are subject to the same political and legal systems. Even if generalization about the kinship practices of 'the English' is possible (and this may now be difficult), this could not apply to the whole population living in England. The ethnic diversity of the United Kingdom is well known. From 1991 to 2011, in England and Wales, the 'white' ethnic group dropped from 94.1 per cent to 86.0 per cent of the population (and within this the 'white British' declined still further, being replaced by other 'white' groups, especially from Poland) while other ethnic groups, especially people identifying as Pakistani and Indian, increased.[12] This diversity extends into family practices. For example, Kathleen Kiernan has shown from data in the Millenium Cohort Study that Asian groups were more likely to be married when they had a baby than either white or black groups.[13] But even these distinctions are breaking down, with an increase from 7 per cent in 2001 to 9 per cent in 2011 of people in England and Wales living in an inter-ethnic relationship.[14]

It is important not to build stereotypes, or exaggerate differences between groups, because there are variations within groups themselves

---

[10] M Strathern, *After Nature: English Kinship in the Late Twentieth Century* (Cambridge University Press, 1992) 83.

[11] Ibid 30.

[12] Office for National Statistics, *Ethnicity and National Identity in England and Wales 2011* (December 2012).

[13] K Kiernan and K Smith, 'Unmarried Parenthood: New Insights from the Millenium Cohort Study' (2003) 114 *Population Trends* 23.

[14] Office for National Statistics, *2011 Census Analysis: What Does the 2011 Census Tell Us about Inter-Ethnic Relationships?*

(minorities within minorities), depending on facts such as religion and social class, as well as significant commonalities between them.[15] This was well illustrated in a 2004 study on how people viewed their family obligations.[16] The study found that ethnic minority respondents tended to marry out of deference to their culture or their parents, whereas the white British were more likely to marry for pragmatic reasons or because they felt it was a symbolic way of showing their commitment. The minority groups tended to see their duties to their partners as originating in the institution of marriage, in contrast to the white British group who were more likely to see their obligations as resting on an independent ethical principle (such as doing good to someone who does good to you). Despite these differences, it was concluded that the end result could look very similar. For example, while many ethnic minority respondents thought it was important that their relationship should develop within the framework of marriage, they saw it as reaching complete fullness on the birth of a child. In a similar way many of the white British saw their relationship being confirmed or transformed by the birth of a child. And while the white British were less willing than the minorities to admit that marriage imposed duties on them towards their 'in-laws', they derived such duties from an alternative route. They saw it as part of their duties to their partner.[17]

This diversity makes understanding the pattern of the exercise of power within our society more difficult. But the power is there nevertheless. The way this is exercised with regard to family behaviour will be examined in detail in 'The welfarism thesis', later in the chapter. However, this book is not only about the way these systems of power are exercised. Its purpose is also to reflect on values which should inform the system of governance in matters concerning what at this stage one can broadly call family living. It is therefore necessary to explain the basis for a fundamental assumption that underlies the approach taken in this book when evaluating institutional and social behaviour.

---

[15] See A Phoenix and F Hussein, *Parenting and Ethnicity*, Review Paper for the Joseph Rowntree Foundation (2006).

[16] M Maclean and J Eekelaar, 'The Significance of Marriage: Contrasts between White British and Ethnic Minority Groups in England' (2005) 27 *Law & Policy* 379.

[17] J Eekelaar and M Maclean, 'Marriage and the Moral Basis of Personal Relationships' (2004) 31 *Journal of Law & Society* 510.

THE OPEN SOCIETY

It is an important feature of institutional lawmaking and law appliance that the lawmakers and law appliers should be susceptible to argument about the values which underpin their activities. Argument is another form of power. This is particularly so where the lawmakers themselves subscribe to sets of values which can act as constraints on the exercise of power. So the themes pursued in later chapters operate as a counterpoint to the exercise of power. My discussion is premised on the assumption that we wish our society to be 'open'. The 'open society' was the expression used by the Austrian philosopher Karl Popper when he looked across the world from New Zealand during his temporary sojourn there in the early 1940s at the threatening clouds of Fascist and Communist totalitarianism.[18] He saw the intellectual seeds of this disaster in the philosophies of Plato, Hegel, and Marx, which he denounced as a *trahison des clercs*. They, he claimed, had sought to deprive people of the possibility of making independent moral judgements by proclaiming that the past determines the future, and that we should not, indeed cannot, deviate from the power of the group morality set for us by our predecessors.

Whether or not one accepts his analysis of those writers, nevertheless his was a rallying call to the human spirit. His 'open society' is not a creature of sophisticated political analysis. It is sketched in stark and simple terms, but confronts the deepest political issues. It is one in which people believe they can make their own decisions for themselves, freed from the belief that their futures are determined by the past. 'The future depends on ourselves, and we do not depend on any historical necessity.'[19] 'We must become the makers of our fate.'[20] With this intellectual liberation comes the responsibility of 'true rationalism', which is 'awareness of one's limitations, the intellectual modesty of those who know how often they err ...'.[21] If we go wrong, we pick ourselves up and start again. 'We must learn to do things as well as we can, and to look out for our mistakes.'[22] It is a society where minds are open, and individuals will not yield meekly to the demands of the

---

[18] K Popper, *The Open Society and Its Enemies*, vols 1 & 2 (Routledge and Kegan Paul, 1945, 4th edn, 1962).

[19] Ibid vol 1, 3.   [20] Ibid vol 2, 280.   [21] Ibid vol 2, 227.

[22] Ibid vol 2, 280.

tribe or community and the belief that the structure of a community automatically takes precedence over personal well-being.

An 'open society' will require to be governed in a certain way; or, at least, it will be antagonistic to certain modes of government. I have used the expression 'open society' in the way Popper used it rather than 'liberal society'. Liberalism is a complex political theory, with strong protagonists and critics, particularly the 'neo-liberalism' which became dominant in western countries from the 1980s, although with origins often associated with Popper's contemporary, Friedrich von Hayek.[23] But neo-liberal views of the role of markets and the state go much further than necessary for a society to be 'open'. Similarly, the liberal ideal described by Ronald Dworkin that the government should not impose any 'sacrifice or constraint on any citizen in virtue of an argument that the citizen could not accept without abandoning his sense of equal worth'[24] also requires more than is necessary for openness. On the other hand, Dworkin's precept that the state should not impose requirements on individuals simply on the basis of the 'external' preferences of other people about what those individuals should do[25] is more important for an 'open society', for such a society is likely to hold that a person should not be forced to do or abstain from actions (which may affect their own well-being or that of others) for no other reason than that others want them to act otherwise. This is because people who take charge of their fate will not readily do the bidding of others for no other reason than that the bidding takes place.

But things are not often so stark. People in power will not often reinforce their commands with a simple: 'because we say so'. They will point to other factors, usually of a 'societal' nature, as Lord Devlin did when he argued that toleration of homosexuality could threaten social stability.[26] 'Societal' arguments of this kind are usually couched in broad terms and focused on the character of a society, and seldom on the well-being of individuals within it, or, if this was adverted to, individual well-being is simply assumed with scant examination to

[23] F von Hayek, *The Road to Serfdom* (Routledge, 1944); for a useful account, see D Harvey, *A Brief History of Neoliberalism* (Oxford University Press, 2005).

[24] R Dworkin, *A Matter of Principle* (Clarendon Press, 1986) 205.

[25] Ibid 196; 359–72.

[26] P Devlin, *The Enforcement of Morals* (Oxford University Press, 1965) ch IV.

coincide with social conformity.[27] In an 'open society' general assertions about the need to conform to the claims of the group will never
be allowed to go unchallenged.

THE WELFARISM THESIS

Since the way the law interacts with family life in an open society is a
matter of governance, it is necessary to understand something of the history of this interaction in Britain. I have proposed a theoretical understanding of this history which I will briefly set out.[28] For convenience,
I will call it the 'welfarism' thesis, although the idea about the role of
welfarism is only a part (but the most important part) of it.

The thesis maintains that, in the period before the eighteenth-cen-
tury Enlightenment, in so far as the law concerned itself with families at all, it was designed to maintain a particular social structure.
In western Europe, the marriage law of the Church[29] gradually displaced the practices of the indigenous populations, so as to enable
it to exercise 'a large measure of control in the domestic domain',[30]
thereby increasing its landholdings and authority. While its insistence
on consent to marriage appears emancipatory, the wide circle of forbidden degrees for marriage, the distinction between agreement to
marry now and agreement to marry in the future, and (after some
uncertainty) the indissolubility of marriage subjected individuals to
extensive institutional control.[31] It has been noted that the application

---

[27] This is discussed further in J Eekelaar, 'Law, Culture, Values' in A Diduck, N
Peleg, and H Reece (eds), *Law in Society: Reflections on Children, Family, Culture and
Philosophy: Essays in Honour of Michael Freeman* (Brill Nijhoff, 2015) 33–4.

[28] The general argument is presented in J Eekelaar, 'The End of an Era?' (2003) 28
Journal of Family History 108 and applied with specific reference to child welfare law
in J Eekelaar, 'Child Endangerment and Child Protection in England and Wales' in
MK Rosenheim, FE Zimring, DS Tanenhaus, and B Dohrn (eds), *A Century of Juvenile
Justice* (Chicago University Press, 2002) ch 14.

[29] This law was a complex mix of compendia of conciliar canons, synodal decrees,
papal decisions, and dicta of church fathers synthesized in books such as the *Decretum*
of Gratian in the mid-eleventh century. See J Brundage, *Medieval Canon Law*
(Longman, 1995) ch 3.

[30] J Goody, *The Development of the Family and Marriage in Europe* (Cambridge
University Press, 1983) 59.

[31] The literature is extensive and complex. For a few sources, see: ibid; F Pollock and
FW Maitland, *History of English Law Before the Time of Edward I*, vol 2 (Cambridge

of religious norms is a significant exercise of power through ideology.[32] But marriage law also underwrote secular power structures,
whether by consolidating land holdings or forming alliances, so that,
in the words of Lawrence Stone, by the end of the seventeenth century
'the husband and father for a time became the family despot, benevolent or malign according to temperament or inclination.'[33] Rebecca
Probert has described how the the law (including the Marriage Act
1753), the ability to place conditions on financial provisions, and the
wardship jurisdiction provided the means for fathers to control the
marriages of children, primarily girls, in propertied families during
the eighteenth and into the nineteenth centuries.[34]

The character of the law produced in this way can be described as
designed primarily to maintain a particular social structure, rather than
to respond to the interests, or well-being, of individuals. Or, to put it
in a more nuanced way, the interests and well-being of individuals are
identified with, or submerged into, the maintenance of the social structure. The form of English (indeed, European) family law largely had this
feature until the last quarter of the last century. Its provisions were supported by what I have earlier called 'societal' reasons: that is, justifications primarily based upon an appeal to maintaining identified social
structures, rather than an appeal to the well-being of individuals.[35] Since
individual well-being was subsumed into the maintenance of social
structures, I call this the era of Instrumentalism.

Under this dispensation, the legal relationships of subordinate
family members (women, children) were designed to promote the
interests of the dominant member, the husband (father), and often
his family line. Hence the wife's property passed to the husband[36] and

University Press, 1895); C Morris, *The Papal Monarchy: The Western Church from 1050
to 1250* (Oxford University Press, 1989); M Sheehan, *Marriage, Family and Law in
Medieval Europe* (Toronto University Press, 1996); F Pedersen, *Marriage Disputes in
Medieval England* (Hambledon Press, 2000); D d'Avray, *Medieval Marriage: Symbolism
and Society* (Oxford University Press, 2005).

[32] For a full discussion, see Mann, n 1.
[33] L Stone, *The Family, Sex and Marriage in England 1500–1800* (Weidenfeld and
Nicolson, 1977) 158.
[34] R Probert, 'Control over Marriage in England and Wales, 1753–1823' (2009) 27
Law and History Review 413.
[35] See pp 7–9.
[36] As Dicey put it: 'Marriage was an assignment of the wife's property rights to her
husband at any rate during coverture. Much of her property, whether possessed by her
at or coming to her after her marriage, either because absolutely her own, or during

she was expected to be subservient to his wishes. He could determine their standard of living, where they lived, and the terms of their separation (should he agree to it); control the property; claim damages from someone with whom she had committed adultery; and even compel her to have sexual relations with him. Social norms may have generated certain constraints on the way that power was exercised. Thus, despite their legally underwritten power, husbands and fathers were expected to behave benevolently, and to provide sustenance for their families. But these social norms had little or no legal reinforcement. Apart from the general criminal law, there were hardly any institutional constraints on the way parents treated their children until the late nineteenth century, and on how husbands treated their wives until the late twentieth century, however much social norms may have demanded restraint (and they were by no means clear even on that).

Similarly, a father's legal interest in his children was in their labour, and their marriage was perceived as a way of furthering his interests. However, it did not follow that the husband (father) was not expected to look after the interests of his wife and children. Despite the opinions expressed by some historians,[37] it seems that parents have usually loved their children[38] and were expected to do so (although their ways of showing this have varied substantially). But during the pre-Enlightenment era, the power of kings and fathers was seen to be constrained by morality, not law. So William Blackstone observed that a parent's duty to support his children was 'a principle of natural law', so not therefore directly enforceable in the courts, though if they became a charge on parish funds (thereby threatening the social order) a court could order payments by their 'father and mother, grandfather or grandmother', but only for necessaries.[39] There was

---

covature might, if he chose, be made absolutely his own, so that even if his wife survived him it went to his representatives': AV Dicey, *Law and Public Opinion in England during the Nineteenth Century* (Macmillan, 1963) 371–2.

[37] E Shorter, *The Making of the Modern Family* (Collins, 1976); L de Mause, *The History of Childhood* (Collins, 1976).

[38] L Pollock, *Forgotten Children: Parent–Child Relations from 1500 to 1900* (Cambridge University Press, 1983); S Shaher, *Childhood in the Middle Ages* (Routledge, 1990).

[39] Blackstone's *Commentaries on the Laws of England* (ed HW Ballantine) (Blackstone Institute, 1915) 310. In *R (Kehoe) v Secretary of State for Work and Pensions* [2006] 1 AC 42, Baroness Hale explained the obligation as being legal rather than moral. But the legal duty was only to reimburse any costs incurred by the parish.

no legal supervision over the way parents brought up their children. Blackstone justified this by speculating that it might be sufficient punishment of neglectful parents that their 'uninstructed' children were likely to cause them grief in the long run,[40] as if the main purpose of bringing up children properly was to further the parents' interests. This system was mirrored in the political world. The populace were subjects of the king's purposes. The structure and content of the law was directed at maintaining institutional and social power relationships. True, this may well have been regarded as promoting the common good; a good king (and father) was expected to behave benevolently, but there was no legal restraint on their authority, nor was it expected that there should be any.

Enlightenment writers,[41] however, following on from John Locke, argued that a king could only *legitimately* exercise power if done in the subjects' interests, and extended this idea to parental power. The effects of this began to be felt as the nineteenth century progressed. The courts of equity, reinforced by the Custody of Children Act 1839, began to override a father's right to custody of his children if he harmed their interests. A father's obligation to support his wife and children slowly became directly enforceable by family members.[42] Legislation protecting children at work, and later within their own families, began to impose duties on public authorities to protect the welfare of children. All this constitutes 'welfarism'. It will be evident that the term 'welfarism' as used here is far wider than the expression 'welfare state'. This is usually taken to refer to centralized governmental provision for citizens' welfare, originating in nineteenth-century social insurance schemes designed initially to protect individuals against the vicissitudes of industrial capitalism, and moving in the mid-twentieth century to provide education and at least essential cover against ill-health and destitution on the basis of citizenship

---

[40] Blackstone, n 39, 1.16.1.

[41] See J Israel, *A Revolution of the Mind* (Princeton University Press, 2010) 90, observing that according to the radical thinkers 'tyranny' was now perceived as any exercise of power that was not in the best interests of the people.

[42] The Poor Law Amendment Act 1844 (later the Bastardy Laws Amendment Act 1872) allowed a mother to take direct action against the father of her illegitimate child, but regarding legitimate children it was not until the Married Women (Maintenance) Act 1920 that courts could add tiny sums for the children to the orders made in favour of wives. See S Cretney, *Family Law in the Twentieth Century: A History* (Oxford University Press, 2003) 449, 556–60.

alone, all of which involves a substantial proportion of national expenditure. Since this patently requires the benevolent use of institutions, the welfare state is a significant manifestation of welfarism, but is only one such manifestation.

Welfarism as used here refers to a particular way in which power over others is exercised. An important feature is that it did not destroy existing social institutions, but acted through them. The reaction to the excesses of the French revolution ensured that the more radical aspects of the Enlightenment's assault on the *ancien régime* failed to take hold. The married father retained his authority over his wife and legitimate children, but was now legally obliged to exercise it in their interests, or, at least, not against their interests. The French sociologist Jacques Donzelot,[43] following the ideas of Michel Foucault, memorably described the process in France whereby, from the nineteenth century, philanthropic institutions and medical professionals used the help they gave to working-class mothers as a means of acquiring leverage to impart behavioural norms: a process he called 'normalization' through 'medical-hygienism'.[44]

In England these processes were supplemented by the strong desire of the Evangelical movement of the late nineteenth century to save children from moral corruption. It was considered that this was best achieved by removing them entirely from corrupting influences, including those of their family. The Poor Law Amendment Act 1889 therefore allowed the poor law guardians to remove such children into the care of guardians.[45] This 'uprooting' power was later transferred to local authority social services committees, extended, and used, until removed by the Children Act 1989. The Children Act 1948 repealed the old duty to 'set to work' the children of the poor (which had in practice long been replaced by education) and required local authorities to further the children's best interests. Dedicated Children's Departments were established to achieve this. There was, however, a change in what people thought served children best. The experiences of evacuee children during the war, and theories about the importance of attachment between babies and their mothers,[46]

---

[43] J Donzelot, *The Policing of Families* (Hutchinson, 1980).

[44] See R Dingwall, J Eekelaar, and T Murray, *The Protection of Children: State Intervention and Family Life* (Basil Blackwell, 1983) 215–17.

[45] The power was exercisable by resolution; the parents might appeal to a magistrates' court, but were often not told of this right.

[46] J Bowlby, *Child Care and the Growth of Love* (Pelican Books, 1953).

had undermined the view that deprived children were best 'uprooted' from a contaminating environment, and replaced it with the policy of rehabilitating them into their families with the assistance of social casework.

Welfarism reached its high point during the 1970s and early 1980s. During the 1960s proposals were made (but only partially implemented) to treat most children who had committed offences in the same way as children who were victims of neglect or ill-treatment.[47] In 1970 the House of Lords interpreted the word 'paramount' in the test that courts were to apply in deciding disputes about a child's upbringing (that the child's welfare was to be the 'paramount' consideration) as if it meant the 'sole' consideration, all other considerations being relevant only if they affected the child's welfare, and extended its application beyond disputes between parents to disputes between a parent and a non-parent.[48] Ten years later it decided that a local authority was not obliged to return a child whom it was looking after on a voluntary basis, even if the parents requested this,[49] and two years later that whether parents would be allowed to visit a child of theirs who was in its care was entirely within the discretion of the authority.[50] In the meantime the Children Act 1975, consolidated in the Child Care Act 1980, expanded local authority powers to take compulsory measures for removing children from home by permitting them to do so on the sole ground that the child had been in the care of the authority or a voluntary association for more than three years.[51] The period from 1945 to 1975 has also been called the 'golden age' of the welfare state. The weighted average of the percentage of gross domestic product of seven major OECD countries described as social expenditure rose from 12.3 to 21.9 from 1960 to 1975.[52]

No one can deny the vast humanitarian benefits of welfarism and the conceptual break from intrumentalism. But it had its dark side. The duty to advance the interests of the vulnerable carried with it the power to decide what those interests were. It is easy for those with

---

[47] J Eekelaar, R Dingwall, and T Murray, 'Victims or Threats? Children in Care Proceedings' (1982) 3 *Journal of Social Welfare Law* 68.

[48] *J v C* [1970] AC 668. See further p 57.

[49] *London Borough of Lewisham v Lewisham Juvenile Court Justices* [1980] AC 273.

[50] *A v Liverpool City Council* [1982] AC 363.

[51] See generally Cretney, n 42, chs 19 and 20.

[52] C Pierson, *Beyond the Welfare State?* (Polity Press, 1998) 124. The countries are Canada, France, West Germany, Italy, Japan, the United Kingdom, and the USA.

such power to convince themselves that the interests which they are supposed to protect coincide with their own interests and the social structures that maintain them. In other words, instrumentalist objectives could be sought under the guise of welfarism and supported by societal justifications. A tragic example occurred in the United States in the twentieth century, where some parents were prepared to allow their children to suffer, and sometimes die, untreated and in great pain, because they believed this was for their spiritual welfare.[53] They were allowing adherence to the structures of a belief system to determine their view of the welfare of the children. Nineteenth-century courts were convinced that children would usually be better off with their fathers than with their mothers.[54] This was not based on any careful evaluation of the children, but rather on a preconception of an exclusively male judiciary about the way societies should order their family relations.

Most dramatically, over the period 1850 to 1960, about 100,000 young children were separated from parents whom denominational 'child rescue' organizations deemed to be morally unfit to look after them and sent to Canada and Australia.[55] The children barely participated in these decisions about their lives, and many were falsely told that their parents were dead. These policies served the interests of those who sent them by passing responsibility for looking after them to others, relieving them of the problems of dealing with their parents and, for some, promoting the cause of British colonization. The Independent Inquiry into (historic) Child Abuse established in July 2014 has focused on the extent to which there may have been knowledge of the abuse of these children. Yet many of its proponents, especially those in the Evangelical child rescue movement, genuinely believed they were doing what was best for the children, one writing:

> The children themselves are saved, with thousands of miles of sea and yellow cornlands and glorious forests putting their old associations out

---

[53] A Rogers, *The Child Cases: How America's Religious Exemption Laws Harm Children* (University of Massachusetts Press, 2014).

[54] See the statement in re *Agar-Ellis* (1883) 24 ChD 317 at 334: 'When by birth a child is subject to a father, it is for the general interest of families, and for the general interest of children, and really for the interest of the particular infant, that the court should not, except in very extreme cases, interfere with the discretion of the father but leave him the responsibility of exercising the power which nature has given him by birth of the child' (Cotton LJ).

[55] Barnardos was the most significant.

of the field of vision … Successfully organised (emigration) … may be regarded as the chief glory and most consoling feature of the work of rescue.[56]

The secrecy that surrounded adoption for many years after its introduction in 1926 provides another example.[57]

The welfarism thesis maintains that the last two decades of the twentieth century saw a movement away from welfarism of such significance as to amount virtually to its collapse. The gist is that people were less willing to allow designated persons, whether family members or institutional authorities, to define what their interests were. They demanded the power to decide this for themselves. This feeling was mirrored by a political ideology which favoured reducing state power in favour of individual responsibility and choice, an aspect of what has been characterized as the birth, or re-birth, of neo-liberalism. It found expression in the language of individual rights, to be examined in detail in chapter 2. Early indications of change can be found in the criticisms of social casework in the 1970s by radical social work theory, which argued that, instead of trying to adapt people to 'the system', the system should change in response to people's demands. Social workers should act as facilitators to assist people to achieve their rights. A natural outcome was the growth of 'rights' movements during the 1970s, such as Family Rights Group, the Children's Legal Centre, and the pressure group for divorced men and their new partners, the Campaign for Justice in Divorce. Research emphasized the antagonism parents felt to social work intervention.[58] Government policy became suspicious of the claims of social casework, and public confidence in social workers was shaken by a series of highly

---

[56] Cited in J Eekelaar ' "The Chief Glory": The Export of Children from the United Kingdom' (1994) 21 *Journal of Law and Society* 487, 496. That article explores the historical origins of the practice, the 'mind-sets' that explain it, and, in particular, the failure of government to fulfil its responsibility properly to supervise the private sector. In 2009 the Australian Prime Minister, and in 2010 the British Prime Minister, formally apologized to these children.

[57] The degree to which adoptive parents delayed telling children of their adoption, or did not do so at all, and the adverse effects of this on the children was first demonstrated in the ground-breaking research of A McWhinnie, *Adopted Children: How They Grow Up* (Routledge & Kegan Paul, 1967) and J Triseliotis, *In Search of Origins: The Experiences of Adopted People* (Beacon Press, 1975).

[58] J Packman, *Who Needs Care? Social Work Decisions about Children* (Blackwell, 1986); S Millham et al., *Lost in Care: The Problems of Maintaining Links between Children in Care and Their Families* (Gower, 1986).

publicized cases in which the social welfare services appeared to damage people's interests, either through failing to intervene adequately to protect a child[59] or by intervening apparently unnecessarily.[60]

In fact, social intervention into families had long been significantly influenced by the medical profession. Early in the twentieth century concerns over the population's health were thought to be best met by improving nutrition and living conditions, and reducing the damage perceived to be caused by alcohol consumption. There was little appreciation that some parents deliberately hurt their children until in the 1960s American radiographers noticed that some babies suffered bone fractures which must have been deliberately inflicted. This 'discovery' of a 'battered baby syndrome' developed into wider recognition of child abuse and neglect, in which medical professionals played an important role.[61] The 'medicalization' of child protection produced a significant welfarist orientation, backed by a strong assertion of professional power. It reached a high point in the Cleveland affair, when two consultant paediatricians claimed to have discovered a medical 'test' which indicated sexual abuse, on the basis of which social workers were persuaded to remove and isolate children from their parents, as if they were at risk of the contamination of disease. The resulting inquiry,[62] which demonstrated the fragility of the evidential value of the test, was an important step in the process of developing controls designed to inhibit the power of welfare and medical professionals in child protection, and enhance the gatekeeping functions of the courts and legal professionals. Jonathan Herring has succinctly described how the almost unquestioned respect given by the courts to the discretionary power of the medical profession to make decisions affecting children has further reduced over the first fifteen years of the twenty-first century.[63]

The lack of confidence in welfare institutions was reflected in assertions that primary responsibility for children lay with parents, rather

---

[59] The cases of Maria Colwell (1974), Jasmine Beckford (1985), and Kimberley Carlisle (1987) were the most well-known.

[60] Allegations of excessive and unnecessary intrusion into families as a result of medical 'misdiagnosis' of sexual abuse in Cleveland in the mid 1980s received much publicity. See E Butler-Sloss (chair), *Report of the Inquiry into Child Abuse in Cleveland*, CM 412 (HM Stationery Office, 1987).

[61] See N Parton, *The Politics of Child Abuse* (Macmillan, 1985).

[62] See Butler-Sloss Report, n 60.

[63] J Herring, 'Medical Decisions about Children' in J Eekelaar (ed) *Family Law in Britain and America in the New Century: Essays in Honor of Sanford N Katz* (Brill, 2016) ch 9. See *Montgomery v Lanarkshire Health Board* [2015] UKSC 11.

than with the state.[64] Thus, a Department of Health Review into safe-guards for children living away from home in foster care, children's homes, and boarding schools proclaimed that 'parents deciding to place a child away from home are ... responsible for satisfying themselves that arrangements for keeping their children safe exist and are likely to prove effective ... [T]he decision about placement is ultimately their responsibility. In making it, parents should possess all the information they need about the arrangements for keeping their children safe.'[65] Intervention into families should be allowed only on strictly defined, and established, criteria. This legalism replaced social workers and medical professionals with the legal profession as the dominant gate-keepers to the exercise of coercive powers over the family. It was encap-sulated in the Children Act 1989, which reduced the powers of local authorities to intervene into families, and defined more restrictively the circumstances in which courts could authorize such intervention.

Similar movements were seen in private family law. An example is the change in the basis upon which courts made financial and prop-erty orders on divorce, explained in chapter 2.[66] The 'welfare principle' which dominated judicial decision-making concerning children came under pressure from fathers' rights activists, who claimed that it was being used unfairly to benefit mothers, and an attempt was made in 2014 to regulate the use of that principle by the courts by requiring them to presume that, unless the contrary is shown, involvement of that parent in the life of the child concerned will further the child's wel-fare.[67] Claims by, or on behalf of, children conceived by artificial means to knowledge of their father were conceded by the government.[68]

THE CASE OF DIVORCE

The story of divorce diverges in some respects from the welfarism thesis. The reason is that the prohibition against the dissolution of

---

[64] See J Eekelaar, 'Parental Responsibility: State of Nature or the Nature of the State?' (1991) *Journal of Social Welfare & Family Law* 37.

[65] W Utting (chair), *People Like Us* (HM Stationery Office, 1997) 72.

[66] See p 44.   [67] Children and Families Act 2014, s 11. See further pp 129–32.

[68] Department of Health, Press Release, 21 January 2004, announcing that as from April 2005, children born from donations after that date would have a right of access to the identity of the donor. See further p 50.

marriage dates from pre-welfarist times, and its foundations in the doctrines of the Church rendered it relatively immune from the humanistic values of the Enlightenment. The Protestant concession to permit divorce on the ground of adultery, which pre-dated the Enlightenment, was not a feature of welfarist concern, but a manifestation of a penal mentality which, at its extreme form, decreed death for adultery between married people in Calvinist Geneva, and in Puritan England, death for a wife and three months' imprisonment for a husband. Adultery remained the only basis upon which a divorce could be granted in England until 1938.

Thus the origins of the matrimonial offence doctrine, which dominated English law until 1971, rested on an instrumentalist notion that broken marriages were to be maintained, if not for the welfare of the parties concerned, then at least for the benefit of wider society, unless one party deserved exclusion from the union as a matter of punishment. This implied, however, that the other party was innocent and would have held to the marriage were it not for the offence. If that assumption could not be made (e.g if the petitioner had also committed a marital wrong, or encouraged the other's wrongdoing, or had invented the wrongdoing in collusion with the other) the petition would be dismissed. The bizarre consequence was that the more hostile the parties were towards one another, or the more mutual the desire for divorce, the less likely it was to be granted. A government official, the King's (Queen's) Proctor, was created to try to ensure that people were not given divorces they did not deserve, and the courts exercised a general supervisory role to prevent this happening. In 1956, the majority of the Royal Commission on Marriage and Divorce who successfully recommended that the matrimonial offence doctrine should be kept argued that 'the inevitable result' of allowing parties to divorce by consent would be to allow divorce if there was no 'real necessity for the remedy'. They predicted that to allow this would create a very real risk that divorce would become widespread and this would destroy the concept of life-long marriage and endanger children. The wishes, and indeed the well-being, of the couple were to be sacrificed to maintain a social structure that was assumed to be for the general good.

Welfarism, however, had brought about some amelioration of the obstacles to divorce. It allowed divorce to be granted by judicial remedy in 1858, whereas before that it needed an Act of Parliament. But this only extended its availability to a small section of the population who had access to the High Court, and the grounds for divorce remained very narrow. A more significant measure occurred in 1878 when concerns over violence against women prompted the enactment of the Matrimonial Causes Act 1878, under which poor women could obtain a non-cohabitation order from a magistrates' court (then known as a 'police' court) which relieved them of their duty to live with a husband who had been convicted of an aggravated assault on them. The husband could also be ordered to provide limited financial support. But the marriage remained intact. In 1895 these courts were empowered to make such orders on the broader grounds that a husband had been guilty of persistent cruelty that caused the wife to leave, or had wilfully neglected to provide reasonable maintenance. These 'poor person's divorces' exceeded the number of 'real' divorces that were granted in the High Court. In 1900 there were 9,553 such orders in magistrates' courts. Between 1900 and 1905 the annual average for High Court divorces stood at 546. The grounds for divorce were themselves extended from 1938 by the Matrimonial Causes Act 1937, allowing petitions by either party to be based on cruelty, desertion for three years, and unsoundness of mind.

Although the majority of the 1956 Royal Commission clung to the instrumentalist, fault-based, ideology of divorce, the heightened welfarism of the 1960s prevailed with the Law Commission, which in 1966 recommended that divorce should become available on the sole ground of irretrievable breakdown of the marriage. One reason for the proposal was that the current procedure caused distress and humiliation. Another was the belief that there were some 180,000 illegitimate children who could become legitimate if the divorce law was changed. The Divorce Reform Act 1969 (effective from 1971) therefore replaced the primarily fault-based divorce law by divorce based on irretrievable breakdown. The law manifested many of the fingerprints of welfarism. It stopped short of empowering the parties to bring the marriage to an end by reason only of their own decision. They still needed to comply with the conditions laid down by the law. Divorce by consent was indeed now possible, but only after a two-year period of separation. It was even possible for someone to be divorced against their wishes after separation for five years. If the parties wished to divorce more quickly, it was still necessary to allege wrongdoing: either adultery or 'unreasonable behaviour'. But it did not matter that they had agreed on this course, or that both had committed such wrongs. The court could reject a petition if it felt the conditions were not established, but as the requirement for a hearing was abolished in the mid 1970s, in the overwhelming majority of cases where the petitioner's statement is not contested by the other party the court can proceed on the basis that the conditions have been established without requiring supporting evidence. Furthermore, a duty, introduced in 1958, that the courts should be satisfied that the arrangements for the children were satisfactory or the best that could be devised was removed by the Children Act 1989. It seems that now the judicial role in divorce is no longer one of regulation, but of regularization, in effect—an entirely administrative process, albeit one which expects an allegation of adultery or some form of 'unreasonable behaviour' to be written down if the parties do not wish to wait the required time periods, and which can be subverted if one of them wishes to oppose the petition, as vividly demonstrated in *Owens v Owens*.[69]

The final chapter in the story of divorce in the twentieth century centres on the reform enacted in the Family Law Act 1996 but never implemented. In 1990, the Law Commission expressed the view that the remnants of the fault system in the reformed 1971 law could give rise to confusion and in some cases injustice. This was because the natural desire to obtain divorce quickly once a marriage has broken down leads most people to use the adultery and 'unreasonable behaviour' facts, even though these either might not have occurred or might not represent the full story of the marriage. But it would be contrary to the interests of either party to contest such allegations, for to do so risks removing the case to court for a hearing, which neither may desire, and could increase friction between them. The Commission preferred to substitute a period of time which had to pass after an application for divorce was lodged as being the most convincing evidence that the breakdown of the marriage was irretrievable. This proposal would have allowed either party, with the consent of the other, or unilaterally, to have brought the marriage to an end, albeit that the legal dissolution would follow after the effluxion of a period of time.

Such a radical empowerment of married people was in keeping with the ideological position of the post-welfarist era. However, the reform was never implemented. The reasons are complex. As the idea developed within government, it began to be viewed as an opportunity to deter people from divorce, and to promote mediation.

---

[69] [2017] EWCA Civ 182. See p 70.

Thus government consultative documents suggested that the process should be preceded by one or both parties attending an information meeting which would, among other things, explain to the parties the effects of divorce on children, and point out the 'helpfulness' of mediation. With these new (welfarist) goals in place, the government was disappointed when pilot studies revealed that the information meetings did not sufficiently steer participants away from legal advice and towards mediation, and may not have been successful in inducing them to reconsider their desire for divorce. This was enough to sink the scheme. While it was perhaps remarkable to find this resurgence of welfarist policy in the mid 1990s, it may also be significant that it was thought unlikely to succeed. And it could be said that, although welfarist, the policy differed from such policies which prevailed during the welfarist era. During that time the outcomes deemed to be in people's interests were simply imposed on them. In the case of the 1996 abortive reform, the policy was to construct procedures which were designed to prompt people to seek the desired outcomes themselves.

The holy grail of post-welfarist policy could be said to be to enhance people's freedom to pursue goals of their own choosing, but to exercise state power surreptitiously by influencing them to choose goals which the state believes to be in their interests, or those of the community. People were to divorce 'responsibly'.[70] The experience of the Family Law Act 1996 was not an encouraging omen for the quest. As a consequence, even in 2017 English divorce law retains the vestigial traces of the fault-based system. This is probably not an impediment to divorce, but causes additional complication, and could aggravate tension unnecessarily. In practice, however, granting a divorce has largely become an administrative matter.

THE NEW ERA: FROM FAMILY LAW TO PERSONAL LAW?

Taken as a whole, family law in the 1960s was much closer to the family law of the 1890s than the family law of the 1990s and beyond. John Dewar and Stephen Parker have gone as far as to characterize the

---

[70] See H Reece, *Divorcing Responsibly* (Hart Publishing, 2003).

present era, in the case of family law, as one of 'chaos'.[71] They describe the
period from 1858 (when judicial divorce was introduced in England and
Wales) to the late 1960s as the 'formal' era when the marital relationship
was seen as an institutional matter for the state. This period emphasized
rights, form, principle, and the public. This gave way to a 'functional-
ist' era when the law became more utilitarian, favoured substance over
form, became more pragmatic (thus preferring discretion to rules), and
retreated from the public domain. This was a preparatory stage for a
'complex' (or chaotic) era, which emphasizes the fact of parenthood over
the status of marriage, shifts away from discretion back towards rules,
and recognizes greater freedom for parties to order their family lives,
each type of relationship generating its own legal form. I have described
this change similarly as the law moving from trying 'to maintain, or even
create, a type of social structure [by] rewarding conformity with that
structure, and penalizing aberrations from it' to resolving, or merely
managing, people's problems on an individualized basis.[72]

What can account for these changes? They are clearly linked to the
changes in family living of the 1970s which Francis Fukuyama has
called 'the great disruption',[73] or, more technically, the 'demographic
transition'. The facts can be simply stated.[74] Of men and women born
in 1930 in England and Wales, 90 per cent of men and 94 per cent of
women had married by age 40 whereas of those born in 1970, 63 per
cent of men and 71 per cent of women had married by the same age.
Of those born in 1930, 51 per cent of men and 74 per cent of women
were married by the age of 25, compared with only 5 per cent of
men and 11 per cent of women born in 1987.[75] The marriage rate for

[71] J Dewar, 'The Normal Chaos of Family Law' (1998) 61 *Modern Law Review* 467;
S Parker, 'Rights and Utility in Anglo-Australian Family Law' (1992) 55 *Modern Law
Review* 311.

[72] J Eekelaar, 'Then and Now – Family Law's Direction of Travel' (2013) 35 *Journal
of Social Welfare and Family Law* 415.

[73] F Fukuyama, *The Great Disruption* (Profile Books, 1999).

[74] See C Gibson, 'Changing Family Patterns in England and Wales over the last
Fifty Years' in SN Katz, J Eekelaar, and M Maclean (eds), *Cross Currents: Family Law
and Policy in the US and England* (Oxford University Press, 2000) ch 2.

[75] Office for National Statistics, *Marriages in England and Wales (Provisional) 2012*,
section 8: http://www.ons.gov.uk/peoplepopulationandcommunity/birthsdeaths
andmarriages/marriagecohabitationandcivilpartnerships/bulletins/marriagesin
englandandwalesprovisional/2014-06-11#proportion-of-men-and-women-who-
have-ever-married (accessed 30 May 2017).

women (marriages per 1,000 unmarried population over 16) dropped from 60.5 in 1972 to 20.0 in 2012.[76]

This seems to be partly cause and partly consequence of social and demographic events like decline in fertility (down from 2.42 children for women born in 1935 to 1.91 for women born in 1969[77]), postponement of childbearing, greater longevity, increased female workforce participation, and contraception. But there has also been a weakening of regard for the importance of marriage, or, at least, of the need to be married before starting a life together. A survey of the evidence available in 2007 has shown that 'in the early 1960s in Britain fewer than one in a hundred adults under 50 are estimated to have been cohabiting at any one time, compared with one in six currently'.[78] People now standardly live together without marrying,[79] though, perhaps unsurprisingly, the more this has occurred, the likelihood of this leading to marriage has declined. In 1976, only 4.9 per cent of children were born to a couple living together outside marriage. By 2012 this had risen to 31.2 per cent.[80] The consequence is a greater variety of 'family' forms: people living together without being married, with or without children, or living with second or subsequent partners, or living as a single adult with children.

The increase in divorce from 3.2 divorces per 1,000 marriages in 1966 to 14.0 per 1,000 in 2004 must be seen as part of this wider picture. It is not *simply* a fulfilment of the prediction of the majority of the Royal Commission of 1956 that weakening the divorce law would destroy the concept of life-long marriage. Studies show that there is only a weak relationship between the rate of divorce and the nature of the divorce law, and that the rate of divorce is independent from the extent of marital breakdown.[81] The causes of marital breakdown

---

[76] Ibid section 4.

[77] Office for National Statistics, *Childbearing for Women Born in Different Years, England and Wales: 2014.*

[78] É Beaujouan and M Ní Bhrolcháin, 'Cohabitation and Marriage in Britain since the 1970s' *Population Trends* 145 (Autumn 2011) 2.

[79] Four in five people marrying between 2004 and 2007 had lived together before marrying: Beaujouan and Ní Bhrolcháin, n 78, 8.

[80] Office for National Statistics, *Statistical Bulletin, Live births in England and Wales by Characteristics of Mother 1* (January 2013).

[81] DW Allen, 'The Impact of Legal Reforms on Marriage and Divorce' and I Smith, 'European Divorce Laws, Divorce Rates, and their Consequences' in AW Dnes and R Rowthorn (eds), *The Law and Economics of Marriage & Divorce* (Cambridge University Press, 2002) chs 11 and 12; T Fahey, 'Divorce Trends and Patterns: An

go much deeper than the nature of the divorce legal regime. This is apparent from the fact that, while making divorce legally easier in 1971 did probably contribute to the increase in divorce in England, the divorce rate steadily *decreased* after 2004 (from 14.0 per 1,000 marriages in 2004 to 10.8 per 1,000 marriages in 2011) without the law becoming more restrictive. It cannot be said with certainty why this is so. The downward trend started before the recession of 2007/8, so the impact of economic conditions is unclear. Perhaps the fact that fewer people are marrying, and doing so later, has led to more secure marriages. This seems to be supported by the increase in the median duration of marriages at the time of divorce from 10.1 years in 1981 to around 11.5 years from 2004 to 2011, suggesting that people may be trying harder to preserve their marriages, although the result is to put longer-established marriages at greater risk.[82]

These changes in behaviour have obviously been accompanied by changes in attitudes. Some attitudinal changes are easy to detect, for example disapproval of pre-marital cohabitation has dropped significantly.[83] Attitudes about personal relationships are harder to pin down. Some writers[84] have suggested that people now pursue the goals of individual self-fulfilment and the quest for 'pure' relationships at the expense of commitment to others. Others have suggested a more nuanced picture where relationships are only provisionally accepted and continually 'renegotiated' on a basis of 'reciprocity'.[85] But the implication that such negotiations take place between self-interested individuals in isolation from social and moral expectations seems implausible. Carol Smart and Bren Neale[86] concluded that the separated parents they interviewed were articulating their wishes within an ethical framework. For the mothers it was an 'ethic of care';

Overview' in J Eekelaar and R George (eds) *Handbook of Family Law and Policy* (Routledge, 2014) ch 2.2.

[82] Office for National Statistics, *Statistical Bulletin, Divorces in England and Wales, 2011* (20 December 2012).

[83] J Haskey, 'Cohabitation in Great Britain: Past, Present and Future Trends—and Attitudes' (2001) 103 *Population Trends* 4.

[84] RE Bellah, R Madsen, WM Sullivan, A Swider, and SM Tipton, *Habits of the Heart: Individualism and Commitment in American Life* (University of California Press, 1985 and 1996).

[85] U Beck and E Beck-Gernsheim, *Individualization* (Sage, 2001); A Giddens, *The Transformation of Intimacy: Sexuality, Love and Eroticism in Modern Society* (Polity Press, 1992).

[86] C Smart and B Neale, *Family Fragments?* (Polity Press, 1999).

for the fathers, an 'ethic of justice'. But they were talking about child-care matters. Mavis Maclean and I found the reverse when separated parents talked about financial support: there the mothers stressed the fathers' obligations in justice to their biological children, while the fathers stressed their new supportive roles in their second families.[87] But whether expressed by women or men, both these 'ethics' demand that attention be paid to interests beyond those of the immediate agent.

These studies concerned only separated parents. In a later study, referred to earlier,[88] Maclean and I explored the extent to which couples who were living together either married or outside mar-riage considered they had obligations to one another, and to their partner's family, and, if so, why. Our interviewees did not seem to regard themselves as being in a position of self-interested negoti-ation and renegotiation with their partners. Some (but not all) of the married thought that the institution of marriage imposed obliga-tions on them. Others, including some of the married, saw the very fact of being in a relationship as generating a kind of obligation to 'work at' its sustenance: the relationship itself exerted a 'normative pull'. Others, also including the married and unmarried, appealed to independent principles, such as that one should treat people well if they have treated you well,[89] or build trust, or treat people with love, respect, and care. The conclusion was that the evidence showed that married and cohabiting unmarried people share many values, indeed that the 'similarities in the normative determinants of their behaviour may be greater than the dissimilarities'. This also seemed to be the case when the ethnicity of the interviewees was taken into account.[90] These findings should remind us that, even though out-wardly people may seem to behave in different ways, at a deeper level they may share many values.

But the fact remains that, since the 1970s and 1980s, many fewer people are willing to allow the way they behave in their personal lives to be dictated to them by social institutions, including marriage. Yet

---

[87] M Maclean and J Eekelaar, *The Parental Obligation: A Study of Parenthood across Households* (Hart Publishing, 1997) 141–2.

[88] Eekelaar and Maclean, n 17.

[89] This is not the same as the 'reciprocity' referred to earlier because the benefits received were perceived as generating a long-term obligation, not one which was con-stantly under view.

[90] Maclean and Eekelaar, n 16.

marriage has lost its oppressive nature, having become an optional structure which can assist in, though it is not necessary for, the development of loving and caring relationships. But no sooner had welfarism made marriage benign than it suffered a relative decline. The French sociologist Irène Théry called the process 'démariage': whereby marriage changed from being a public representation of a social ideal to being a private matter.[91] It is reflected in the widely held view that the fact of parenthood is assuming more legal importance than the status of being married.[92] Why, then, has there been this diminution in conformity with institutional practices? Could it be that revelations of past (sometimes present) abuses within institutions (domestic violence within marriage, institutional child abuse) have bred distrust? Is there a link to the contemporaneous decline, or restructuring, of the welfare state, following economic conditions of the mid 1970s, which saw reduction in economic growth, high unemployment and high inflation, and the rise of 'neoliberal' social and economic policies?[93] Can an alleged decline in the standards of civic virtue in the public domain[94] have affected institutions which formerly dominated our private lives? Whatever the reasons, the result creates a problem concerning the legitimacy of authority, which is a central feature of governance.

The welfarism thesis suggests that this change is part of the attack on welfarist power structures, which gave persons in authority discretion to determine outcomes they believed to be in the interests of others. The decline of welfarism and the diminution of public institutional power does not mean that the exercise of power has disappeared. Much of it has been transferred to individuals, who may exercise it through private institutions (as is evident by the dominance of global business corporations) or simply as wealthy individuals. The greater 'individualization' of family law has also exposed individuals to the exercise of power by other individuals, for example, as they seek more scope to determine the nature and consequences of their relationships, either by contract (eg through increasing acceptance of the use of pre-nuptial contracts), or when couples live together without the 'protection' of the marriage law, or where individuals seek children through international adoption or surrogacy, or where one simply

---

[91] I Théry, *Le Démariage* (Editions Odile Jacob, 1993).
[92] Maclean and Eekelaar, n 87, 8–11.   [93] Pierson, n 52, 138ff.
[94] As argued, for example, by D Marquand, *Decline of the Public* (Polity Press, 2004).

dominates the other. In these complex scenarios the need to reconcile the 'rights' of all concerned becomes of paramount importance, and will be considered in the next chapter.

This scenario raises new problems. One is to find a legitimate basis for such rights and entitlements. Of course they often originate through the usual sources of law-creation, the legislature and the courts. But these are institutions, and therefore afflicted with the institutional distrust of the post-welfarist era. As in the case of the first Enlightenment, there can be appeal to norms beyond the positive law: to universal rights. Such appeals are assisted by the presence of international human rights instruments, such as the United Nations Convention on the Elimination of All Forms of Discrimination against Women 1979 (hereafter CEDAW), the United Nations Convention on the Rights of the Child 1989 (hereafter UNCRC) and, more importantly for the United Kingdom, the European Convention on Human Rights and Fundamental Freedoms (hereafter ECHR), enacted into domestic law from October 2000 by the Human Rights Act 1998. The difficulty is that it is not clear that the legitimacy of such instruments is very secure in wider society, or even among the legal or political community. In 2012 the majority of a Commission set up following criticisms by the then Prime Minister, David Cameron, and others, of decisions by the European Court of Human Rights recommended that the United Kingdom should withdraw from the European Convention and enact its own Bill of Rights,[95] and this was a manifesto commitment of the Conservative Party, elected to government in 2015. The role of human rights will be considered further in the next chapter. The other problem lies in the means available to secure protection of these rights, which governments may consider to be purely a private matter for which they have no responsibility. This will be considered further in chapter 7.

This greater emphasis on individual rights has thrown up another issue which is particular to family law. Legal rights within family relationships have tended to be defined by reference to formal definitional categories, such as those who have 'family life' under the European Convention, or are married, or are members

---

[95] Commission on a Bill of Rights, *A UK Bill of Rights? The Choice before Us?* December 2012. The issue was put on hold pending the withdrawal of the United Kingdom from the European Union.

of a 'family', or are legally recognized parents. For example, in *Fitzpatrick v Sterling Housing Association*,[96] in order to qualify for recognition, a same-sex couple needed to be characterized as a 'family' for the purposes of the relevant legislation. Similar problems could arise when considering in what way, if at all, relationships between unmarried heterosexual people living together without a sexual relationship, or heterosexual people with a sexual relationship but who are not living together should be subject to special legal attention. Do we need to try to bring these under some concept of 'family'?

In truth, we are dealing with the role of the law in relation to what is usually referred to as people's 'personal', or 'private', lives. People's 'private' life can of course include many matters other than relationships with others, but in this context will be understood as referring to such relationships. These relationships can be very complex, and disputes and problems that can arise difficult to resolve by legal means. We may not need a unifying concept such as that of the 'family', as the South African Constitutional Court recognized when it decided that the absence in the 1996 draft Constitution of a reference to a right to marry or to family life did not invalidate the Constitution,[97] since 'families come in many shapes and sizes. The definition of the family also changes as social practices and traditions change.'[98] Yet it has still proved possible to protect the rights individuals have to family life and to protect family values through individuals' rights to equality, non-discrimination, and respect for dignity.[99]

It could therefore perhaps be liberating to abandon the label 'family' law and replace it with the expression 'personal law'. In many jurisdictions, especially those which include communities with strongly distinctive religious traditions, 'personal law', or 'personal status law', is used to refer to laws which attach to individuals because of their membership of a religious or ethnic community and which cover

---

[96] [2001] 1 AC 27.

[97] *Certification of the Constitution of the Republic of South Africa* 1996 (4) SA 744.

[98] *Rahim Dawood v Minister of Home Affairs* 2000 (3) SA 936, para 31.

[99] See *Minister of Home Affairs v Fourie* 2006 (1) SA 524 (CC) (confirming a right to same-sex marriage). See A Sachs, 'Foreword: Unfamiliar Families—the Strange Alchemy of Life and Law' in C Lind, H Keating, and J Bridgeman (eds) *Taking Responsibility, Law and the Changing Family* (Ashgate/Routledge, 2010).

matters covered by family law as we understand it. This is not the sense in which it is used here. Rather, it refers to laws, whether applicable on the basis of an individual's communal allegiance or not, which purport directly to regulate their private life. This usage will therefore be adopted for the rest of this book.

2

Rights

RIGHTS AS A COUNTERVAILING FORCE TO POWER

The previous chapter described the history of English family law in terms of the power it gave to those who designed and administered it, and the way it distributed power within society. It recognized that this power was sometimes mitigated by social norms requiring its benevolent exercise, but noted that this was not legally underwritten until the growing force of welfarism began to be felt. But then welfarism also involved the exercise of power and could revert to instrumentalism. Towards the end of the last century, social changes and the emergence of the rhetoric of rights introduced a countervailing force against the power structures that preceded it.

This chapter explores in more detail this role played by rights in attenuating the structure of power created by the earlier family law. It then moves to consider the role of rights in the post-welfarist context where they are relevant to relationships between individuals in regard to their personal lives. But it is necessary to start by setting out an understanding of the idea of 'rights' in this context.

WHAT ARE RIGHTS?

The language of rights is replete with ambiguity. If I say that 'I have a right to x', do I mean that I think that as things stand I expect some person or persons to make x available to me? If so, do I expect such person or persons to drop everything and present me with x, disregarding what anyone else may say about the effects of doing this on

Family Law and Personal Life. Second edition. John Eekelaar. © John Eekelaar 2017.
Second edition published 2017 by Oxford University Press.

them? Do I expect to have some form of redress if none of this is done? Or am I expressing only the ardent wish that the world should be ordered in a fairer way, and if it was, x would become available to me? It becomes more complicated if I say, 'My grandfather had a right to x which was denied to him.' Am I saying that had my grandfather, during the last century, sought x (which he might have done), he could have expected x to be made available to him? Or that, although he could never have expected it in his society, a better organized, or more moral, world would have made it available? And if I say that women have a right to x, am I saying that I think x should be made available to them, even though some may not expect it, or want it? And in any of these cases, am I restricting my observations to what I think the *legal system* provides, or should provide, or am I looking beyond the law to how people in general should behave towards one another?

It is possible that I might mean any of these things. It is not surprising therefore that there is so much disagreement about what rights are. Indeed, it is arguable that the fact that there is no stable basis in which the concept can be grounded means that its meaning will inevitably be contested.[1] This does not mean that one should not attempt to defend a particular version of it if it is believed to be useful. It is clear that references to rights are now widely made in relation to family matters. This has caused some alarm, especially when applied to children. A perceptive writer on children, Michael King, has warned that the promotion of children's legal rights is unlikely to make a better world for children, and may even cause harm;[2] and it has been suggested that it would be better to talk of 'doing right' for children rather than about children's 'rights'.[3] On a wider level, Mary Ann Glendon has argued that talk about rights has promoted a perception that society is constituted of self-interested individuals,[4] a theme taken up by Tony Blair shortly after he became British Prime Minister

---

[1] See WB Gallie, 'Essentially Contested Concepts' (1955–6) 56 *Proceedings of the Aristotelian Society* 167.

[2] M King, *A Better World for Children?* (Routledge, 1997). See also M Guggenheim, *What's Wrong with Children's Rights* (Harvard University Press, 2005), reviewed by M Freeman in (2006) 2 *International Journal of Law in Context* 89.

[3] RE Goodin and D Gibson, 'Rights, Young and Old' (1997) 17 *Oxford Journal of Legal Studies* 15.

[4] MA Glendon, *Rights Talk: The Impoverishment of Political Discourse* (The Free Press, 1991).

when he told the Labour Party Conference in September 1997 that 'a decent society is not based on rights. It is based on duty. On duty to each other.' The judge Sir John Laws expressed a widely held view of rights when he argued that inter-personal morals should be based on the language of duty, not rights.[5]

Yet the language of rights has been of great significance in fashioning the way in which individuals, institutions, and the state treat other people. So, against those sceptical views, I wish to argue that one particular way of thinking about rights is very important in the context in which personal law operates. Or perhaps it should be put this way: using the concept of rights in a particular way helps in the understanding and exposition of an approach to the application of personal law which I would wish to defend. The approach is one which both promotes and appropriately limits the different interests which are affected by personal law. Above all, it provides pathways by which power can be more appropriately distributed within the population. But before I can start the attempt, I must set out the particular way I propose that the concept of rights should be understood. It must be stressed that at this stage my concern is with the *structure* of claims about rights, not their content: not with what rights people should have, but with the kind of claim that is made when people claim them, and hence what is implied by recognizing claims as rights.

The central case of rights

The understanding of rights I will set out must take its place alongside many others. It is not intended to be a useful way of analysing *legal* rights. Such analyses, which usually take as their starting point the work of Wesley Newcombe Hohfeld,[6] are helpful in assisting more precise understanding of legal relationships. But their range is narrow, and can lead to extreme reductive outcomes, such as Albert Kocourek's conclusion that legal rights ultimately boil down to powers to initiate legal proceedings,[7] or Herbert Hart's formulation that a legal right exists when there is a legal system, under whose rules

---

[5] Sir John Laws, 'Beyond Rights' (2003) 23 *Oxford Journal of Legal Studies* 265.

[6] WN Hohfeld, *Fundamental Legal Conceptions as Applied in Judicial Reasoning* (Yale University Press, 1923).

[7] A Kocourek, *Jural Relations* (Bobbs Merrill, 1927).

some person is obliged to do or abstain from action and this is made by law dependent on the choice or authorization of another.[8] Even Ronald Dworkin, who broke down conceptual distinctions between legal and moral sources of law, in his early work advanced the disappointing proposition that it was only after a court had weighed up all the consequences of the possible decisions available to it, and made its choice between them, that it could be said that the successful litigant had a 'right' to its decision.[9] This idea of having a right is much more restricted than the 'right to moral independence' for which Dworkin later argued.[10] My concern will be with the idea of rights in this second, wider, sense.

It is useful to distinguish between two senses in which it can be said that a person 'has' a right. One sense is where we say (for example) that slaves in ancient times 'had' rights even in a world which did not recognize them. There the appeal is to a contemporary moral principle believed to be of universal value, holding even in societies, or a whole world, remote from ours for which the principle may be foreign. I call this a 'weak' sense of the usage, for in its fullest sense saying that someone 'has' a right is not simply to state a moral proposition: the whole point is to bring about social action. This of course cannot be done for times gone by. Similarly, to say that someone who does not want a particular outcome 'has' a right to it is also to use it in a weak sense, for such a person is not likely to seek to bring about the change, or is likely to resist it. A claim to a right is about the way power is distributed in society: normally it is a call for its *redistribution* in some way. Hence the stronger the claim of right and the greater the degree of social recognition the claim receives, the stronger the sense in which it can be said that the claimant 'has' the right. It is perhaps at its strongest when the right is incorporated in legal or social instruments.

But what is recognized, or claimed, in the case of rights? Joseph Raz gives a clear answer, which is widely accepted: 'Rights themselves are

---

[8] 'Definition and Theory in Jurisprudence' (1953), re-published as ch 1 in HLA Hart, *Essays in Jurisprudence and Philosophy* (Oxford University Press, 1983). Later Hart examined a much wider concept of rights in 'Are There Any Natural Rights?' (1955, re-published in J Waldron (ed), *Theories of Rights* (Oxford University Press, 1984) ch 4.

[9] R Dworkin, *Taking Rights Seriously* (Duckworth, 1977) 303–5.

[10] R Dworkin, 'Do We Have a Right to Pornography?' (1981) 1 *Oxford Journal of Legal Studies* 177.

grounds for holding others to be duty bound to protect or promote certain interests of the right-holder.'[11] There are, however, difficulties with this encapsulation. It is not obvious that what constitutes the right are the *grounds* (reasons) for imposing duties rather than the state of affairs the claimant seeks to achieve (eg an interest like good health), or even the actions or abstentions of others designed to achieve or protect that interest for which there are grounds for holding others bound to bring about. I have called the results of such actions or abstentions 'end-states'.[12] The end-state may be the interest to be protected, or the act or abstention necessary to achieve it. It seems better to see rights as being a *complex amalgam comprising a claim of entitlement to an end-state necessary to protect an interest and an implication that the interest possesses sufficient weight to impose a duty to activate the means contemplated to achieve the necessary protection.*[13] Each of these elements itself requires elucidation. They will therefore be considered in more detail.

End-states

Famously, Neil MacCormick claimed that rights must be seen as protecting interests rather than giving effect to expressions of will, because if we thought about rights in the second way, very young children could not have rights, since they are incapable of exercising choice.[14] This seems reasonable, until we consider the position of people who *can* articulate their interests. Formulations of rights in terms of 'interests' are notably reticent in stating *how* the right holder's interests are constructed, and by whom. MacCormick, for example, wrote that 'to ascribe to all members of a class *C* a right to treatment

---

[11] J Raz, *The Morality of Freedom* (Clarendon Press, 1986) 44.

[12] What follows is a summary of a more detailed exposition of the concept of rights made in the context of advancing a theory of human rights. J Eekelaar, 'Invoking Human Rights' in T Endicott, J Getzler, and E Peel (eds), *Properties of Law: Essays in Honour of Jim Harris* (Oxford University Press, 2006) ch 16.

[13] This formulation derives from 'claim' theories of rights, such as that of Joel Feinberg (see J Feinberg, *Rights, Justice and the Bounds of Liberty: Essays in Social Philosophy*, University of Princeton Press, 1980, 143–55), presented fully in J Eekelaar, 'The Importance of Thinking that Children Have Rights' (1992) 6 *International Journal of Law and the Family* 221.

[14] N MacCormick, 'Children's Rights: A Test Case for Theories of Rights' in N MacCormick, *Legal Right and Social Democracy* (Clarendon Press, 1982) ch 8; see also Goodin and Gibson, n 3.

T is to presuppose that *T* is in all normal circumstances a good for every member of C, and that *T* is a good which it would be wrong to withhold from any member of C.'[15] What was important for him was that the good of the rightholders was seen as an end in itself, and not a means to advance other people's projects. He seemed content that the presupposition might be made by people with de facto power over others, for, while he thought people should be free to waive their rights so determined, he insisted that this power was merely 'ancillary' to the existence of the right.

The interests must surely be in some way beneficial to the right holder, or allow the right holder to perform some function more efficiently. But what is beneficial or efficient can be very subjective. Are we to allow some people to define the interests of others, ignoring the way those others do in fact articulate their interests, and label these as rights? If I (and likeminded academic commentators) agree that certain interests of certain people justified requiring certain actions to be taken regarding them even though those people did not see their interests in the same way, we could still refer to them as holding rights in a weak sense. But strong rights imply social recognition and demand social and institutional action designed to produce end-states which can change people's lives. It is not enough simply to say that the action is what well-meaning people have decided should be done. If this were so, powerful social actors could proclaim what they deem to be in the interests of others, establish institutional mechanisms for promoting or protecting those interests, and claim to be protecting the rights of those others, whether or not the others approved or even knew that their interests were being constructed in that way. If that were so, the language of rights would be nothing other than a ruse for the assertion of power over others.

It is true that many rights socially recognized through international instruments and legal decisions are probably unknown to large populations. Sometimes the rights are said to be inalienable. But, even though people may not constantly articulate claims to these rights, even to themselves, many of these proclaimed rights can be viewed as rights in the strongest sense because they specify interests or end-states which it can safely be assumed anyone would want protected: conditions such as freedom from torture, provision of education and health

---

[15] MacCormick, n 14, 161.

care, and freedom of speech and to practise their religion.[16] In the
same way we can speak of unconscious people, or very young children, as having rights in the strong sense even if they are not capable
of articulating them. They refer to protection of interests which the
claimant perceives or can reasonably be assumed to perceive, as an
element of his or her well-being. *This upholds the centrality to this
view of rights that the interests protected must be defined from the viewpoint of the right holders.*

This reflects the value of autonomy. While no one can be completely unaffected by the society in which they live, the extent to which
people are deprived of scope to determine what is of value to them
affects their autonomy. Joseph Raz's statements that 'significantly
autonomous agents are part creators of their own moral world' and
that 'people's well-being is promoted by having an autonomous life'[17]
are judgements of value. A society can be imagined whose members
consider that autonomous self-determination is deemed to be in no
one's interests. But such a society would not be an open society. It
is a precondition for an open society that the exercise of autonomy
by an agent is assumed to be in that agent's interests, and it is a precondition of believing that people have rights to hold that they have
a right to achieve competence and articulate their own self-interest.
For surely if people are prevented from formulating what is in their
interests, they lose much of their humanity. It then becomes possible
to regard an actual claim by such an agent to entitlement to exercise
that autonomy as a claim to a right in the strong sense.

As a corollary, if the evidence were to show that people con-
sciously repudiated an alleged interest, its protection could not be
said to be in furtherance of their rights. These would be rights only
in a minimal, weak sense, lacking the force of articulated rights-
claims. This does not mean that people could never waive a right.
But whereas MacCormick considered a waiver to be 'ancillary' to

---

[16] It follows that where in a specific case an individual rejects the perception of
their interest represented by a right, they must be allowed to do so. So when Diane
Pretty sought legal permission to be assisted in her suicide when her disease made her
life unbearable, and failed, it seems perverse to see this outcome as an enforcement
of *her* right to life. The outcome must have *diminished* the total sum of her rights. See
Pretty v United Kingdom (2002) 35 EHRR 1.

[17] Raz, n 11, 154, 191. For excellent discussions of the value of autonomy, see KA
Appiah, *The Ethics of Identity* (Princeton University Press, 2005) ch 2, and F Ahmed,
Religious Freedom under the Personal Law System (Oxford University Press, 2016) ch 3.

the existence of the right, on the view taken here, the choice whether to claim an end-state or not is the core of the right. As I have written before, 'if individuals were compelled to live, marry, vote etc against their will, these would not be rights but duties. But they are rights because they may be chosen. Choice implies the possibility of rejection.'[18] Hence, the central case of rights advanced here is premised on the capacity of the individual to have a genuine appreciation of his or her goals: it is assumed that the individual is fully competent to make the choice and acting in conditions of freedom (the unconscious or non-competent can be included if the process of imputation described earlier can reasonably apply). If talking about people having rights is to have any force at all, we must believe they have a right to be freed from oppression and to achieve competence as far as possible so that they can comprehend and articulate their own self-interest. That is consistent with what Hart appeared to argue when he stated that 'in the case of special rights as well as of general rights, recognition of them implies the recognition of the equal right of all men to be free.'[19] In so far as competence and freedom are always imperfectly achieved, then rights are correspondingly less fully realized.

It is also necessary to emphasize that, while the recognition of claims as rights in the full sense implies accepting individuals' capacity to define their own self-interest, and thus is consistent with the goal of enhancing individual 'empowerment', it in no way implies a society where individuals are left to fend for themselves without state support, nor that their interests are not normally instantiated through personal relationships. To the contrary, it demands support, including by the state,[20] of all, especially the vulnerable, in achieving their well-being as understood according to the 'capability' approach, in which, as Amartya Sen puts it, the focus is on enhancing 'the freedom that a person actually has to do this or that—things that he or she may value doing or being.'[21] In itself, the approach recommends no specific policies, but provides a critique for such policies focusing on

---

[18] Eekelaar, n 13, 226–7.

[19] Hart, 'Are There Any Natural Rights?', n 8, 90.

[20] See M Eichner, *The Supportive State: Families, Government and America's Political Ideals* (Oxford University Press, 2010).

[21] A Sen, *The Idea of Justice* (The Belknap Press of Harvard University Press, 2009) 231–2. See M Nussbaum, *Women and Human Development: The Capabilities Approach* (Cambridge University Press, 2000). For discussion of 'relational' rights, see pp 166–7.

individual opportunities. It therefore *presupposes* a moral system in the same way as Hart showed that claims to legal rights presuppose the existence of a legal system.[22] The moral system will fashion the values that individuals hold and it is the task of that system to promote virtuous values. It is therefore evident that the present account of rights does not in itself tell us what rights people should have. It is simply an account of the structure of claims to rights. The strength of rights claims is that, like legal cases in common law systems, they focus on fact situations which apply, interpret and, often, extend the *application* of moral principles through the extension of duties. Such accretions can be strongly contested, of course, as the history of rights claims shows. But the overall result is the expansion of the scope of obligations.[23]

The social base

Claims of right are claims for the distribution of power as a matter of entitlement. They must therefore be supported by justificatory reasons. I will call the first element of this justification the *social base* for the right. It is a consequence of the fact that claims to entitlement must be generalizable. Hence if a person claims that they are morally entitled to a specific end-state, they are committed to holding that any other person experiencing a relevantly similar position will be entitled to it too. In this sense, entitlement includes the fundamental principle of justice that like cases must be treated the same way. The position will characteristically be some social category, event, condition, or activity with which the claimant identifies and which the claimant claims to ground an entitlement. Victims, prisoners, patients, fathers, and so on are obvious examples. This important implication is much neglected in contemporary rights analyses. Indeed, the failure to recognize it accounts for the misleading picture of the nature of rights expressed by all those who seem to view rights discourse as a manifestation of selfish individualism.[24] In fact, recognition of claims to

---

[22] Hart, 'Definition and Theory in Jurisprudence', n 8.

[23] This explains why the rhetoric of rights appears to be most important in circumstances where the right is threatened or contested. See J Donnelly, *Universal Human Rights in Law and Practice* (Cornell University Press, 1989).

[24] See Glendon, n 4, ch 3.

rights is an inclusive exercise more characteristically associated with assertions of sectional interests.

Weight

The second element to be considered as a ground for entitlement is whether the claim is strong enough to impose an obligation. This is an evaluative and empirical matter. Since the claim is that social action should be taken, its strength will depend on an evaluation of its importance in the context of other claims, resources, and other social demands. Certain disability rights (such as for access to buildings) may be an example.

In assessing the weight of an interest it is important to remember that the claim is to an end-state which the claimant perceives as an element of his or her well-being. Is it possible to evaluate the importance of various end-states to the well-being of different claimants? The concept of rights in itself cannot generate measures for assessing the relative weights of different interests. But that does not mean that there can be no standard against which rights claims can be measured. We could assess the impact they have on an individual's life. It is normally more important for someone to attend a job interview than that another should attend a sporting event, so while both may be claimed as rights in some contexts, if only one can be achieved, the former should be chosen. The decision about with whom a child should live is more important to the child than it is for either adult who disputes it because of the potential long-term effects on the child's life. A woman's decision about whom she wishes to marry is more important to her than it is to any of her family members.

The weight of the justification may also be related to the extent to which the exercise of the right is bound up with responsibilities. There is no *necessary* linkage between rights and responsibilities of this kind. It is conceptually possible to claim a right, and indeed to have one, without undertaking any corresponding responsibility. Rights to humane treatment are perhaps of this kind: claiming such rights necessarily implies recognizing the rights of others to humane treatment, but does not necessarily imply that you owe any other duties to those you expect to act humanely towards you. The rights not to suffer violence, or to be afforded freedom of marriage, demand no payment in return, other than recognition of the same rights in others. To link children's rights with responsibilities imposed on them could be highly oppressive.[25] However, though there is no *necessary* linkage, such a linkage may be important. One could characterize the rights, claimed by men over their wives, of fidelity and domestic subservience through traditional marriage law and custom as being part of a compact under which husbands, in return, undertook to provide lifelong economic support to their wives. Of course such rights expressed a patriarchal system of domination. But consider what the position would have been if husbands undertook no such reciprocal responsibility. Such linkages, then, may play an important part in the grounds for justification of rights. Even such claims as those for economic well-being and good environmental standards raise issues of the responsibility of the claimant, among others, towards achieving those goals. This is, therefore, another way in which rights-discourse promotes community morality.

HUMAN RIGHTS

A claim that a right is a human right is best understood in the same terms as explained above for all rights claims, except that the social base is the whole of humanity: that is, the claimant claims to be entitled by virtue of his or her identification with the human race. Such an approach avoids unsatisfactory attempts to define, a priori, certain features as being essential to human well-being.[26] This is not just a theoretical matter, for if anyone claims to be owed an end-state because they are human, then they must believe all human beings have the same entitlement as they are claiming.

But that establishes human rights only in the weak sense. They become rights in the strong sense to the extent that they are claimed, or can reasonably be assumed to be claimed, also by others, and the claims are recognized. There is much discussion whether human rights initiatives represent a project to impose 'western' values globally. The need for the subjects of the rights themselves to claim their

---

[25] A James, 'Responsibility, Children and Childhood' in J Bridgeman, C Lind, and H Keating (eds), *Responsibility, Law and the Family* (Ashgate/Routledge, 2008) ch 8.

[26] See J Eekelaar, 'Naturalism or Pragmatism? Towards an Expansive View of Human Rights' (2011) 10 *Journal of Human Rights* 230.

protection if the right is to possess the character of a 'strong' right responds to this view, although it is important that there should be freedom to make such claims. This focus on individuals is important for dialogue about human rights. Kwame Appiah has commented on the difficulty of conducting such dialogue internationally in terms only of principle. 'It isn't principle that brings the missionary doctor and the distressed mother together at the bedside of a mother of a child with cholera: it is a shared concern for this particular child.'[27] So human rights spring from a response to specific, local, issues involving the well-being of individuals, and recognition of these as being the common experience of mankind.[28]

Such recognition should lead to practical action, as is often observed in the works of international organizations, and, legally, through international human rights instruments. Of course, not all international instruments purport to deal with rights which it is believed everyone in similar circumstances would claim, but are specific to certain nations: for example, the European Council Regulation concerning recognition and enforcement of child custody decisions in the European Union.[29] There is, however, a tendency for cross-fertilization between bodies which interpret and apply specific human rights instruments, such as the ECHR, and those of specific jurisdictions like Canada, India, South Africa, New Zealand, and the United States,[30] which supports the view that the belief that a right is a human right implies belief that it is something everyone is entitled to claim.

How such rights are protected is a matter of governance. They may only create obligations for the state under international law, breach of which could entail censure by international institutions, but not confer rights on individuals that are directly enforceable against the state,

---

[27] Appiah, n 17, 256.

[28] See M Freeman, 'Human Rights, Children's Rights and Judgment: Some Thoughts on Reconciling Universality and Pluralism' (2002) 10 *International Journal of Children's Rights* 345; J Eekelaar, 'Law, Culture, Values' in A Diduck, N Peleg, and H Reece (eds), *Law in Society: Reflections on Children, Family, Culture and Philosophy: Essays in Honour of Michael Freeman* (Brill, 2015), ch 2.

[29] Council Regulation (EC) No 2201/2003, known as Brussels IIA.

[30] See C McCrudden, 'Using Comparative Reasoning in Human Rights Adjudication: the Court of Justice of the EU and the European Court of Human Rights Compared' (2012–13) 15 *Cambridge Yearbook of European Legal Studies* 383; S Fredman, 'Foreign Fads or Fashions: The Role of Comparativism in Human Rights Law' (2015) 64 *International and Comparative Law Quarterly* 631.

except in so far as the domestic judiciary chooses to have regard to them when applying domestic law. CEDAW and the UNCRC operate in this way with respect to the United Kingdom. The ECHR operated in this way until October 2000 when it was incorporated into UK law by virtue of the Human Rights Act 1998.

DEVELOPMENT OF CLAIMS OF RIGHTS IN PERSONAL LAW

I now turn to an account of some of the ways in which rights have been used in personal law to protect the interests of individuals in the area of personal law, sometimes to counteract the power structures described earlier but also in attempts to provide a balance in inter-personal relations.

Rights claimed through political action

During much of the nineteenth and twentieth centuries married women struggled to achieve greater social recognition of their interests and corresponding restraints on the power of others over them: that is, for rights. This is a classic instance of claims for rights. For example, in the 1880s 150 petitions with 15,000 signatories were presented to Parliament in the attempt by women to achieve equal rights with their husbands with respect to their children. This was not so much about keeping the child after divorce or separation (welfarist nineteenth-century thinking had modified the strong rights of the father in that regard, at least in the case of children of 'tender years') but the 'right' of mothers to make decisions about their children during the marriage. The common law ascribed this power to husbands alone. The effort was defeated because it was believed that there should not be 'duality of control' over the family. The rights claimants were bought off by the welfarist provision in the Guardianship of Infants Act 1886 which required a court dealing with disputes over a child's upbringing to have regard to the wishes of the mother as well as of the father, 'having regard to the welfare of the Infant'.[31]

---

[31] See S Maidment, *Child Custody and Divorce* (Croom Helm, 1984) 126–7.

The battle was fought all over again in the 1920s by individual activists (in particular, members of the National Union for Societies for Equal Citizenship: NUSEC), and was again defeated, for the same reason.[32] This time the activists had to be content with an amendment to the 1886 welfarist provision, which now required the court to regard the child's welfare as the 'first and paramount consideration', and that it 'should not take into consideration whether from any other point of view the claim of the father was superior to that of the mother or the claim of the mother was superior to that of the father'.[33] Formal equality was achieved only in 1973.[34] Similar campaigns were undertaken to secure independent property rights for married women, partially achieved by the Married Women's Property Acts of 1870 and 1882,[35] and more specialist lobbying improved the legal protection for victims (mostly women) of domestic violence in the Domestic Violence and Matrimonial Proceedings Act 1976, Domestic Proceedings and Magistrates' Courts Act 1978, and Family Law Act 1996, Part IV[36] and, later, the Serious Crime Act 2015, section 76 of which extends its definition to controlling and coercive behaviour.

In the 1970s it was the turn of married men to become seriously concerned about their rights. This was because in January 1971, when the reformed divorce law came into effect, statute embedded the principle, which had only fleetingly appeared in the cases, that the courts' purpose in dealing with financial consequences of divorce was to try, as far as possible and just, to keep the parties in the position in which they would have been if the marriage continued (sometimes called the 'minimal loss' principle). At the same time the courts acquired extensive new powers to order husbands to transfer their capital to their former wives on divorce.[37] This could include their entire interest in the matrimonial home. It seems that, when recommending this power, the Law Commission did not appreciate its significance. Women, who previously would have had to leave the home on divorce, now had the chance of staying in it (usually with the children). Between 1971 and

---

[32] See S Cretney, *Family Law in the Twentieth Century: A History* (Oxford University Press, 2003) ch 16.

[33] Guardianship of Infants Act 1925, s 1.   [34] Guardianship Act 1973, s 1.

[35] See the account in Cretney, n 32, ch 3.   [36] Cretney, n 32, 752–6.

[37] By the Matrimonial Proceedings and Property Act 1970; subsequently consolidated in the Matrimonial Causes Act 1973, s 24.

1981 the total number of divorce petitions increased by 53.6 per cent; but the increase in petitions by wives was by 85.5 per cent, and by husbands only 5.5 per cent.

It seems that the new power had the effect of giving wives the same freedom to divorce as men had enjoyed earlier, and therefore significantly enhanced the ability of women to exercise their right to divorce. However, in 1978 the Campaign for Justice in Divorce was established to enhance the rights of divorced husbands and their new partners. It was partly rewarded by the Matrimonial and Family Proceedings Act 1984, which repealed the 'minimal loss' principle and encouraged courts to make 'clean break' orders which would eliminate, or at least greatly reduce, the period of time for which a divorced husband could be required to support his former wife.

Later, the focus of male campaigners shifted to a perceived failure of the courts to sustain contact between fathers and their children after parental separation. The movement had started as far back as 1974 when Families Need Fathers was established, but achieved high political profile later through publicity stunts supported by Fathers4Justice. Although both these bodies expressed a commitment to the welfare of the child, they (especially the latter) heavily employed the rhetoric of rights. The articulation of a sectional interest rises to a howl from Bob Geldof: 'A huge emptiness would well in my stomach, a deep loathing of those who would deign to tell me they would ALLOW me ACCESS to my children—those I loved above all, those I created, those who gave meaning to everything I did, those that were the very best of us two and the absolute physical manifestation of our once blinding love. Who the fuck are they that they should ALLOW anything?'[38] Geldof, like others claiming these rights, insisted that there should be a presumption that children should share their time equally between separated parents. This is clearly a claim about justice between the parents, similar to one which was emerging regarding the distribution of property between divorced partners.

How these claims for rights have been accommodated in personal law is considered in later chapters.[39]

---

[38] Bob Geldof, 'The Real Love that Dare Not Speak Its Name' in A Bainham, B Lindley, M Richards, and L Trinder (eds), *Children and Their Families: Contact, Rights and Welfare* (Hart Publishing, 2003) 175, emphases in original.

[39] See pp 108–9, 129–32.

Rights developed through judicial lawmaking

People do not only claim rights through the political process. They also do so through litigation. Perhaps the most dramatic example of this in personal law was the judicial removal of a husband's former immunity from prosecution for the rape of his wife by the Scottish High Court of Judiciary in *S v HM Advocate* in 1989.[40] The court stated:

> By the second half of the 20th century ... the status of women, and the status of a married woman, in our law have changed quite dramatically ... A live system of law will always have regard to changing circumstances to test the justification for any exception to the application of a general rule ... It cannot be affirmed nowadays, whatever the position may have been in earlier centuries, that it is an incident of modern marriage that a wife consents to intercourse in all circumstances, including sexual intercourse obtained only by force.

In the 1950s and 1960s married women found a champion in Lord Denning, who asserted, perhaps created, a right which allowed a deserted wife to remain in occupation of the matrimonial home, even if it belonged to her husband, and even if he had disposed of his interest to a third party.[41] Lord Denning also promoted the view that a wife could acquire a share of her husband's property through looking after the home, so that, if the couple separated, she should be allocated the share she had acquired in that way.[42] This last doctrine would, of course, have effectively anticipated the powers the courts eventually acquired by statute only in 1971 to order the transfer of property between people who divorce, and it is not surprising that the House of Lords rejected it in 1970.[43] After 1971 the courts operated within the framework of the Matrimonial Causes Act (consolidated in 1973). In the Court of Appeal, Lord Justice Ormrod favoured a strongly welfarist approach. He was unwilling to hold wives to agreements they had reached during negotiations,[44] and felt that it should always be possible for them to return to court after an order was made to ask the

---

[40] 1989 SLT 469, 473. This was cited, and followed, by the House of Lords in *R v R* [1991] UKHL 12.
[41] *Bendall v McWhirter* [1952] 2 QB 466.
[42] *Rimmer v Rimmer* [1953] 1 QB 63.   [43] *Pettitt v Pettitt* [1970] AC 777.
[44] *Camm v Camm* (1982) 4 FLR 577; other judges took a more robust line: *Edgar v Edgar* [1980] 3 All ER 887.

court to vary an agreed order if circumstances changed.[45] Later courts were stricter in holding parties to their negotiated agreements,[46] and the 1984 reforms, mentioned earlier, allowed courts to make it difficult for wives to keep extending orders beyond their initial duration. But most significantly, Lord Justice Ormrod 'rephrased' the statutory duty on the courts to take into consideration (among other things) the parties' 'financial needs' with the expression 'reasonable requirements', believing that this allowed the courts to order the husband to meet a wider range of expenses.[47]

As it turned out, this invitation to courts to evaluate a former wife's 'reasonable requirements', made at the culmination of the welfarist era, and intended to lead to more generous orders for wives, in fact opened the way for courts to make wide-ranging judgements about the lifestyle which a divorced wife could reasonably expect to lead, and to assess her moral desert in the light of her activities during marriage, including such matters as entertaining and cooking skills.[48] There was an uncomfortable air of paternalism about a male-dominated judiciary deciding how wives should, or should not, be rewarded at the termination of their marriages, particularly as the courts maintained their view that a married person should not be allocated any part of the business assets of their partner if they had not worked in the business or contributed directly to it.

The reaction came in 2000, when, in *White v White*,[49] the House of Lords repudiated Lord Justice Ormrod's gloss on the statutory text. The wife's needs which the courts were to take into account in deciding how much to order the husband to pay were to be narrowly understood. Once these were dealt with, the issue became one of deciding whether one partner had 'earned' a share in the assets of the other. If they had, then they would be entitled to it, even if it gave them more than their 'reasonable requirements' demanded. This can be called the 'earned share' principle. As Coleridge J said in one case regarding the

[45] *Dipper v Dipper* [1981] Fam 31. This was made much more difficult after the Matrimonial and Family Proceedings Act 1984.

[46] *Xydias v Xydias* [1999] 2 All ER 386, building on *Edgar v Edgar* [1980] 3 All ER 887. See now *Radmacher v Granatino* [2010] UKSC 42.

[47] *O'Donnell v O'Donnell* [1976] Fam 83.

[48] *F v F* [1995] 2 FLR 45; *A v A* [1998] 2 FLR 180.

[49] [2001] 1 AC 596. Alison Diduck describes this change in a detailed examination of the cases over this period in A Diduck, 'What is Family Law for?' (2011) 64 *Current Legal Problems* 287.

awards he would make: 'She has earned it ... so has he.'[50] Furthermore, there would need to be reasons why the sharing should not be equal. So an elderly person with a limited life expectancy after a long marriage could be awarded far more than they could be expected to need to keep them comfortable for the remainder of their life. It was like an entitlement to property: what they did with it was their business. This moves from the weaker sense of having a right under welfarism to a stronger form. For the right under welfarism is only to what another deems that you need, and depends on whether you have conducted yourself properly. The new kind of right reflects the claim people make for just reward for what they have earned. The theoretical basis for making awards on divorce is explored further in chapter 4.[51]

The influence of human rights

While the courts developed certain personal rights through the evolution of the common law and statutory interpretation, as when in 1999 the House of Lords accepted that same-sex partners could be considered a 'family' for certain purposes on the basis of changed social attitudes,[52] human rights instruments, particularly the ECHR, which was incorporated into UK law in 2000 as a result of the Human Rights Act 1998, have provided a significant additional source for personal rights. The proclamations of the Convention most relevant to personal law are that:

1. no one shall be subject to torture or to inhuman or degrading treatment or punishment (Article 3);

2. everyone has the right to respect for his private and family life, his home and his correspondence (Article 8); and

3. men and women of marriageable age have the right to marry and to found a family, according to the national laws governing the exercise of this right (Article 12);

4. (these rights shall be enjoyed) without discrimination on any ground such as sex (which includes sexual orientation[53]), race, colour, language, religion, political or other opinion, national or social origin, association with a national minority, property, birth or other status (Article 14).

---

[50] *RP v RP* [2006] EWHC 3409 (Fam) para 63.   [51] See pp 108–12.
[52] *Fitzpatrick v Sterling Housing Association Ltd* [1999] 3 All ER 705.
[53] *Da Silva Mouta v Portugal* (2001) EHRR 41; *Karner v Austria* (2004) 38 EHRR 24.

Although phrased in terms of a right, the second of these proclamations can perhaps more easily be seen as a statement of background
value, from which concrete rights can be extracted as a consequence
of a judgement involving application of that value in the context of
other values which are set out in Article 8(2), namely national security, public safety, or national economic well-being; prevention of disorder or crime; protection of health or morals; or the protection of the
rights and freedoms of others. They all involve claims which people
actually make or can be assumed to wish to make. These claims are
mediated through the judiciary. While the courts cannot 'strike down'
legislation that is inconsistent with these rights, they must interpret
legislation, where possible, consistently with them and if not they may
make a 'declaration of incompatibility'.[54]

This has the potential of bringing about significant restructuring of
some aspects of personal law, of which the following are a few examples. If an individual's private or family life, or their home, is in issue,
the court will have to give that interest proper weight in applying the
law. So in *Ghaidan v Godin-Mendoza*,[55] the House of Lords interpreted
the phrase 'living together as husband and wife' in legislation concerning the succession of protected tenancies as applying to a same-sex
couple because not to have done so would have been to have discriminated against the claimant with respect to his 'home' on the ground
solely of sexual orientation, contrary to Articles 8 and 14 of the ECHR.
Some decisions of the European Court of Human Rights led directly to
Parliamentary action, such as *Campbell and Cosans v United Kingdom*
(1982)[56] which led to the highly controversial[57] total prohibition of
corporal punishment in state-funded schools in the Education (No 2)

---

[54] Human Rights Act 1998, ss 3, 4, and 10.   [55] [2004] 2 AC 557.
[56] App No 7511/76, judgment 25 February 1982.
[57] The measure passed the House of Commons by a single vote: see HC Deb, 22
July 1986, vol 102, cols 226–78. When in 1978 the European Court held that birching
a child for a criminal offence violated the child's Article 3 rights, the British judge,
Sir Gerald Fitzmaurice, dissented, saying: 'I have to admit that my own view may be
coloured by the fact that I was brought up and educated under a system according to
which the corporal punishment of schoolboys (sometimes at the hands of the sen-
ior ones—prefects or monitors—sometimes by masters) was regarded as the normal
sanction for serious misbehaviour, and even sometimes for what was much less serious … They also not infrequently took place under conditions of far greater intrinsic
humiliation than in (this) case. Yet I cannot remember that any boy felt degraded or
debased': *Tyrer v United Kingdom* App No 555856/72, judgment 25 April 1978, para
12 of the dissent.

Act 1986, and *A v United Kingdom*,[58] where the European Court of Human Rights decision that the acquittal of an adult who had used corporal punishment on a child on the basis of the defence of 'reasonable chastisement' infringed the child's Article 3 protection against 'inhuman or degrading punishment' resulted in section 58 of the Children Act 2004, which limited the defence of reasonable chastisement to prosecutions for common assault. This, however, remains inconsistent with the UNCRC,[59] despite the United Kingdom having ratified that Convention. Although, unlike the ECHR, it has not been incorporated into UK law, some judges think that the UNCRC could have legal force in the United Kingdom, either simply because the United Kingdom has ratified it, or because aspects of that Convention (in particular the 'best interests' principle of Article 3) have been imported by the European Court of Human Rights into the way the ECHR's right to family and private life is applied.[60]

The cardinal principles that any interference that engages Article 8 rights must be 'proportionate', that permanent removal of a child from parents, or even family, requires strong justification,[61] and that when children are removed from their parents, welfare services must seek family reunification where appropriate[62] are now becoming embedded in judicial reasoning.[63] The Gender Recognition Act 2004 also followed a European Court of Human Rights decision that the inability to have a change in sexual identity legally recognized breached the applicant's rights under Articles 8 and 12.[64] The right

---

[58] (1999) 27 EHRR 611.

[59] See Committee on the Rights of the Child: Forty-ninth session: Consideration of Reports submitted by States Parties under Article 44 of the Convention: Concluding Observations: United Kingdom of Great Britain and Northern Ireland, CRC/C/GBR/CO/4, 20 October 2008, para 40.

[60] See *R (on the Application of SG) v Secretary of State for Work and Pensions* [2015] UKSC 16.

[61] *Johansen v Norway* (1996) 23 EHRR 33, *K and T v Finland* (2001) 36 EHRR 18, *R and H v United Kingdom* (2012) 54 EHRR 2, and *YC v United Kingdom* (2012) 55 EHRR 33.

[62] *KA v Finland* [2003] 1 FLR 696.

[63] J Eekelaar and M Maclean, *Family Justice: The Work of Family Judges in Uncertain Times* (Hart Publishing, 2013) 149. *Re B (Care Proceedings: Appeal)* [2013] UKSC 33; *re B-S (adoption: leave to oppose)* [2013] EWCA Civ 1146. See B Sloan, 'Adoption Decisions in England: *Re B (A Child) (Care Proceedings: Appeal)* and Beyond' (2015) 37 *Journal of Social Welfare and Family Law* 437.

[64] *Christine Goodwin v United Kingdom* App No 28957/95, judgment 11 July 2002.

of a child to know his or her parentage has been more influenced by the UNCRC than the ECHR. Article 7 of the UNCRC provides 'that a child has, as far as possible, the right to know and be cared for by his or her parents'.[65] The Human Fertilisation Authority (Disclosure of Donor Information) Regulations 2004 give all children born after 1 April 2005 as a result of donation the opportunity to obtain identifying information about the egg or sperm donor, but only when they reach 18.[66]

However, neither the legislation for civil partnerships enacted in 2004 nor that for same-sex marriage, enacted in 2013,[67] was instigated in reaction to court decisions about human rights, but rather by a desire to avoid hardship and injustice and recognition of a right to equality that had long been asserted by campaign groups.[68] In fact it seems that, in 2004, the ECHR was not thought to require civil partnerships for same-sex couples to be introduced, though in 2015 the European Court of Human Rights changed its position on that as a result of the growing acceptance of civil partnerships in Europe, and because not to do so discriminated against them.[69] But it still did not think that there was a right to same-sex marriage under the Convention,[70] and in 2017 such marriages were constitutionally banned in ten European countries.[71] This history illustrates the dialogue that can occur between democratic developments and the principled application of human rights norms, which, it will be argued later in the chapter, is an important feature of the way such norms are developed.

---

[65] See B Sloan, 'Conflicting Rights: English Adoption Law and the Implementation of the UN Convention on the Rights of the Child' (2013) 25 *Child and Family Law Quarterly* 40.

[66] See pp 151–6.   [67] Marriage (Same Sex Couples) Act 2013.

[68] See J Eekelaar, 'Perceptions of Equality: The Road to Same-Sex Marriage in England' (2014) 28 *International Journal of Law, Policy and the Family* 1.

[69] *Oliari v Italy* App Nos 18766/11 and 36060/11, judgment 21 July 2015. It seems that if a state (like the UK) provides civil partnerships *and* marriage for same-sex couples, but marriage alone for opposite-sex couples, this would contravene the non-discrimination requirement of Article 14, as the Court of Appeal held in *Steinfeld and Keidan v Secretary of State for Education* [2017] EWCA Civ 81, although the Court (perhaps generously) held that this discrimination was justified for the moment while the government decided how best to resolve the issue.

[70] *Oliari v Italy*, n 69, para 192.

[71] See I Curry-Sumner, 'Same-Sex Relationships in a European Perspective' in JM Scherpe, *European Family Law*, vol III (Edward Elgar, 2016) ch 4.

In the United States, by contrast, reform was driven by judicial decisions. After the Supreme Court of Hawaii threatened to hold the exclusion of same-sex marriage unconstitutional in 1993,[72] a series of constitutional attempts to embed man–woman marriage in state constitutions followed, and a federal statute defined marriage for federal purposes as being only between a man and a woman and authorized states not to recognize same-sex marriages contracted in other states.[73] However in 2003, in *Goodridge v Department of Health*,[74] the Supreme Judicial Court of Massachusetts held that denial of marriage to same-sex couples infringed Article 1 of that state's Constitution, which requires that '[e]quality under the law shall not be denied or abridged because of sex, race, color, creed or national origin.' The court decided that there was no rational basis for confining marriage to opposite-sex couples. In 2015 the US Supreme Court, by a 5–4 majority, held that bans on same-sex marriage were unconstitutional[75] because the right to marry was protected by the Due Process and Equal Protection Clauses of the Fourteenth Amendment. The core of the difference between the majority and the dissentients was the view of the latter that this was a matter for elected legislatures, not the courts, Justice Scalia calling the majority decision a 'threat to American democracy'.[76]

Human rights and judicial power

As the remark of Justice Scalia indicates, some have objected to giving judges powers which can override, or seriously impede, legislative or government action and thus seem to remove or diminish the democratic rights of ordinary citizens to participate in the lawmaking process.[77] In considering this issue it is important to remember that, while emerging from specific social cultures, human rights standards are also partially autonomous from them. This is evident in

---

[72] *Baehr v Lewin* 74 Hawaii 530; 852 P 2d 44 (1993).
[73] Defense of Marriage Act 1996.
[74] 440 Mass 309; 798 NE 2d 941 (2003).
[75] *Obergefell v Hodges*, 576 US ___, 135 S Ct 2584, 2594 (2015).
[76] See SN Katz, *Family Law in America* (Oxford University Press, 2nd edn, 2015) Introduction and 54–7.
[77] There is extensive literature on this, notably J Waldron, *Law and Disagreement* (Oxford University Press, 1999) chs 10–13; R Dworkin, *Sovereign Virtue: The Theory and Practice of Equality* (Harvard University Press, 2000) ch 4; R Bellamy, *A Republican Defence of the Constitutionality of Democracy* (Cambridge University Press, 2007).

their appearance in so many international instruments and the 'cross-fertilization' between jurisdictions referred to earlier.[78] The influence of European Enlightenment writers on the formation of the US Bill of Rights is well known. Human rights standards possess a sufficient degree of 'externality' from individual political entities for them to be used as a critique for a culture and its laws.[79]

Yet can it not be said that interpretations of these standards often give rise to dispute, and that these can be resolved fairly only by giving equal weight to the views of all citizens, implying the need for majoritarian decisions rather than judicial resolution?[80] However, the normal democratic legislative process is usually more complex than through referendum, and we do not expect legislators elected through a democratic process always to use their powers, or refrain from using them, in the way desired by a majority of electors on a specific issue. To resolve human rights disputes only by referendum or a similar procedure would not only be impractical, but put at risk those groups whose human rights require protection from communal majorities. A more moderate position is that the resolution of such controversial issues revert to the legislators. But many disputes concern the actions of legislators and governments (which often control legislatures), so it would be futile for them to be constituted as adjudicators in their own cause. It would also lose the profoundly important feature that these values are relatively autonomous from the polity concerned.

The mechanism within which the resolution of such issues occurs should also be relatively autonomous from the political process, and must therefore allow for reflection, analysis, and consideration of evidence, a form of public reasoning which independent and uncorrupt courts have the best chance of providing.[81] However, citizens are not totally excluded from the forensic process because arguments of this kind are not conducted in a vacuum, free of influence from opinions expressed outside the courtroom, as the influence of legal developments in member states on the decisions of the European Court of Human Rights shows. In the United States, by the time *Obergefell* was

---

[78] See Fredman, n 30.

[79] This is why it is misguided to talk about a purely 'British' Bill of Rights as a replacement for more internationally accepted standards.

[80] See Waldron, n 77, 297; T Gyorfi, 'Between Common Law Constitutionalism and Procedural Democracy' (2013) 13 *Oxford Journal of Legal Studies* 317.

[81] For a similar argument, see D Kyritsis, 'Constitutional Review in Representative Democracy' (2012) 32 *Oxford Journal of Legal Studies* 297.

decided, thirty-six states had already legalized same-sex marriage[82] and public opinion was moving in favour of such recognition, especially among the young.[83]

Stephen Gardbaum has supported what he calls a 'new' model for protecting human rights through 'the twin mechanisms of judicial *and* political rights review of legislation, but with the legal power of the final word going to the politically accountable branch of government rather than the courts'.[84] This is the structure in the United Kingdom, where courts cannot set aside legislation, but may declare it incompatible with human rights provisions. The conflict is usually resolved through an iterative process, whereby the courts indicate in general terms what needs to be done if the rights of the claimants are to be satisfied, and Parliament, through the democratic process, brings the law into line with human rights standards, as was illustrated earlier. So, even if, as in the United Kingdom, conflicts between the courts and democratic representatives on human rights issues could ultimately be resolved by the latter, this should be a difficult and exceptional event, giving maximum opportunity for the public reasoning described earlier. It appears that in systems using this model it is indeed rare for the legislature to override a judicial decision on human rights.[85]

Without such a process *the dual claim people make to popular self-determination coupled with entitlement to laws which comply with explicit standards would have to be abandoned.* And it would be a great loss, because we should have learned to be very fearful of the unrestricted exercise of power in the name of popular self-determination.

Court decisions are not necessarily irreversible, and decisions on human rights provide a forum for reasoned debate, and an important sounding board by which to measure the extent to which democratic laws reflect values expressed in human rights instruments and satisfy human rights claims.

---

[82] J Zorthian, 'These Are the States Where SCOTUS Just Legalized Same-Sex Marriage', *Time*, 26 June 2015, http://time.com/3937662/gay-marriage-supreme-court-states-legal/ (accessed 13 June 2017).

[83] Pew Research Center, *Changing Attitudes on Gay Marriage*, 29 July 2015, http://www.pewforum.org/2015/07/29/graphics-slideshow-changing-attitudes-on-gay-marriage/.

[84] S Gardbaum, *The New Commonwealth Model of Constitutionalism: Theory and Practice* (Cambridge University Press, 2013) 2 (emphasis in original).

[85] See R Dixon, 'Weak-Form Judicial Review and American Exceptionalism' (2012) 32 *Oxford Journal of Legal Studies* 487.

Rights

CHILDREN'S RIGHTS AND THE 'BEST INTERESTS' (WELFARE) PRINCIPLE

Rights and welfare

Children's rights have the same structure as rights described earlier, namely as a claim of entitlement to an end-state necessary to protect an interest seen from the child's viewpoint and possessing sufficient weight to impose a duty to activate the means contemplated to achieve the necessary protection. But there are special features in the way the structure is applied. This is because, first, the Children Act 1989 demands that when a court determines any question with respect to the upbringing of a child 'the child's welfare shall be the court's paramount consideration', and the UNCRC that 'in all actions concerning children, whether undertaken by public or private social welfare institutions, courts of law, administrative bodies or legislative bodies, the best interests of the child shall be a primary consideration'.[86] Secondly, children may be too young to articulate a claim, or to do so with proper understanding of the relevant issues. Self-determination under a mistake is a cruel illusion.

The major constraints on children's competence to make the requisite claims are insufficient understanding of the workings of the world, instability in the child's appreciation of its own (at least medium term) life-goals, and the presence of excessive or improper pressure. In such circumstances decisions must be made in accordance with the 'best interests' principle. But does this mean that such children therefore have no rights? As we have seen,[87] Neil MacCormick thought the solution lay in equating children's rights with presuppositions about their interests, and from that concluded that *all* rights were suppositions about what was good for people. But another solution is to say that the rights of non-competent children are grounded not merely in suppositions about what is good for them, but in what it can reasonably be assumed a child would choose if fully competent. It can, for example, be reasonably assumed that children would want decisions to be made in their best interests and (following from this) that those interests be viewed *from their perspective*. In most cases the result

---

[86] Children Act 1989, s 1(1). UNCRC, Art 3. The Convention has some legal force in the UK: see n 59.

[87] MacCormick, n 14.

would be uncontroversial. This does not treat children differently from adults *just because they are children*. Adults with similar lack of capacity would be treated in the same way.

There is another consequence of this approach. Children of limited competence can be regarded always as *potential* right holders, in the strong sense. This means that, in deciding what is best for children, the child must be viewed as someone entitled to exercise autonomy and claim rights as soon as full competence is achieved. This is hardly a novel proposition. It is an aspect of autonomy that goes back at least as far as JS Mill.[88] It was advocated over thirty years ago by Joel Feinberg[89] and Michael Freeman.[90] I reformulated it about ten years later with the label 'dynamic self-determinism'.[91] The duty of a child's carers is to establish the most propitious environment in which the child will be able in due course to make a decision that is in accord with the personality growing within him or her. It is dynamic because it allows for revision of outcomes in accordance with the child's developing personality, and involves self-determination because of the scope given to the child to influence the outcome. Its operation involves a range of complex practical factors. This is indistinguishable from the 'capability' approach, described earlier.[92] Of course it doesn't expect a frantic process of seeking to involve a child in all possible influences and experiences, any more than it excludes respect for the rights of others and compliance with social duties, including receiving guidance and training, but does include openness of the child to a range of influences and opportunities appropriate to the child's age. For, in Amartya Sen's words: '[T]he idea of freedom also respects our being free to determine what we want, what we value and ultimately what we decide to choose. The concept of capability is thus linked closely with the opportunity aspects of freedom, seen in terms of

---

[88] See JS Mill, *On Liberty* (1865) especially ch 3.

[89] J Feinberg, 'The Nature and Value of Rights' in J Feinberg (ed), *Rights, Justice and the Bounds of Liberty: Essays in Social Philosophy* (Princeton University Press, 1980).

[90] M Freeman, *The Rights and Wrongs of Children* (Frances Pinter, 1983) 57.

[91] J Eekelaar, 'The Interests of the Child and the Child's Wishes: The Role of Dynamic Self-Determinism' in P Alston (ed), *The Best Interests of the Child: Reconciling Culture and Human Rights* (Oxford University Press, 1994) 54. See also F Kaganas and A Diduck, 'Changing Images of Post-Separation Children' (2004) 67 *Modern Law Review* 959.

[92] See Sen, n 21. See also N Peleg, 'Reconceptualising the Child's Right to Development: Children and the Capability Approach' (2013) 21 *International Journal of Children's Rights* 523.

"comprehensive" opportunities, and not just focusing on what happens at "culmination".[93]

This is a central feature of an open society, and, while assessments of children's interests and well-being need to be grounded in evidence and approached from the child's perspective, it should be assumed that it is in a child's interests to participate in an open society, and therefore not unduly cut off from other members of society, or from developing alternative identities. This approach could have been used in a case where the Court of Appeal decided to return a ten-year-old Zulu boy, who had been brought to England when he was six, to his parents in Soweto, South Africa, despite his vehement opposition to the move. The court thought it was his 'right' to be brought up in Zulu culture.[94] If he was not fully competent to make the decision, his current position could have been maintained, but in communication with his parents, until such time as visits would be possible and he would be in a position to decide where his future lay. In *re G (Children)*[95] Munby LJ endorsed this approach in a custody dispute where he found in favour of a mother who was proposing to send the children to a school that would have given them more opportunities to choose their own lifestyle than the education the father was proposing, saying that the objective must be 'to bring the child to adulthood in such a way that the child is best equipped both to decide what kind of life they want to lead—what kind of person they want to be—and to give effect as far as practicable to their aspirations'.

The 'best interests' principle (like welfarism generally) has been very beneficial for children. It developed a discourse which focused on children's interests, making it possible to move away from treating children as instruments of adults' interests. But, important though it was, it only made the move possible; it did not ensure it. For, like welfarism generally, as explained in the previous chapter,[96] it has its dark side. It might mean only defining the child's interests in such a way as to coincide with a favoured social structure. Recall

---

[93] Sen, n 21, 232.

[94] *M v M* [1996] 2 FLR 441. The child was returned to England after six months.

[95] [2012] EWCA Civ 1233, para 80. But a different result would be reached if this arrangement would be harmful to the children in other respects: *J v B and The Children* [2017] EWFC 4.

[96] See p 13.

the statement in *re Agar Ellis* in 1883 cited in chapter 1: 'When by birth a child is subject to a father, it is for the general interest of families, and for the general interest of children, and really for the interests of the particular infant, that the court should not, except in very extreme cases, interfere with the discretion of the father but leave him the responsibility of exercising the power which nature has given him by birth of the child.'[97] As recently as 1968 a judge authorized the severance of the relationship between a child and his father because the father was not married to the mother, and it was better for the child to become a 'respectable' member of society.[98] Helen Reece, citing earlier cases where courts were hostile to children being brought up by gay parents, argued that the principle was socially harmful as it contributed to entrenching dominant social attitudes.[99] Robert van Krieken goes as far as to say that a central characteristic of the welfare principle has been to operate as a 'code' or 'proxy' for 'other' concerns.[100]

The principle is also open to the opposite objection: that it is unfair to adults if it is applied in such a way that no one's interests except the child's are given any weight, which would be the case if the child's interests overrode all others. Yet a parent's relationship with a child is part of the parent's private and family life. Its value must therefore be reflected in the decision. The problem is magnified if the child's best interests are to be 'a primary consideration' not just in matters concerning the child's upbringing, but in 'all actions concerning children, whether undertaken by public or private social welfare institutions, courts of law, administrative authorities or legislative bodies' as required by Article 3 of the UNCRC. Must every decision be directed at achieving what someone in charge thinks is the very best for children who may be affected by it at the expense of other goals, such as public safety and economic development?

One way to resolve this is to draw a distinction between cases which can be characterized as being directly about a child (for example, with

---

[97]   *Re Agar-Ellis* (1883) 24 ChD 317, 334 (Cotton LJ).

[98]   *Re E (P) (An infant)* [1968] 1 WLR 1913. On the consequences of this attempt to uphold a social structure on mothers and children, see J Robinson, *In the Family Way: Illegitimacy between the Great War and the Swinging Sixties* (Viking, 2015).

[99]   H Reece, 'The Paramountcy Principle: Consensus or Construct?' (1996) 49 *Current Legal Problems* 267.

[100]   R van Krieken, 'The "Best Interests of the Child" and Parental Separation: On the "Civilizing of Parents"' (2005) 68 *Modern Law Review* 25.

which parent a child is to live) and cases affecting children indirectly (for example, whether a parent should be deported or imprisoned, or where a case is to be heard).[101] Decision-makers need to choose which characterization best reflects the nature of the issue at hand. This may sometimes be difficult (and is of course contestable). For example, in *R (on the Application of SG) v Secretary of State for Work and Pensions*,[102] which concerned the impact of a benefits 'cap' on children, the Ministerial decision was primarily concerned with limiting welfare payments, and therefore affected children 'indirectly' (though importantly). Other examples concern the deportation, or imprisonment, of adults where this affects children, and decisions whether to return children who have been abducted, either under the procedure of The Hague Convention on the Civil Aspects of International Child Abduction 1980 or (within the European Union) the Brussels Regulation II bis. The primary issue in such proceedings is *in which jurisdiction the future of the child (and therefore its best interests) should be decided*, so those interests are only indirectly affected at this stage.

In cases which can be characterized as affecting children only *indirectly*, the focus of the decision-maker should be on reaching the *'best' solution to the issue to be decided* rather than on what outcome would be best for the child in question. However, the child's interests do remain a primary consideration, so that they could lead to a modification of the 'best' solution to the issue at hand, or even its abandonment if that solution is sufficiently detrimental to the child's interests. But that is not inevitable because the nature of that outcome may be so important that it must be achieved notwithstanding its detrimental effect on the child's interests. In *Neulinger and Shuruk v Switzerland*[103] the European Court of Human Rights treated a case under The Hague Convention more like one directly about the child, resulting in considerable confusion.[104] The English courts once treated disputes in

---

[101] This is fully discussed in J Eekelaar, 'Two Dimensions of the Best Interests Principle: Decisions about Children and Decisions Affecting Children' in EE Sutherland and L-AB Macfarlane (eds), *Implementing Article 3 of the United Nations Convention on the Rights of the Child: Best Interests, Welfare and Well-being* (Cambridge University Press, 2016); See *HH v Deputy Prosecutor of the Italian Republic* [2012] UKSC 25, para 11 (Baroness Hale).

[102] [2015] UKSC 16.   [103] App No 41615/07; [2010] ECHR 1053.

[104] See P Beaumont, K Trimmings, L Walker, and J Holliday, 'Child Abduction: Recent Jurisprudence of the European Court of Human Rights' (2015) 64 *International and Comparative Law Quarterly* 39.

'relocation' cases (where one separated parent wishes to move to another country with the child) as if they were decisions primarily about the reasonableness of that parent's decision, affecting the child only indirectly, but later moved to treating them primarily as decisions directly about the child's upbringing.[105]

For decisions that are *directly* about children (most usually, where the child should be brought up, or whether a medical procedure should be performed or withheld), the focus should be on seeking the *best outcome for the child in question* through a holistic examination of a wide range of possible outcomes, and choosing what is best for *this* child in *these* circumstances. This requires full consideration of evidence about the consequences of any decision on the child's well-being, viewed from the child's standpoint, and adopting the 'capability' approach.[106] Seeing the application of the 'best interests' principle *as the child's right,* and not solely a duty on decision-making authorities, means that those interests must always be viewed from the child's perspective. Duties alone are not enough, even if they are to act virtuously,[107] for it is not clear that those with the duties will *necessarily* interpret them as requiring them to adopt the child's perspective in the way described, rather than to follow their own perception of virtue, or benevolence, as under the welfarist approach discussed in chapter 1.

The centrality of the child's perspective is underlined by Article 12 of the UNCRC, which says that 'the child shall in particular be provided the opportunity to be heard in any judicial and administrative proceedings affecting the child'. This does not mean that children should always be participants in court proceedings, or even be interviewed by the judge, but a range of procedures for representing children's views should be available.[108] But even if children are not

---

[105] See R George, *Relocation Disputes: Law and Practice in England and New Zealand* (Hart Publishing, 2014) 31ff.

[106] Sen, n 21. For illustrative decisions, see *Wyatt v Portsmouth NHS Trust* [2005] EWCA Civ 1181, especially para 87; *Re B-S (Children)* [2013] EWCA Civ 1146; *Bradford County Council v M* [2014] EWCC B4 (Fam).

[107] L Ferguson, 'The Jurisprudence of Making Decisions Affecting Children: An Argument to Prefer Duty to Children's Rights and Welfare' in A Diduck, N Peleg, and H Reece (eds), *Law in Society: Reflections on Children, Family, Culture and Philosophy: Essays in Honour of Michael Freeman* (Brill, 2015) 141. The result could of course be the same if acting virtuously was to be construed in this way.

[108] See T Gal and B Duramy (eds), *International Perspectives and Empirical Findings on Child Participation* (Oxford University Press, 2015).

directly represented, treating the application of the 'best interests' principle as a child's right and not merely a way of acting beneficently towards the child should reduce the risk that it will be applied entirely from an adult point of view.

The danger of conflating the child's perspective with upholding social structures must be minimized by reference to empirical evidence on the impact of various options on the individual child. In decisions directly about a child, the interests of others are also relevant, and could influence the resultant decision, but the principle that the child's interests are ' paramount',[109] or 'primary',[110] operates to privilege, or give greater weight to, the children's interests over the equivalent interests of others. This is often justified on the basis of children's vulnerability, but other reasons include the likely longer-term impact of most decisions on children than on the adults involved, and the likelihood that the children bore no, or less, responsibility than the relevant adults for the circumstances that have arisen.

Given the range of individual circumstances which can arise, it may frequently be impossible to determine outcomes without careful consideration of individual circumstances. In 1975, Robert Mnookin famously objected to the 'best interests' principle in disputes between parents because of its inherent indeterminacy,[111] and he has more recently reiterated that view, preferring a presumption in custody cases that time with the child should approximate the way it was allocated between the parents when they were together.[112] But legal decisions are often based on indeterminate standards, such as in deciding issues of 'reasonableness' or 'proportionality'. Over-reliance on presumptions risks giving too much weight to compliance with social convention and too little to the circumstances of the case in question.[113]

The rights of competent children

Usually parents will make decisions on behalf of children in matters over which they lack full competence, since they will normally have

---

[109] Children Act 1989, s 1(1); *YC v United Kingdom* (2012) EHRR 33.

[110] UNCRC, Art 3.

[111] RH Mnookin, 'Child Custody Adjudication: Judicial Functions in the Face of Indeterminacy' (1975) 39 *Law and Contemporary Problems* 226.

[112] R Mnookin, 'Child Custody Revisited' (2014) 77 *Law and Contemporary Problems* 249.

[113] See the discussion on separated parents in chapter 5, pp 129–32.

'parental responsibility' enabling them to do so,[114] subject to the operation of the 'best interests' principle.[115] But could this happen even if children are competent? Statute[116] provides that children aged sixteen and seventeen have the right to consent to medical treatment without the consent of a parent, and in *Gillick v West Norfolk and Wisbech Area Health Authority* Lord Scarman was willing to allow this for a children aged sixteen or under if sufficiently 'competent', competence being understood as ability to understand fully what is proposed and make a wise choice in the matter.[117] Yet courts have been unwilling to follow the wishes of children, even if 'competent', if this would seriously harm them, for example if they would lead to the child's death. The child's apparent 'right to decide' could be overridden, either by the child's parents, or the court (if the parents refuse), applying the 'best interests' test.[118] This does seem to be treating children differently from adults *just because they are children*. It has been suggested that this can be avoided by applying a deeper test of competence if a child refuses *all* treatment rather than specific treatments, so the child could be treated as non-competent in that regard.[119] But it may not always be practical to make this distinction.[120] Another approach, which avoids delving into whether the child has requisite competence regarding the issue, is to say that, while everyone is influenced by their social circumstances (and in that sense 'pure' autonomy is impossible[121]), family members (especially parents) or other adult

---

[114] See chapter 5, pp 115–7, 123 on parenthood and parental responsibility.

[115] *LCC v A* [2011] EWHC 4033 (Fam) (court orders immunizations for children where parents had refused). But the courts will not necessarily side with medical opinion: See J Herring, 'Medical Decisions about Children' in J Eekelaar (ed), *Family Law in Britain and America in the New Century: Essays in Honor of Sanford N Katz* (Brill, 2016) ch 10.

[116] Family Law Reform Act 1969, s 1(1).   [117] [1986] AC 112.

[118] See the English and Australian cases discussed in J Seymour, *Children, Parents and the Courts: Legal Intervention in Family Life* (The Federation Press, 2016) Part 2. This dilemma is the subject of the novel by Ian McEwan, *The Children Act* (Jonathan Cape, 2014).

[119] See S Gilmore and J Herring, ' "No" Is the Hardest Word: Consent and Children's Autonomy' (2011) 23 *Child and Family Law Quarterly* 3 for a detailed discussion of the issues and the case law.

[120] E Cave and J Wallbank, 'Minors' Capacity to Refuse Treatment: A Reply to Gilmore and Herring' (2012) 20 *Medical Law Review* 423. See also the cases discussed in Seymour, n 118; M Freeman, 'Re-thinking *Gillick*' (2005) 13 *International Journal of Children's Rights* 201.

[121] As Farrah Ahmed has put it, 'An autonomous person is not one who has no external pressures upon her, nor one who insulates herself from these pressures, but

figures can exercise a unique influence on children during childhood (some of which operates in complex ways detectable only by family therapy) and this renders suspect a decision by an apparently competent child which severely damages the child's 'basic' interests to health and survival. Therefore, in such circumstances, those interests should be protected until the child reaches adulthood and has had further opportunities for reflection and until then the 'best interests' principle should be applied (either through the parents or the court), treating the child's decision as being relevant, but not necessarily determinative. In such cases the competent child would be denied the rights an adult would have to make such a decision[122] but would be subject to a decision based on the 'best interests' principle where his or her views would be relevant but not decisive. However, this would only happen where the consequences of the child's decision would have severely deleterious consequences, which, fortunately, is not usually the case when medical treatment is sought, or sometimes even when refused.

There are other circumstances where competent children are denied rights adults have (although not necessarily replaced by the 'best interests' principle), such as when a minimum age is set regarding receiving education and in what manner, the acquisition of a driving licence (given the higher risk of driving accidents by young people), buying alcohol, engaging in hazardous activities, or even voting. While a purely interests-based theory of rights, such that of MacCormick,[123] might characterize the imposition of treatment, education, and protection from exposure to the risks of driving, consuming alcohol, or working in dangerous conditions on unwilling but competent children as examples of enforcing their rights, it is better to accept them as occasions when rights are withheld even if the child is 'competent', rather than to try to adapt a view of children's rights so as to embrace them as rights, or to use different tests of competence from those used for adults. Looking at it in this way underlines the seriousness of such decisions.[124] They may well be necessary and justifiable in the interests of children or society generally, but should always be taken with care and a thorough understanding of the circumstances.

one who against the background of these pressures is able to make decisions that make her life her own': Ahmed, n 17, 120.

[122] For an opposing view, see Freeman, n 120.   [123] MacCormick, n 14.

[124] Hence a 'competent' child under 18 may not be free to decide where to live: see *Re W (a child)* [2016] EWCA 804.

RIGHTS AND VALUES

It will be necessary to revert to the role of rights when the role of the community in personal law is addressed in the final chapter. But before then, attention will be directed at four values that play an important part in the nature and application of personal law: respect, friendship, responsibility, and truth.

3

Respect

Since the implementation of the Human Rights Act 1998 from
October 2000, the ECHR has become part of UK law. All our family
law therefore has to measure up to the standards set by the relevant
articles of the Convention. Article 8 is one of the most important. It
states that 'everyone has the right to respect for his private and family life'. A public authority may not 'interfere with the exercise' of this
right except in defined circumstances. The wording is unhappy. How
can one *exercise* a right to respect? The drafters must have meant that
public authorities should not interfere with the exercise of the right
to family life and might even have positive duties to promote it.[1] But
why talk about respect at all? Why not simply say that 'everyone has
the right to private and family life'? Does 'respect' add or subtract
anything?

I want to argue that the idea of respect is a pivotal value in personal
law, and I want to do this by looking at the values which come into
play if the law is to be respectful.

WHAT IS RESPECT?

Rather unexpectedly, the idea of respect was propelled into British
political rhetoric when the third Blair government placed in
the Queen's Speech on 17 May 2005 the line: 'My government is

---

[1] Such positive duties are now well established: for example, to assist parents to
maintain contact with their children: *Hokkanen v Finland* (1995) 19 EHRR 139, and
many subsequent cases.

Family Law and Personal Life. Second edition. John Eekelaar. © John Eekelaar 2017.
Second edition published 2017 by Oxford University Press.

committed to creating safe and secure communities, and fostering a culture of respect.' What had been called the 'respect agenda' of that Labour government was derided as nothing more than an alternative phrase for 'law and order',[2] and the linkage with 'creating safe and secure communities' seems to support this view. But this may be too quick. Law and order could be achieved through a culture of fear. Achieving it through a culture of respect might be significantly different. But in what way?

It is common to trace the concept of respect for individuals to Kant's injunction that people should be treated as ends and not as means. Ronald Dworkin believed that the justification for democracy is that 'it enforces the right of each person to respect and concern as an individual.'[3] Joseph Raz thinks that respect for law can form the basis of a 'quasi-voluntary obligation' of obedience.[4] Multi-culturalists claim that people's distinct identities should be respected.[5] Most people think that we should respect the dead; and this has been extended to the idea that we should respect the body parts of individuals who have perished. The Report into the storage of body tissue at the Alder Hey Hospital in Liverpool (and elsewhere) in 2001 stated that 'in relation to retained organs and tissue, it is the right of surviving relatives to request respectful disposal, and they must be given that opportunity.'[6]

What 'respect' is in these contexts is not easy to discern. Dworkin mentioned a number of ways in which failure to comply with equal respect and concern may be manifested. One is where weight is given in a utilitarian calculation of people's preferences to their preferences about how *others* should behave: he called these *external preferences*. What was wrong about that, in his view, was that to do so caused disadvantage to a person against whom the preferences are directed 'in virtue of the fact that his concept of a proper life is despised by others.'[7] That violated a 'right to moral independence'. He put it another way in saying that self-respect demands the ability to identify and pursue one's conception of living one's life well, and respect requires recognizing this

---

[2] See the columnist EJ Dickson, 'Our Modern Obsession with Respect' in *The Independent*, 29 June 2005.

[3] R Dworkin, *A Matter of Principle* (Clarendon Press, 1986) 196.

[4] J Raz, *Ethics in the Public Domain* (Oxford University Press, 1994) 354.

[5] C Taylor, 'The Politics of Recognition' in A Gutman (ed), *Multiculturalism* (Princeton University Press, 1994) 25–75.

[6] *Report of The Royal Liverpool Children's Inquiry* (The Stationery Office, January 2001), para 1.9.

[7] Dworkin, n 3, 366.

in others. Put plainly, people should not be expected to act as others tell them for no other reason than that those others want them to because of who they are, or expect that of others. For if people did that, they would have lost their dignity as humans.[8] Yet again the idea of respect seems redundant. It could simply be that we should accept people's right to moral independence. In fact, in both instances Dworkin referred to the prescriptions as a feature of *equality*.[9] To treat people as equals requires recognizing their right to moral independence.

Colin Bird discussed this difficulty in finding 'work' for the concept of respect in abstract statements about equality.[10] He tried to find it by drawing on Stephen Darwall's[11] distinction between 'recognition respect' and 'appraisal respect'. Appraisal respect occurs when we hold individuals in high regard for features of special excellence (eg a talented musician); as such it is not owed to everyone. Recognition respect describes what occurs when we give appropriate recognition to people as people, and are willing to constrain our behaviour accordingly. That process does not involve admiration or approval, but a 'deliberative disposition'. But Bird recognized that this still did not completely account for the notion of 'respect', for one may restrain one's behaviour with regard to others without necessarily respecting them, and Bird sought to complete the account through the idea that the deliberative disposition leads us to recognize that people have a 'status' before which we 'submit' in the same way as we demonstrate respect through submission to higher authority.

It is not clear that it is necessary to try to construct a kind of metaphysical hierarchy in order to make sense of the notion of respect. Nor is Darwall's distinction between recognition and appraisal respect completely convincing. The two share a common element which is more important than the differences: namely, that respect for something or someone lies in acknowledging that a feature of that entity has value in and of itself, the value usually not being assessable in monetary terms.[12] This may involve admiration, as in

---

[8] R Dworkin, *Justice for Hedgehogs* (The Belknap Press of Harvard University Press, 2011) 208.

[9] Dworkin, n 3, 196 ('The decision invades rather than enforces the right of citizens to be treated as equals') and 205.

[10] C Bird, 'Status, Identity, Respect' (2004) 32 *Political Theory* 207.

[11] S Darwall, 'Two Kinds of Respect' (1977) 88 *Ethics* 36.

[12] This looks similar to the proposition advanced by Carl Cranor, and criticized by Darwall, that respect involves judging a person as having a characteristic which is a 'good thing': 'Toward a Theory of Respect for Persons' (1975) 12 *American*

appraisal respect. But one can respect something without admiring it for instance the dogged determination of someone to persist in a view one holds to be misguided. One respects the dead, but we do not admire them for being dead. In those cases respect acknowledges a value: dedication and consistency in the first case; in the second, remembering that we are to some extent all beneficiaries of the efforts of our forebears, and acknowledging our own mortality. A remarkable case occurred in 2004 when a woman, tracing her ancestry, discovered she was descended from a notorious murderer of the early nineteenth century. As was the custom, the murderer had been executed and his body given to medical research. His skeleton was subsequently publicly displayed by the Royal College of Surgeons and the relative demanded the cremation of the skeleton.[13] Trivializing or desecrating human remains affronts the value which they, albeit symbolically, hold of recalling the gift of life, and the role of our forebears in passing it down to us, even if they be people of disrepute.

Bird[14] distinguished between respect for persons and respecting difference between people. It is a good distinction. His reason for making it is that the object of respect must bear 'an independent significance and weight', which difference alone does not have. This can be explained well in terms of value. The fact that A is of a different culture from B, speaks a different language, or worships a different god, is not in and of itself a matter of value. Some might disagree, believing that diversity in itself is valuable, and it can certainly be enriching. However, it is very contingent on its consequences. In some circumstances they may be beneficial, but a proliferation of languages, religions and other cultural practices within a society could sow discord. The point about respect for difference is that the common attributes of humanity, including speech, belief, and so on, should be valued *irrespective of differences between them*. What is then valued is the *ability to exercise* the variety of ways in which cultures give expression to the human goods, rather than the fact of difference itself. The

Philosophical Quarterly 303. It is different, though, in that Cranor's idea of a 'good thing' implies something which is morally desirable, whereas I use 'value' simply in the descriptive sense as referring to something which is (highly) valued in its own right.

[13] http://news.bbc.co.uk/1/hi/england/suffolk/3573244.stm (accessed 13 June 2017).

[14] Bird, n 10, 216.

respect due to this freedom demands that this ability to exercise is protected and welcomed.

We can now suggest a sense in which couching a 'law and order' agenda in the language of respect might be different from expressing it in terms, say, of deterrence. The reference to respect suggests that the policy goal is to try to instil in the members of the community a perception of the value of the community and the people living in it. The hope would be that from that sense of value individuals would not only desist from harming the community and its participants, but perhaps contribute to it in a positive way. We can also see that the addition of the term 'respect' in Article 8 does add a dimension which would be lost without it. If the provision merely read 'everyone has the right to private and family life' and that a public authority must not 'interfere with the exercise' of that right, except in specified circumstances, it would indeed have imposed a defeasible obligation on the state. The insertion of the word 'respect' gives the provision the character of a statement that family life has a timeless quality and is to be held to have value in and of itself. That value does not disappear even if in some circumstances its breach is justified. It persists in a world of many values. So Article 8 seeks to entrench family life as a value. It goes further, of course, in setting up its exercise as a protected legal interest. There are other values which may not have similar protection.

RESPECT AND THE INTIMATE

What values, then, does personal law need to acknowledge if it is to be respectful? I want to argue that, if personal law is to be respectful, it must be informed throughout by recognition of the value of the intimate. This is essential because without it love is unlikely to flourish and the scope for moral behaviour is reduced. By 'the intimate' I do not refer to a geographical or temporal space. I mean by it that there is, or should be, a sphere of personal interaction, whether between adults with one another, or between adults and children, which is privileged in the way I will describe. I have in mind behaviours ranging from everyday communication and modes of dealing with routine events, and the allocation of domestic roles, to emotional interactions, strategies for coping with difficulties and crises, mutual participation in diversionary activities, modes of care, and so on. My claim is that, while individuals of course draw upon moral and social norms in their conduct in these contexts, they should do so free from institutional constraint and censure. I will call this the 'privileged sphere'.

How does personal law show that it values this? I can start by showing how it has failed to do so. The early feminist cry, 'the personal is political', has been valuable in exposing the significance which domestic circumstances have had for the ordering of public affairs.[15] But the conclusion sometimes drawn that this revelation should put all aspects of intimate relationships into the public domain is too swift.[16] The intimate has in fact been regulated from time immemorial. One could start with the early church laws on marriage, of which Pollock and Maitland wrote: 'When we weigh the merits of the medieval church and have remembered all her good deeds, we have to put into the other scale as a weighty counterpoise the incalculable harm done by a marriage law which was a maze of flighty fancies and misapplied logic.'[17] The harm referred to is primarily that caused to loving relationships.

Wives have been placed under a legal or social duty to obey their husband.[18] In our recent history, nullity law has defined and investigated 'incurable' impotence.[19] Penetration without ejaculation,[20] or coitus interruptus,[21] consummates a marriage; ejaculation without penetration does not.[22] In *L v L*,[23] a wife persisted for six years while her husband attempted therapeutic means to overcome his impotence, and had herself inseminated by his sperm. After much argument, the court decided that she was not to be prevented from seeking annulment because she had not accepted this 'abnormal' relationship.

---

[15] For a discussion, see K O'Donovan, *Sexual Divisions in Law* (Weidenfeld & Nicolson, 1985) 1–20.

[16] See SM Okin, *Justice, Gender and the Family* (Basic Books, 1989) 127–33.

[17] F Pollock and FW Maitland, *History of English Law before the time of Edward I*, vol 2 (Cambridge University Press) 389. See further J Eekelaar, 'Family Law and Love' (2016) 28 *Child and Family Law Quarterly* 289.

[18] See chapter 1, pp 9–10.

[19] *S v S* [1962] 1 All ER 33 (questioning whether it is necessary to submit to an operation to cure it).

[20] *R v R* [1952] 1 All ER 1194.   [21] *Cackett v Cackett* [1950] 1 All ER 677.

[22] *Clarke v Clarke* [1943] 2 All ER 540.   [23] [1949] 1 All ER 141.

In divorce law, the definition of adultery,[24] and the whole edifice of fault-based law, including the doctrines of connivance, condonation, provocation, and recrimination, all provided opportunities for extensive judicial analysis of what went on in people's private lives, and for pronouncements to be made approving or condemning the way they dealt with crises in their emotional lives. Stephen Cretney has given many examples, including the decision in 1962 that a wife had to put up with her drunken husband because there was no evidence of 'any disgusting behaviour such as vomiting or being unable to control his bladder'.[25] All this was of course inherent in the nature of the conditions which the legal regime laid down for the establishment and dissolution of such relationships. Even today, in the much attenuated version of the previous fault-based system which makes up the English divorce law, when undefended divorce is sought on the basis of unreasonable behaviour, statements about behaviour in people's personal lives must be written down for (at least theoretical) evaluation by a judge (though this is minimal in practice). If the case is defended, courts may have to pronounce on how someone should handle living with another person of a very different disposition.[26] As recently as 2017, in such a case in which matrimonial squabbles were pored over in detail up to the Court of Appeal, the President of the Family Division observed that 'it is not a ground for divorce that you find yourself in a wretchedly unhappy marriage', and castigated the 'hypocrisy' of the law.[27]

What is the value which is not being respected here? It could not be the actions themselves, which range across all manner of intimate behaviours, including a variety of sexual practices (and attempts). It is the value of having space to develop one's personality and personal interaction free from the external gaze. Susan Moller Okin is right to claim that there must be matters which legitimately should be kept beyond the reach of public scrutiny and knowledge. Thomas Nagel,

---

[24] Sexual gratification less than full penetration does not count: *Sapsford v Sapsford* [1954] P 394.

[25] S Cretney, *Family Law in the Twentieth Century: A History* (Oxford University Press, 2003) 262, citing *Hall v Hall* [1962] 1 WLR 1246.

[26] *Birch v Birch* [1992] 1 FLR 564.

[27] *Owens v Owens* [2017] EWCA Civ 182, paras 84, 93–5. The operation of the law is subject to investigation by Liz Trinder, Caroline Bryson, and Penny Mansfield, supported by the Nuffield Foundation: http://www.nuffieldfoundation.org/finding-fault-divorce-law-practice-england-and-wales (accessed 13 June 2017).

writing angrily in the wake of the humiliation of President Clinton, argues that public life would be impossible if the space for public figures to exercise intimacy is not respected.[28] A stronger argument could be made: that love itself demands such a space if it is to sustain a lifelong partnership. The value of the privileged sphere lies in the freedom to engage in unregulated activity that is not harmful *irrespective of the inherent capacity of the activity to advance the well-being either of the actors or of others.* Such activities may have much, little, or no value. Compared to Picasso's solitary jottings, my idle efforts have no value, either for me or others. I would be better off reading philosophy. Compared to the value of intercourse resulting in pregnancy, some other types of sexual activity may have little or none. At least, whatever value they have is irrelevant to the recognition of the value of allowing unregulated space to perform them. That value is violated when the most intimate aspects of adult relationships are measured against the prescriptions of a legal or social norm.

This value is similar to, but not the same as, the value of privacy upheld by the US Supreme Court in cases from *Griswold v Connecticut*[29] to *Lawrence v Texas*.[30] The value of privacy covers a wider range of activities. It also seeks to protect against *intrusion, external observation, or disclosure.* The behaviour I am considering is valued by reason of its freedom from external *regulation.* This may imply freedom from observation or disclosure, but not always. It could take place very publicly, and I will argue that privileged behaviour in parent–child relationships should in principle always be open to observation. Some intimate behaviour may warrant public disclosure, for example if there is a public interest in such disclosure.[31] The behaviour is also interactional. Privacy, on the other hand, can protect solitary actions. Nor is respect for the privileged sphere based on the good of autonomy. This is partly because the value of autonomy extends beyond the privileged sphere, but also because some argue that an autonomous life is valuable only if it is worthwhile. Why should we value an autonomous life if it is misspent? As Joseph Raz

---

[28] T Nagel, *Concealment and Exposure & Other Essays* (Oxford University Press, 2002) ch 2.

[29] 381 US 479 (1965) (prohibition on use of contraceptives held unconstitutional).

[30] 539 US 558 (2003) (Texas sodomy laws held unconstitutional).

[31] See the controversial Supreme Court judgment in 2016 upholding an injunction restraining the disclosure of the names of celebrities alleged to be living as a 'threesome': *PJS v News Group Newspapers* [2016] UKSC 26.

writes: '[W]e value autonomous choices only if they are choices of what is valuable and worthy of choice.'[32] In contrast, my argument is that recognition of the privileged sphere is a value *whether the activities (if not harmful) that take place within it have value or not.* This creates the conditions necessary for flourishing (love) and the living of a worthwhile, autonomous, life, but it is not the same as those. Nicholas Bamforth stresses the unique centrality of sexual activity to an individual's well-being.[33] This may be so (though people can lead fulfilled lives without engaging in sexual relationships), but is of no relevance to the value of recognizing the privileged sphere.

I must not be misunderstood. The personal sphere is privileged, not licensed for irresponsibility. The general legal norms of criminal law, or of tort law, are not displaced. In particular, the value that is respected by conferring freedom in the privileged sphere is defeated if the behaviour harms anyone within or outside that sphere. This is a further difference from the good of autonomy, for it can be argued that autonomous persons should be free to undergo consensual, and therefore victimless, harm.[34] Whatever view may be taken on that, I am not arguing that respecting the privileged sphere in itself demands acknowledging freedom to engage in consensual harmful activity. If prevention of harm is to allow intrusion into the privileged sphere, harm must be understood in terms of violations of physical integrity, or of emotional oppression. Behaviour cannot become harmful simply by assertion.[35] Victims of domestic violence sometimes resist

---

[32] Raz, n 4, 120.

[33] N Bamforth, 'Same-sex Partnerships and Arguments of Justice' in R Wintemute and M Andenaes, *Legal Recognition of Same-sex Partnerships: A Study of National, European and International Law* (Hart Publishing, 2001) especially 41–3.

[34] See Raz, n 4, 124.

[35] J Finnis, 'Law, Morality and Sexual Orientation' (1994) 69 *Notre Dame Law Review* 1049 describes homosexual acts as being 'manifestly unworthy of the human being and immoral', and 'morally worthless'. 'Whatever the generous hopes and dreams and thoughts of giving with which some same-sex partners may surround their sexual acts, those acts cannot express or do more than is expressed or done if two strangers engage in such activity to give each other pleasure, or a prostitute pleasures a client to give him pleasure in return for money, or (say) a man masturbates ... after a gruelling day on the assembly line.' The worthlessness of the activity would not matter under my argument. However, Finnis goes further in claiming that same-sex relationships are actually harmful to the participants because the partners' bodies do not fit together in the same way as a man and a woman's do and are 'deeply hostile to the self-understanding of those members of the community who are willing to commit themselves to real marriage'. Of course, some intimate actions can be harmful, but they do not become so by mere assertion.

protective intervention because they claim they love the perpetra-
tors. They may well do. But they surely love them despite, not because
of, the violence. The protection of the privileged sphere is not to be
bought at such a price. Love would surely grow, not fail, were the violence to be eradicated. Respect for the privileged sphere may therefore
demand intervention where harm is inflicted within it, though the
effectiveness of the manner of intervention is a matter of pragmatic
assessment.[36] But this does not refer to the upsets and heartaches that
are the sadly frequent accompaniments of the joys of intimate lives,
and the capacity of individuals to cope with and be enriched by personal relationships would be reduced by social or legal regulation in
such matters.

Furthermore, legal norms could guide the *consequences* of behaviours within the privileged sphere. As discussed in chapter 5, they do
so by allocating broad responsibilities which arise as a consequence
of such behaviours. For example, post-divorce settlements may reflect
the fact that the wife looked after the children while the husband provided income; child support obligations may arise whether a child's
conception was deliberate or not. An important feature of modern
marriage law is that it provides a framework within which intimate
behaviours and love can flourish, but the law does not lay down how
the couple should divide their labour or attempt to control their fertility. This is a perhaps overlooked value of marriage in many modern societies. That is, marriage law itself does not lay down how the
couple should carry out most aspects of their lives. Indeed, any agreements about such matters will generally not be legally enforceable as it
is unlikely that the couple would have intended this.[37] The law usually
steps in only if the relationship finishes. This is in contrast to 'con-
tractual' models for relationships, such as that suggested by Martha
Fineman, which could open a wide range of behaviours in the intimate realm to legal scrutiny and interpretation.[38]

The case of homosexual behaviour warrants special mention,
for here the intimate sphere was not only not respected, but legal

[36] For a trenchant statement of the justification for state intervention in cases of
domestic violence, see S Choudhury and J Herring, 'Righting Domestic Violence'
(2006) 20 *International Journal of Law, Policy and the Family* 95.

[37] *Balfour v Balfour* [1919] 2 KB 571. This is also one consequence of the element
of friendship within marriage: see p 100.

[38] MA Fineman, 'The Meaning of Marriage' in A Bernstein (ed), *Marriage
Proposals: Questioning a Legal Status* (New York University Press, 2006) 58.

and social norms assumed their most terrible punitive and repressive aspects in the way Michel Foucault described as characterizing all penal law during the *ancien régime*. Its goal was to remove the offender from the body politic, through death, transportation, or social ostracism.[39] But, while penal law (in Foucault's analysis) later moved towards working on the criminal's mind, in order to try to instil desired modes of behaviour, in the case of homosexuals, for the most part (and particularly in the case of males), it maintained its punitive posture. This was achieved both through inflicting punishment for homosexual activity and through social practices which denigrated homosexual relationships. The cruel deployment of institutional and social power against individuals for no reason other than their consensual sexual behaviour in private has only very recently been attenuated (but not universally). This seems to be part of the general realignment of power, in which the concept of rights has played an important part, in what may be a new era in the interaction between the law and personal relationships.

The progression of homosexual behaviour from criminality into the protection of the privileged sphere has been quite rapid. Criminalization of sodomy between adults was lifted in Britain in 1967;[40] the Texas sodomy laws were held to be unconstitutional only in 2003.[41] Writing in 1994, John Finnis[42] defended what he called the 'standard European position' regarding homosexual conduct. Under that dispensation, while it was 'unjust for A to impose any kind of disadvantage on B simply because A believes that B has sexual inclinations towards persons of the same sex', it was acceptable for the *state*, in its supervision of the public realm, to discourage the expression of such inclinations through sexual activity by allowing disadvantage and discrimination against homosexuals in order to manifest its judgement that 'life involving homosexual conduct is bad even for someone unfortunate enough to have innate or quasi-innate homosexual inclinations'. Such 'acceptable' discrimination included a higher age of consent for homosexual than for heterosexual intercourse, forbidding

---

[39] M Foucault, *Discipline and Punish: The Birth of the Prison* (Penguin Books, 1991). See further DF Greenberg, *The Construction of Homosexuality* (University of Chicago Press, 1988).

[40] Sexual Offences Act 1967. For a full discussion, see S Cretney, *Same Sex Relationships: From 'Odious Crime' to 'Gay Marriage'* (Oxford University Press, 2006) ch 1.

[41] *Lawrence v Texas* 539 US 558 (2003).   [42] Finnis, n 35.

homosexuals to adopt children or marry one another, and the prohibition the United Kingdom Parliament once placed on local authorities against promoting 'the teaching in any maintained school of the acceptability of homosexuality as a pretended family relationship'.[43]

Whatever opinion one might hold of Dworkin's view[44] that respect for autonomy requires the state to be neutral as to what constitutes the good, recognition of the privileged sphere does not require abandonment by the community of common ideals. My argument does not suppose that the activities within the privileged sphere need to be treated as being valuable (though they should not be harmful). On the contrary, some might be valueless. But there is no reason for the community to be neutral between valuable and valueless activities. Suppose two friends indulge their spare time in a harmless, useless, activity (say, planespotting); another two play tennis (equally harmless, marginally less useless). The community may choose to promote tennis over planespotting (to encourage exercise, socialization, national achievement, and pride) without inhibiting the activities of planespotters. Indeed, it must make such choices. In open societies these choices will be accompanied by debate and criticism in the public domain. Unless criticism occurs in a context where it is an element in social forces which create burdens likely to obstruct the activities, it is consistent with respecting the privileged sphere. Pro-natalist policies favour some kinds of activities in the privileged sphere without impeding those unlikely to lead to procreation. Iconic images of sports stars with their babies as much as paternity leave encourage greater involvement of men in childcare without imposing constraints upon those who adopt a more old-fashioned division of labour. Marriage and partner counselling is premised on the desirability of the endurance of relationships, but imposes no burdens on those who choose against it. Policy might encourage marriage provided its consequences do not discriminate harmfully against people taking a different option. Nor does it disrespect a form of intimate life to provide alternatives outside that realm, as the Children's Aid Society thought the provision of school meals did at the beginning of the last century in England.[45] So providing civil partnerships as an alternative to marriage does not disrespect marriage.

---

[43] Local Government Act 1988, s 28.

[44] R Dworkin, 'Liberalism' in *A Matter of Principle* (Clarendon Press, 1986) ch 8.

[45] See H Hendrick, *Child Welfare in England 1872–1989* (Routledge, 1994) 105.

But there is a significant difference if encouragement of some activities implies, or leads to, denigration, stigmatization, and social ostracism for engaging in others. These penalties would then amount to institutional constraint and censure within the intimate sphere and be disrespectful of it. The 'standard European position' in regard to same-sex relationships as described by Finnis crossed that line,[46] and has since disintegrated. The European Court of Human Rights gradually accepted that discrimination on the basis of sexual orientation is a breach of human rights,[47] and in the United Kingdom the age of consent to sexual activity has been equalized,[48] joint adoption by gay couples permitted,[49] gay cohabitants held to have been living together 'as (if) man and wife',[50] and the prohibition against 'promoting' homosexuality as a 'pretended' form of family living repealed.[51] The introduction of civil partnerships for same-sex couples and same-sex marriage was described in chapter 2.[52] It is now widely recognized that the value of love between same-sex partners should indeed be promoted, and that institutional support, such as marriage, is an appropriate way to do this. A Brazilian court expressed this when Justice Marco Aurelio stated that the 'right to life' implied the right to a 'decent' life, and this included the right to live one's life according to one's 'life project':

> The dignity of life requires the possibility of concretizing goals and projects. From that premise, the issue of existential harm arises when the State restricts the citizens in this aspect. It is worthy to be said: that the State is obligated to guarantee that individuals search for their own happiness, as long as they do not violate the rights of others, which does not occur in the present case. It is true that the life project of those attracted by the same sex would be harmed with the absolute impossibility of creating a family. To expect from them a change of sexual orientation so that they are capable of reaching that legal situation shows a lack of appreciation of dignity. It is also

---

[46] See the examples of deleterious consequences of the policy for homosexuals given in Wintemute and Andenaes, n 33.

[47] *Da Silva Mouta v Portugal* (2001) EHRR 41; *Karner v Austria* (2004) 38 EHRR 24; *EB v France* App No 43546/02, judgment 22 January 2008.

[48] Sexual Offences Act 2003, ss 9–22.

[49] Adoption and Children Act 2002, s 144(4).

[50] *Ghaidan v Godin-Mendoza* [2004] 2 AC 557.

[51] Local Government Act 2003, s 122.   [52] See p 50.

faced with the constitutional objection to prejudice by reason of sexual orientation.[53]

It follows from the same principles that marriage or equivalent institutions should be available to people who identify neither as male nor female.[54]

CARE AND NURTURE

Over time, various reasons have been given for affording parents the entitlement to care for and nurture their children. One is the sentiment that parents in some sense 'own' their children, which might still be reflected in continued references to 'my' children, but, whatever may have been the view in past times, which cannot be taken seriously today.[55] It may seldom have been literally followed.[56] More significant, historically, has been the perception, described in chapter 1, that children, certainly during minority, and frequently beyond that, were a means by which parents promoted their own interests, and through whom the community promoted its interests. These are unappealing reasons. The justification is best seen as grounded in respect for the privileged sphere, in this case, one in which caregivers interact with children.

The justification starts with the scheme for identifying which adults have primary responsibility for caring for the children. This is discussed in chapter 5.[57] We hope those to whom this task is allocated, usually the parents (whether biological or social), will love their children. If they do not, the law cannot make them. That simply intrudes too deeply into the dynamics of our behaviour in the intimate realm.

---

[53] See Inter-American Commission on Human Rights, *Legal Standards Related to Gender Equality and Women's Rights in the Inter-American Human Rights System: Development and Application*, Updates 2011–2014, para 179.

[54] See J Herring and P-L Chau, 'Assigning Sex and Intersexuals' (2001) 31 *Family Law* 762.

[55] For discussions, see D Archard, *Children: Rights & Childhood* (Routledge, 1993) 98–102 and, generally, JG Dwyer, *The Relationship Rights of Children* (Cambridge University Press, 2006).

[56] Even the original power of the Roman *paterfamilias* to kill a child or sell a child into slavery became heavily circumscribed.

[57] See pp 122–9.

Societies have been wise enough therefore to allow alternative provision for caring for and nurturing children where parents have felt
unable to bear the burden. But while the 'allocation' of a child to a parent is a matter of social organization, the interaction between them,
like that between adult partners, falls within the privileged sphere,
and is to be valued in the same way.

David Archard perceptively and sensitively expresses doubts about
drawing this parallel between parent–child and adult relationships.
He points out that, unlike intimate partners, children have no choice
in the relationship; it is not a relationship between equals.[58] But
Archard is criticizing the invocation of 'privacy' as a means to protect intimacy, and I am not arguing for privacy in itself, but for space
for unregulated action within intimate relationships. Between adults,
privacy may sometimes be necessary to allow this to occur. It is, however, never necessary in the case of the parent–child relationship.
Indeed, it is undesirable. All actions between parents and children
must in principle be open to scrutiny because of children's vulnerability to harm and exploitation. However, the practice of such scrutiny
is subject to a number of practical constraints. The first results from
what has been called the 'rule of optimism', which is the presumption professionals make that parents treat their children well.[59] This
means that possible indicators of the infliction of harm may initially
be given a benign interpretation as a way of limiting intrusion into the
private sphere. Imagine if agencies adopted a 'rule of suspicion'.[60] Like
all interpretations, those of indicators of harm will be contextualized,
resulting in a form of relativism so that, for example, physical injury
to a child in a middle-class environment is likely to be read as acci-
dental, whereas the same injury to a child in a rougher neighbour-
hood may be assumed to be deliberately inflicted. Likewise, signs of

[58] Archard, n 55, 124–5.
[59] This term is used in R Dingwall, J Eekelaar, and T Murray, *The Protection of
Children: State Intervention and Family Life* (Basil Blackwell, 1983) ch 4. For further
discussions, see Postscript (by Robert Dingwall) to the second edition (Avebury,
1995) and R Dingwall, 'The Jasmine Beckford Affair' (1986) 49 *Modern Law
Review* 489.
[60] The consequences of doing this can be glimpsed by the dawn raids and the holding and interrogation of children when moral panic over feared satanic or ritual abuse
gripped some social services departments in the early 1990s: see C Lyon and P de
Cruz, *Child Abuse* (Family Law, 1993) 52–7. Such events, which sometimes occur after
a high-profile failure in child protection, are clearly exceptions to the operation of the
'rule of optimism'.

neglect are more likely to be considered suspicious in a well-off area than a poorer one. Social workers are important for, as Nigel Parton has observed, 'social work plays the key role in putting into operation the state's legal basis for intervening into some families where there are concerns about children while trying to ensure that not all families become clients.'[61]

Another constraint is found in libertarian principles which restrain intrusion into private space in the absence of evidence-based, formal authorization. These should be seen as designed to protect individuals against excessive official intrusion into their domestic space (such as their dwellings), and not as protecting them against surveillance of their interaction with their children, although it will partially do that. That is to say, the fact of surveillance of that interaction should not in itself be objectionable, though some circumstances may make it so. For this reason there should be no objection in principle to monitoring a parent's interaction with a child in a public place, such as a hospital.[62]

But tensions will always arise in regard to the extent to which privacy interests of parents should override opportunities to monitor parent–child relationships. For example, a database (ContactPoint) initiated in England in 2004 in response to cases of child abuse and launched in 2009 as an online directory containing basic information on all children in England and accessible to frontline professionals such as teachers and social workers was shut down in 2010 because of privacy and security concerns. An ambitious scheme was launched in Scotland in 2016 under which all children and young people from birth to 18, or beyond if still in school, were to have access to a Named Person to help support their well-being. The Named Person could be in the health or education services, and is seen as a central point of contact if a child, young person or their parent(s) wants information or advice, or if they want to talk about any worries and seek support.[63] Since it is often thought that children in difficulty often feel a lack of someone to turn to, this scheme (if it can be effectively implemented)

---

[61] N Parton, 'Social Work, Child Protection and Politics: Some Critical and Constructive Reflections' (2014) 44 *British Journal of Social Work*, 2042, 2053.

[62] This has caused controversy: see N Shabde and A Croft, 'Covert Video Surveillance: An Important Investigative Tool or a Breach of Trust?' (1999) 81 *Archives of Diseases in Childhood* 291.

[63] Children and Young People (Scotland) Act 2014.

appears to cover an important need, but provoked strong opposition from groups defensive of family privacy who argued that having such a person without the consent of the child or his or her parents and without there being any assessment as to whether there was a pressing social need sufficient to justify such appointment contravened Articles 8 and 9 of the European Convention. Although the Scottish courts held that the mere creation of a Named Person, available to assist a child or parent, 'no more confuses or diminishes the legal role, duties and responsibilities of parents in relation to their children than the provision of social services or education generally', [64] the UK Supreme Court held that it was defective in its current form, largely because it failed to take properly into account the need to keep parents and children informed about how information would be shared, and various legal provisions were too imprecisely drafted. [65]

A third constraint is that, since there can be a degree of uncertainty over what behaviours are harmful to children, there is a danger that preventive intervention could cause greater harm than the parental behaviour. Therefore the legal threshold for forcible intervention should allow a degree of latitude to parental behaviour. This is demonstrated by the requirement in English law that state intervention is restricted to instances where the harm is thought to be 'significant'. [66] And to rule out harms originating in causes beyond the parents' control, it must be a result of a failure of care. Where harm has not occurred to a child, but is feared, the matter becomes one of calculation of risk. [67] These are aspects of a 'liberal compromise' between the community's duties towards children and other values. It needs to be recognized that an inevitable consequence of this compromise is that some cases of child mistreatment will go undetected. But that is not necessarily because of systemic or individual failures. It is an indication that the compromise is working.

If the significant harm threshold is crossed, justifying intervention, this does not mean that the child will necessarily be removed from the parents, or, if so, that it will be permanent. That could happen, but there are other options, such as remaining home under supervision,

---

[64] *The Christian Institute v the Scottish Ministers* [2015] CSIH 64, para 68.
[65] *The Christian Institute v The Lord Advocate* [2016] UKSC 51.
[66] Children Act 1989, s 31.
[67] See *re S-B (children)* [2009] UKSC 17; *In the matter of EV (a child) (Scotland)* [2017] UKSC 15.

and the final decision about what action to take will be based on the children's best interests. In chapter 2 it was said that the principle that family reunification should be sought where appropriate was becoming embedded in judicial reasoning,[68] but there must be concern that a twenty-six-week limit for the duration of care proceedings introduced in 2014[69] and government enthusiasm for increased and more rapid adoption of children in care[70] coupled with meagre support for parents having difficulty bringing up their children[71] will weaken this approach. An alternative model is provided by the London Family Drug and Alcohol Court, which (following various US models), actively engages with parents over a period of time in the context of services designed to resolve the problems that have put their children at risk. Initial evaluations indicate an encouraging success rate in resolving the problems and maintaining children with their families.[72] It is, of course, expensive to run, but may well be cost-effective in the longer run.

It is frequently maintained that the need for such drastic intervention will be reduced by enhancing the services provided to families with children in the community. There were considerable efforts to 'refocus' efforts in this way in the 1990s.[73] The Scottish 'Named Person' scheme is an example, and this policy is characteristic of a number of European countries.[74] However, the policy demands considerable resources where those that are available tend to be concentrated on crisis intervention. It also raises the problems about privacy and surveillance discussed earlier, and could divert attention from individual acts of abuse. But it is important not to give up trying because

---

[68] See p 49. [69] Children and Families Act 2014, s 14.

[70] See Department for Education, *Adoption: A Vision for Change* (March 2016). This notably makes many references to the position of prospective adopters, but none at all to the child's parents. Its proposals are enacted in the Children and Social Work Act 2017.

[71] K Broadhurst and C Mason, 'Birth Parents and the Collateral Consequences of Court-ordered Child Removal: towards a Comprehensive Framework' (2017) 31 *International Journal of Law, Policy and the Family* 41.

[72] J Harwin, M Ryan, and J Tunnard, *The Family Drug and Alcohol Court (FDAC) Evaluation Project: Final Report* (Brunel University, 2011).

[73] See N Parton, *Safeguarding Children: Early Intervention and Surveillance in Late Modern Society* (Palgrave Macmillan, 2006). They were not new: see Children and Young Persons Act 1963, s 1.

[74] See N Gilbert (ed), *Combating Child Abuse: International Perspectives and Trends* (Oxford University Press, 1997).

children are mostly threatened by failing families, and families fail for many different reasons, some of which can be obviated before the problem becomes too serious.

In any event, the scrutiny is to detect harm and exploitation, not to impose a favoured ideal of upbringing. It is a difficult distinction to make, but the difficulty is one of application, not of principle. An English decision provides a fine example. A separated father complained that the mother and her new partner sometimes walked naked around the home and bathed communally with the children. The trial judge ordered the children to be returned to the father. The Court of Appeal overturned that decision. Butler-Sloss LJ said:

> A balance has to be struck between the behaviour within families which is seen by them as natural and with which that family is comfortable, and the sincerely held views of others who are shocked by it. Nudity is an obvious example. Both on the beach and in the home some grown ups walk around nude—indeed you see it at one end of Budleigh Salterton Beach—and they bring up their children to do the same. Other parents pass on to their children a more inhibited approach to nudity. Communal family bathing is another example ... [I]n a happy well run family how the members behave in the privacy of the home is their business and no one else's.[75]

The judge clearly did not regard this practice as harmful in itself, as being brought up in a gay or non-marital household was regarded in the examples given in chapter 2,[76] but warned against possible harms that personal conflicts it might stir up could have on the children, which are a relevant consideration even within the privileged sphere.

More far-reaching issues have arisen over the medical treatment of children. We saw in chapter 2 that medical staff (or someone else with a sufficient interest) can seek court authorization where parents refuse such treatment for their children.[77] So while courts will place great weight on the importance of having the parents' approval of treatment given to their children, the parents do not have the final word. We also saw[78] that a decision of the European Court of Human Rights led to section 58 of the Children Act 2004 which removed the defence of 'reasonable chastisement' if hitting a child causes grievous or 'actual' bodily harm, which means some visible injury. It has been

---

[75] *Re W (minors) (residence orders)* [1999] 1 FLR 869 (Butler-Sloss LJ).
[76] See p 57.   [77] See p 61.   [78] P 49.

argued that the use of corporal punishment on children should be seen only as a means of bringing them up, and that making it unlawful is to favour one means over another when there is no empirical proof whether its use or non-use is better for children.[79] Against that, it could be said that the use of corporal punishment on children is wrong in itself (like lying) and therefore improper whether or not it led to 'better' results for the children: more so if the outcome is unclear.

For some, the compromise in the Children Act 2004 is unacceptable. If we hold to the view that the privileged sphere is not one of legal immunity, and that children's vulnerability justifies scrutiny of parent–child interaction, it is hard to see why the law should not treat the physical integrity of children in the same way as it treats that of adults, for whom any unwanted invasion of their physical integrity is unlawful, except in special circumstances. How does it respect children to treat them differently in this matter? The UN Committee on the Rights of the Child regards any form of violence used against children as being contrary to the UNCRC.[80] Introducing such a prohibition into law need not lead to excessive intrusion into the parent–child relationship, for attitudes can be changed through education and exhortation. The prohibition is directed at violence used for punitive purposes, and not, for example, the use of force 'motivated by the need to protect a child or others'.[81] Similarly, the law does not concern itself with trivial incidents. If striking in itself were to be made unlawful, the law would be applied within that context, and that of the 'liberal compromise' referred to earlier. The parents' private space would remain protected; the 'rule of optimism' would put a favourable interpretation on a parent's actions, and punitive legal action be restricted to only significant or flagrant cases. At the same time it would be hoped that a culture would develop in which the use of punitive violence against children, even if minor, would be rejected, as appears to have occurred in Sweden.

---

[79] See R Ahdar and J Allen 'Taking Smacking Seriously: the Case for Retaining the Legality of Parental Smacking in New Zealand' [2001] *New Zealand Law Review* 1.

[80] See Committee on the Rights of the Child, General Comment No 13, CRC/C/GC/13, 18 April 2011, 'The Right of the Child to Freedom from All Forms of Violence', para 17.

[81] Committee on the Rights of the Child, 42nd Session, General Comment CRC/C/GC/8 (2 March 2007), para 15. See *Trust A v X* [2015] EWHC 922 (Fam) on the scope of parents' powers lawfully to 'detain' their children.

RELIGION

Freedom of religion is respected because of the value of allowing human beings to assess the wisdom of the past and find their own answers to questions about the place of mankind in the world.[82] The value is not the same as that described earlier concerning the privileged sphere, which concerns interaction between individuals. But it is akin to it. It was expressed in a wonderful passage of the United States Supreme Court, referring to marriage, procreation, contraception, family relationships, child-rearing, and education, drawing on the liberty and equality interests of the equal protection clause:

> These matters, involving the most intimate and personal choices a person may make in a lifetime, choices central to personal dignity and autonomy, are central to the liberty protected by the Fourteenth Amendment. At the heart of liberty is the right to define one's own concept of existence, of meaning, of the universe, and of the mystery of human life. Beliefs about these matters could not define the attributes of personhood were they formed under compulsion of the State.[83]

The value of freedom of belief does not imply that the belief itself is valuable: for others, it might seem quite absurd. But without that freedom and that space, a creative, psychological need, akin to the need for love, cannot develop. Although religious and other beliefs of the same nature are ultimately private, many demand public manifestation and group participation; respecting such public manifestation and participation is therefore part of the sustenance of private beliefs.

It is widely held that respect for a person's religious or philosophical beliefs requires allowing that person to pass those beliefs on to his or her child. Article 2 of the First Protocol of the ECHR requires states to 'respect the right of parents to ensure such education and teaching in conformity with their own religious and philosophical convictions'. The International Covenant on Civil and Political Rights requires states parties to respect 'the liberty of parents ... to ensure the religious and moral education of their children in

---

[82] For further discussion and a selection of literature, see J Eekelaar (ed), *Family Rights and Religion* (Routledge, 2017).

[83] *Planned Parenthood of Southeastern Pennsylvania v Casey* 505 US 833 at 851 (1992).

conformity with their own convictions'. But what value does this respect? David Archard states the common view that it is 'the liberal ideal of tolerating diversity in adult ways'.[84] But, as suggested earlier, while diversity may sometimes be attractive, its value is purely contingent on its consequences. It can sow discord. Some adult ways may be better than others. Diversity is merely a likely consequence of respecting individual beliefs, which may be attractive or unattractive, not an end in itself. So could the value in respecting a parent passing religious belief to children be the perpetuation of the parent's belief? But why should its perpetuation be valuable? Society might be much better off with a different belief. Could it be the satisfaction of the parent? This may be politically expedient, but it is an unattractive value, resting on the perception of children as mere instruments of their parents' wish to control the nature of the world after their death.

The real value in allowing parents to pass on their religious beliefs to their children is respect for the privileged sphere of the parent–child relationship. The United States Supreme Court appeared to acknowledge this when it said that 'the state cases create a zone of private authority within which each parent, whether custodial or noncustodial, remains free to impart to the child his or her religious perspective.'[85] Seeing the value as being that of interaction in the privileged sphere allows it to cover imparting all kinds of ideas, religious or otherwise, and to extend beyond the parental relationship to that where any person is acting in the parental role. Claims that this authority extends beyond the privileged sphere have met with little success. In the United States such attempts have come up against the Establishment clause of the First Amendment, prohibiting the advancement of religion in schools. English parents are constrained by the school curriculum.[86] More recently, in England, concern over the influence of religious fundamentalism has led the UK government to impose duties on schools to promote 'British' values,

[84] Archard, n 55, 131.
[85] *Elk Grove Unified School District v Newdow* 124 S Ct 2310 (2004) (Stevens J). In that case the court rejected an attempt by an atheist father to challenge the requirement that his daughter should take the Pledge of Allegiance as it contained the words 'under God'. The court held that this was not in fact a religious exercise.
[86] L Lundy, 'Family Values in the Classroom? Reconciling Parental Wishes and Children's Rights in State Schools' (2005) 19 *International Journal of Law, Policy and the Family* 346.

though, as Rachel Taylor[87] points out, these include those accepted by the international community in Article 29 of the UNCRC, among which is 'the preparation of the child for responsible life in a free society, in the spirit of understanding, peace, tolerance, equality of sexes, and friendship among all peoples, ethnic, national and religious groups and persons of indigenous origin'. These values should therefore override any inconsistent wishes of the parents regarding activity outside the privileged sphere.

The European Court of Human Rights has also held that compulsory sex education did not interfere with the parental right, provided it was not done in a doctrinaire manner.[88] Other parents in England[89] and South Africa[90] have been unsuccessful in their attempts to use their religious beliefs to *require* schools to use corporal punishment. However, parents are sometimes able to withdraw their children from exposure to ideas of which they disapprove. In England they are expressly permitted to withdraw them from classes in religion and sex education. The United States Supreme Court allowed Amish parents to withdraw their children from the secular education system.[91]

The only justification for allowing parents to control what happens beyond the privileged sphere is if what happens outside it threatens the ability of the parent to impart his beliefs in that sphere, or if exposure to new ideas threatens the stability of the child. *Instruction in* a different belief (as opposed to instruction *about* different beliefs) might have such consequences, but it should not be easily assumed that exposure to other values and beliefs carries such threats.[92] As the European Court of Human Rights has put it: '[T]he Convention does not guarantee the right not to be confronted with opinions that are opposed to one's own convictions.'[93] The introduction of same-sex marriage in some countries has opened up a new and sensitive area of

---

[87] RE Taylor, 'Responsibility for the Soul of the Child: The Role of the State and Parents in Determining Religious Upbringing and Education' (2015) 29 *International Journal of Law, Policy and the Family* 15.

[88] *Kjelsden, Busk Madsen and Pedersen v Denmark* (1976) 1 EHRR 711.

[89] *R (on the application of Williamson) v Secretary of State for Education and Employment* [2005] 2 AC 246.

[90] *Christian Education South Africa v Minister of Education* (2000) 9 BHRC 53.

[91] *Wisconsin v Yoder* 406 US 205 (1972).

[92] For the United States, see *Mozert v Hawkins County Board of Education* 827 F 2d 1085 (1987); for Europe, see *Efstratiou v Greece* App No 24095/94, judgment 18 December 1996; *Lautsi v Italy* App No 30814/06, judgment 18 March 2011.

[93] *Dojan v Germany* App No 319/08, judgment 13 September 2011.

tension between the value of encouraging tolerance and any parental right to control ideas to which their children might be exposed outside the privileged sphere.[94] But it is important that children should not be shielded from ideas to which their parents may disapprove, such as that same-sex relationships are legally accepted, otherwise they will be less equipped to participate as citizens in an open society, and indeed dangerous tensions within the community could be created.

Respecting the beliefs of adults therefore has only limited consequences with regard to the way children should be taught in the public sphere. But the beliefs of children, too, demand respect, even if we must accept that those beliefs might only be provisional while they are developing their ideas. Thus issues of a child's religious education in the public sphere, and of allowing the child to observe religious practices, should be seen as aspects of the rights of children rather than of parents. Hence the UN Committee on the Rights of the Child has recommended that the United Kingdom should allow children to withdraw from religious worship at school 'independently', that is, without requiring authorization by the child's parents.[95] To be sure, the child is likely to reflect the parents' beliefs and, while the child is young the parent must be taken to speak for them. But this conceptual realignment allows more space for attention to be paid to the emerging views of the child in the manner described in chapter 2.[96] It is part of the developing autonomy of the child. So schools should not compel children to participate in religious worship, or be instructed in a religion against their will, whatever the parents might wish. On the other hand, respect for the privileged sphere precludes preventing parents from passing on religious views to their children within that sphere and thereby influencing them voluntarily to practise and pursue those beliefs outside the home.

While it cannot be that a child's right to 'freedom of thought, conscience and religion', protected by Article 9 (1) of the European

---

[94] RM Vanderbeck and P Johnson, 'The Promotion of British Values: Sexual Orientation, Equality, Religion and England's Schools' (2016) 30 *International Journal of Law, Policy and the Family* 292.

[95] Committee on the Rights of the Child, *Concluding Observations on the Fifth Periodic Report of the United Kingdom of Great Britain and Northern Ireland* (June 2016), para 35. For full discussion, see U Kilkelly, 'The Child's Right to Religious Freedom in International Law' in MA Fineman and K Worthington (eds), *What is Right for Children?* (Ashgate, 2009) 243.

[96] See p 55.

Convention, is violated by exposure to other beliefs, especially as the article proceeds to elaborate that the right 'includes the right to change his religion or belief', *requirements* concerning dress, attendance at religious services, or periods of study which conflict with the child's beliefs may infringe the right to 'manifest' the child's belief, protected by Article 9(2). But this must be balanced against the duty which schools have to promote social harmony within the school. In an important decision the House of Lords held that a school which imposed a uniform dress code for Muslim girls which was considered appropriate by religious figures in the local Muslim community had conscientiously balanced these interests and was therefore justified in not allowing one pupil to wear a *jilbab*, which was not considered a religious requirement in mainstream Muslim opinion.[97] So compromises over the extent to which a child's religious views can be accommodated may be necessary for the sake of providing efficient education and the equal treatment of all children.

Under European human rights law, such infringements may be justified if according to law, in pursuit of a legitimate aim, proportionate, and 'necessary in a democratic society in the interests of public safety, for the protection of ... health or morals, or for the protection of the rights and freedoms of others'. So prohibitions on wearing religious symbols have been upheld where this was necessary on safety grounds.[98] In *Leyla Şahin v Turkey*[99] the European Court of Human Rights allowed a ban on wearing headscarves in Turkish universities on the basis that it fell within a state's margin of appreciation to permit such a ban based on its perception that such symbols might place unacceptable pressures on those who did not wish to wear them, might lead to discord, and needed to be banned in order to protect democracy.

In June 2004 a French law imposed a blanket ban on the display of conspicuous religious symbols in state schools. That ban appeared to be founded on an assertion of a *policy* of secularism (*laïcité*) in

---

[97] *R (on the application of Begum, by her litigation friend Rahman) v Headteacher and Governors of Denbigh High School* [2006] 2 All ER 487. For a good account of the compromises available, and generally, see S Poulter, 'Muslim Headscarves in School: Contrasting Legal Approaches in England and France' (1997) 17 *Oxford Journal of Legal Studies* 43.

[98] See *Eweida v United Kingdom* App No 48420/10, judgment 15 January 2013.

[99] (2005) 41 EHRR 8.

schools.[100] The problem is that this sees the manifestation by children of their religious beliefs in certain contexts as in itself a breach of the policy, without regard to specific social consequences. Nevertheless, in 2009 the European Court of Human Rights held that this was a legitimate reason for the ban.[101] In 2011 France and Belgium went further and banned the wearing of full face veils in public, and the French decision was upheld by the European Court of Human Rights on the ground that the ban was justified to protect the right of others to social communication and interaction. Two dissenting judges, much more convincingly, observed that, while it was true that the face plays an important role in human interaction, it could not be said that human interaction is impossible if the full face is not shown.[102] Further attempted prohibitions in 2016 on the wearing of 'burkinis' (full-body swimwear) by some French local authorities, on the ground that they indicate religious affiliation, supported by the French Prime Minister,[103] may be explained as reactions to recent terrorist acts, but appear to contradict the value of respect promoted by secularism itself and to protect no reasonable countervailing interest. Possibly these heightened community tensions might provide a justification for such bans grounded in the need to prevent discord, although the need to uphold respect for religious expression should result in action against those who sow the discord, and refusal by public authorities to encourage it.

PROCREATION

The privileged sphere of interaction includes decisions taken about conception and actions consequential to them. The US Supreme Court has long recognized the protected status of heterosexual relations, both within[104] and outside[105] marriage, on the basis of the

---

[100] See MM Idriss, '*Laïcité* and the Banning of the "Hijab" in France' (2005) 25 *Legal Studies* 260.

[101] The court ruled a number of challenges to the ban to be inadmissible on this ground: see *Aktas v France* App No 43563/08; *Bayrak v France* App No 14308/08, judgments 17 July 2009.

[102] *SAS v France* App No 43835/11, judgment 1 July 2014.

[103] See *The Guardian*, 18 August 2016.

[104] *Griswold v Connecticut* 381 US 479 (1965).

[105] *Eisenstadt v Baird* 405 US 438 (1972).

right to privacy. If the decision is against procreation, there is no reason for infringing the privileged sphere of intimate relations, although, as suggested earlier,[106] there can be no objection if the community wishes to encourage conception for pro-natalist reasons. But libertarian principles inhibit restraints being placed on decisions to procreate. There are good reasons for such inhibition. The eugenics movement of the late nineteenth and early twentieth centuries produced policies in many countries, especially the United States and Sweden, which forced unwanted sterilization on people thought to be mentally or socially unfit to produce children.[107] The policies were taken to horrific extremes by German Nazism. Forced sterilization is accepted as a violation of human rights. In English law, unwanted sterilization will only be visited on people who are mentally incompetent and if a court has decided that this is in the individual's best interests.[108]

The issue, however, becomes more complicated when it concerns whether to provide or allow the provision of assistance to overcome infertility, or to allow practices such as surrogate birth. Emily Jackson argues that respect for individual autonomy demands that infertile people should, through the provision of medical services, have the same opportunities to procreate as fertile people, since procreation and childbearing are significant aspects of individual well-being.[109] This is an attractive position, but raises broad political and ideological issues, such as upon whom the duty to make such provision should fall, and how the resources needed should be provided. I leave those questions open. But there is a deeper issue. There is perhaps no greater power over others than the power to procreate. The position maintained here is that withholding or obstructing such treatments that are available through standard processes of medical provision would be as much an intrusion into the privileged sphere as making the sale of contraceptives illegal was in *Griswold v Connecticut*.[110] But this does not mean that the consequences of such provision on children born as a result have no relevance, and my argument does not allow the privilege to permit harmful behaviour, or contemplate outcomes

---

[106] See p 75.

[107] See E Jackson, *Regulating Reproduction: Law, Technology and Autonomy* (Hart Publishing, 2001) ch 4.

[108] See *re F (Mental Patient: Sterilisation)* [1989] 2 AC 1; *Re DD (No 4) (Sterilisation)* [2015] EWCOP 4.

[109] Jackson, n 107, ch 1.   [110] *Griswold v Connecticut*, n 104.

that might be harmful. So when the state is involved in the process, either by providing services or allowing their provision, these matters become relevant. Section 13(5) of the Human Fertilisation and Embryology Acts 1990 (amended in 2008) requires that licensed providers of infertility treatment should take into account the welfare of any child who may be born as a result of the treatment. Jackson considers that 'the future welfare of would-be patients' children should be irrelevant when deciding whether to help them to conceive.'[111] The matter, she says, should be left to the parents.

But is it necessary to place the future children so completely at the disposal of infertile parents who seek external assistance to conceive? It is often said that the conditions experienced by a child born through such assistance cannot be deemed harmful because existence, even if in a damaged state and adverse conditions, is always better than non-existence, so that it could never be wrong to bring a child into existence, no matter how debilitating. But a non-existent being has no interests that can be adversely affected, or weighed against those of a born child, so comparison cannot be made between the life the child is likely to lead and its non-existence. The only issue is whether the life the child is actually likely to experience is likely to be sufficiently close to one which a person would reasonably choose as acceptable.[112] If not, there is good reason to withhold the service. So potential harms to the future child, the circumstances of the parents, and other factors (eg costs of provision) may all properly be weighed in the balance. For these reasons controls can rightly be placed on the way reproduction may be assisted through public services. The degree to which such assistance is regulated, or even allowed, varies greatly between countries. In the case of embryo donation, where the children have no genetic link with the parents who bring them up, comparisons have even been made with adoption, with the implication that assessments should be made of the suitability of the prospective parents to receive such a donation

---

[111] E Jackson, 'Conception and the Irrelevance of the Welfare Principle' (2002) 65 *Modern Law Review* 176, 182. For a contrary view, see D Archard, 'Wrongful Life' (2004) 79 *Philosophy* 403.

[112] There is extensive philosophical discussion. For views similar to that taken here, see J Feinberg, 'Wrongful Life and the Counterfactual Element of Harming' (1987) 4 *Social Philosophy and Policy* 164; E Harman, 'Harming as Causing Harm' and B Steinbock, 'Wrongful Life and the Counterfactual Element of Harming' in MA Roberts and DT Wasserman (eds), *Harming Future Persons: Ethics, Genetics and the Non-identity Problem* (Singer, 2009) chs 7 and 8.

similar to those expected for adoption.[113] But care must be taken to avoid improper discrimination, and even the age of the parents-to-be should probably not, in itself, rule out the procedure.[114]

Another context in which these issues have arisen is that of 'saviour siblings', when a child is conceived for the purpose of providing biological material for the benefit of an older sibling. There are potential risks to a child conceived in that way, including possible psychological consequences of a perception of having been conceived as a commodity. Although, as has been pointed out, the duty on clinics to take into account the welfare of such children is probably unenforceable (for it is difficult to see what remedy such a child would have),[115] nevertheless the duty is not meaningless in practice, and the question needs to be faced whether permitting conceptions for collateral purposes should ever be permitted, or (as in the United Kingdom) permitted subject to regulation. It is rather hard to delve into people's purposes when knowingly procreating children: doing so for their own benefit, or that of the wider family (or trying to achieve gender balance among their children) are not unknown. This does not necessarily reduce their commitment to the born child, or unacceptably harm their welfare.[116] Some risks may, however, be too great. What seems important is to try always to imagine as far as possible whether the conceived child would view its position as acceptable.

RESPECTING CHILDREN

So what is it to respect children? Partly, it is the same as for any person. Respect acknowledges the value of those features of individuals which

---

[113] For a broad discussion of these issues, see S Goedeke and K Daniels, 'Embryo Donation, or Embryo Adoption? Practice and Policy in the New Zealand Context' (2017) 31 *International Journal of Law, Policy and the Family* 1.

[114] See E Blyth, 'To Be or not To Be? A Critical Appraisal of the Welfare of Children Conceived through New Reproductive Technologies' (2008) 16 *International Journal of Children's Rights* 505.

[115] See L Cherkassky, 'The Wrong Harvest: The Law on Saviour Siblings' (2015) 29 *International Journal of Law, Policy and the Family* 36 for a general discussion.

[116] See R Boyle and J Savulescu, 'Ethics of Using Preimplantation Genetic Diagnosis to Select a Stem Cell Donor for an Existing Person' (2001) 323 *British Medical Journal* 1240.

allow them to flourish. Physical abuse and neglect clearly contradict this. Allowing any physical striking of a child in circumstances where to do the same against an adult would be unlawful also fails to respect the child. But that cannot be the whole story. Respect for a child demands more than the kind of respect one has for one's pet hamster. It is more than merely providing the child with a happy childhood. As indicated earlier,[117] it involves recognizing the gradual emergence of the child as an individual with an identity and interests and aspirations which are their own. The English Court of Appeal showed this respect when confirming that a person under 16 was owed a duty of confidentiality by the medical profession when provided with medical advice and treatment, including abortion advice and treatment, if they properly understood what was involved. The child's parents had no right to be told if the child did not want this to happen.[118]

This is one aspect of a deeper value. Just as we show respect to our elders by putting value on those things they have achieved and handed down for our benefit, so we show respect to the coming generation by accepting that their contribution to the nature, beliefs, and ideals of the society in which they will live has value. All societies reflect their past, whether transmitted from the previous generation through the intimate sphere or by public means. But we must value the privileged spheres and relationships in which members of the next generation develop new ideas with which to face the new realities which confront them.

---

[117] See p 55.
[118] *R (on the application of Axon) v Secretary of State for Health* [2006] 1 FCR 175.

4

Friendship

During an interview with a married woman as part of a project seeking to explore people's sense of obligation within intimate relationships[1] it emerged that the household contained an unusual individual. Mr Schmid (as I will call him) had come to England from Berlin in the 1930s. He had no family and no possessions. He became a lodger with my respondent's mother-in-law, and when my respondent married, they took Mr Schmid into their home while he looked for somewhere else to live. That was twenty-two years ago. He was still there. He shared meals and living facilities with the family. 'He was a friend,' my respondent said, 'and when we found he had nowhere to live and we had a spare room we agreed he could come and stay with us until he found somewhere else … and he's stayed ever since.' Did they see him as part of the family, I asked. 'Ummm, it's a very unusual relationship,' came the answer, 'he isn't part of the family; he has lived with us for a long time and I guess it is something that just happened.' She was anxious to dispel any idea that this was done out of a sense of obligation, or that any such obligation continued. If he could no longer look after himself, it was expected that he would find care with the welfare authorities.

'He was a friend.' Respondents sometimes talked of family ties as creating stronger duties than friendship ('Not [friends] … it's family and you make that extra effort to help them'), and living in cohabitation likewise ('Being together you should be mutually supportive … otherwise you're just living with a friend') and sometimes as if friendship added something more to a family relationship ('[My

---

[1] This research is reported in J Eekelaar and M Maclean, 'Marriage and the Moral Bases of Personal Obligations' (2004) 31 *Journal of Law and Society* 510. I will refer to this as 'the Personal Obligations research'.

mother and I] are best of friends'). But more often respondents seemed unwilling to distinguish. You could owe the same obligations, or not owe them, to family and friends. 'I have friends I would probably treat more favourably than certain family members, but again I have some family members I would treat better ... it depends on who you're talking about.' So, what do we owe to family? What do we owe to friends?

We must first see if we can define 'family' and 'friend'. Neither is easy. It is perhaps taken as given that family includes 'kin' in a genetic sense (blood relations), but of course 'kinship' is a social construction, manifested mostly through institutions instituted by formal acts such as marriage and adoption. But it is not confined to such institutions, and it seems we can now include adults, whether of the opposite or the same sex, who live together in an intimate relationship over a period of time as constituting a family.[2] For example, in 1997 the European Court of Human Rights said: 'When considering whether a relationship can be said to amount to "family life" a number of factors may be relevant, including whether the couple live together, the length of their relationships and whether they have demonstrated their commitment to each other by having children together or by other means.'[3] But if this happens does this mean that they are no longer friends? Were they ever friends? How does one cross the line between friendship and family membership in the absence of a calculated act demonstrating a clear intention to move from one type of relationship to another? Do these questions even matter?

I am going to suggest that we should reflect on the role of friendship in personal relations in order to see whether this might help in approaching some of the issues currently under discussion with regard to their legal regulation. Discussion of such regulation tends to start with the paradigm of marriage, and to ask how far its legal incidents should be extended beyond its confines. This leads naturally to such concerns as to whether the law should 'impose' marriage on the non-married,[4] and whether to do so might 'undermine' marriage, and

---

[2] *Fitzpatrick v Sterling Housing Association* [2001] 1 AC 27.

[3] *X, Y and Z v United Kingdom* App No 21830/93, judgment 22 April 1997.

[4] The classic example is R Deech, 'The Case against the Legal Recognition of Cohabitation' in J Eekelaar and SN Katz (eds), *Marriage and Cohabitation in Contemporary Societies: Areas of Legal, Social and Ethical Change* (Butterworths, 1980) ch 30. For a thorough discussion, see EE Sutherland, 'Unmarried Cohabitation'

indeed what the legal consequences of marriage are. If, however, we see the core relationship as one of friendship, we might find a new perspective on the issue of legal regulation and ask whether legal regulation of the married and the unmarried can be justified on the basis of a different relationship which has been important to people across the centuries: friendship.

FRIENDSHIP AND BROTHERLY LOVE

We face, however, a formidable conceptual problem at the outset. Defining 'friendship' is possibly even more difficult than defining 'family'. The literature is vast, stretching into ancient times, and my examples are chosen only to give a sense of the perenniality of the issue and to illustrate a few selected themes. It is clear that the concept changes over time and between cultures. I am not going to be concerned about labelling: that is, whether the term 'friendship' is properly applicable only to one particular behavioural concept. I am content to note its diverse range. But I will be interested in some more than others.

A strong seam in western thought uses words usually translated as friendship (Greek: *philia*; Latin: *amicitia*) as describing the bond that can exist between all humans, or at least all members of a political community. In Pythagorean and Stoic thought, friendship not only links all humans with one another, but identifies them with the natural world in a reflection of the divine.[5] There is a striking instance in the Christian gospel. Immediately after recounting the parable of the vine (where Jesus says: 'I am the vine; you are its branches'), St. John records Christ saying to the disciples:

> This is my commandment: that you should love one another, as I have loved you. This is the greatest love a man can show, that he should lay down his life for his friends (philoi); and you, if you do all that

---

in J Eekelaar and R George (eds), *Routledge Handbook of Family Law and Policy* (Routledge, 2014) ch 1.5.

[5] J McEvoy, 'The Theory of Friendship in the Latin Middle Ages'; EG Cassidy, 'Classical and Christian Perspectives on the Limits of Friendship' in J Haseldine (ed), *Friendship in Medieval Europe* (Sutton Publishing, 1999) chs 1 and 2.

I command you, are my friends. I do not speak to you any more as my servants; a servant is one who does not understand what his master is about, whereas I have made known to you all that my Father has told me; and so I have called you my friends.[6]

And shortly later:

At the time I speak of, you will make your requests in my name; and there is no need for me to tell you that I will ask the Father to grant them to you, because the Father himself is your friend, since you have become my friends ...[7]

It is possible that these utterances refer to a deep personal relationship between Jesus (God, in Christian belief) and the disciples, but it is also plausible that the friendship exists not only between the disciples and Jesus, but between all Christians. The Pauline references to the members of that community as parts of the same body, which is also Christ's 'mystical body',[8] suggest a much wider concept of friendship binding people who may not even know each other, making them one through communion with the divine. ('I am the vine. You are the branches'). Today we might prefer an expression such as brotherly love, or love of humankind, to express such an idea. Its importance is not in question. It is the foundational motivation behind human rights claims. But it is not the aspect of friendship with which I am here concerned. For this I will turn first to Aristotle.

'FULL' FRIENDSHIP AS A PARADIGMATIC VALUE

To be sure, Aristotle nods in the direction of this idea of universal friendship.

So we praise those who love their fellow men. And one notices in one's travels how everybody feels that everybody else is his friend and brother man. Again, it is pretty clear that those who frame the constitutions of states set more store by this feeling than by justice itself. For their two

---

[6] John 15: 12–16.   [7] John 16: 26–28.
[8] 1 Corinthians 12: 12; Romans 12: 5.

prime objectives are to expel faction, which is inspired by hate, and to produce concord, concord being like friendship.[9]

But the bulk of Aristotle's discussion examines a much more personal type of friendship. He regards it as of immense personal importance: 'No one would choose a friendless existence on condition of having all the other good things in the world.'[10] He is not one to oversimplify. He recognizes that the term can cover different types of relationship. Three in fact. In one, the friendship is grounded on the utility it brings to the friends; in another, it is the pleasure it brings them. Both are forms of friendship, capable of inspiring concern for the good of the other, but the friendship is contingent on the utility or the pleasure. But full friendship exists between the good, in the sense that they want nothing else except the good of the other.

> It is those who desire the good of their friends for their friends' sake who are most completely friends, since each loves the other for what the other is in himself and not for something he has about him which he need not have. Accordingly, the friendship of such men lasts as long as they keep their goodness—and goodness is a lasting quality.[11]

For Aristotle, the distinction between these categories has important consequences, which I will deal with a little later. But I need to dwell a little on the nature of what I will call 'full' friendship thus described. It is indeed deeply personal, and Aristotle says that 'besides goodness, (men) need time and intimacy to establish perfect friendship.' A similar notion of friendship was famously expounded by Michel de Montaigne in the sixteenth century:

> If a Man should importune me to give reason why I lov'd him, I found it could not otherwise be expres't, than by making answer, because it was he, because it was I.[12]

This type of relationship, Montaigne averred, could only be found between men (though he was careful to say that it was not sexual), not because it was a theoretically impossible experience between a man and a woman, but because no woman had apparently yet been

---

[9] Aristotle, *Nichomachean Ethics* (trs JAK Thomson) (Penguin Classics, 2004) Bk 8, ch 1.
[10] Ibid Bk 8, ch 1.   [11] Ibid Bk 8, ch 3.
[12] *Essays of Michel, Seigneur de Montaigne* (trs Charles Cotton, London, 1685), Bk I, ch 27, 332.

found with the quality of constancy of mind to endure 'so hard and durable a knot'. Were one miraculously to appear, so that 'not only the Soules might have their entire fruition, but the Bodies also might share in the Alliance ... the Friendship would certainly be more full and perfect'. But he clearly thought marriage was inimical to such an outcome:

> That is a Covenant, the entrance into which is only free, but the continuance in it is forced, compelled, having another dependence, than that of our own Free will, and a Bargain commonly contracted to other ends, there almost always happens a Thousand Intricacies in it, to unravel, enough to break the Thred, and to divert the Current of Lively Affection: whereas Friendship has no manner of Business or Traffick with any but itself.[13]

Writing in 1960, CS Lewis put friendship on a less elevated plane. For him, friendship was centred upon a sharing of common interests. It was an escape from the affairs of everyday life. Lewis never quite convinces how this is distinct from companionship (a kind of *camaraderie*), and he sees it as very possible for it to be shared between a number of people.[14] Because it is contingent upon shared interests,[15] he observes that, though such a relationship might arise between a man and a woman, the social worlds of women and of men were then sufficiently separate to make that difficult. But he did accept that it was possible for such friendships to arise between women. At the end of the twentieth century, Ray Pahl detected the opening up of new possibilities of communication, and therefore of intimacy, between men and women.[16] However, like Aristotle, he writes of a very wide range of types of friendship, some crudely utilitarian (he calls them 'commodified'), such as where we try to 'win friends and influence people', but others where secrets are shared and 'each soul-mate is closely responsive to the direction and interpretation of the other'.[17]

While 'friendship' can therefore cover many types of relationship, I am concerned mainly with 'full' friendship, of a kind similar or close to that described by Aristotle and Montaigne. It can be seen as a paradigmatic altruistic value. Lawrence Blum argues, similarly

---

[13] Ibid 331.   [14] CS Lewis, *The Four Loves* (Fontana, 1960).
[15] 'Friendship must be about something, even if it were only an enthusiasm for dominoes or white mice': ibid 63.
[16] R Pahl, *On Friendship* (Polity Press, 2000).   [17] Ibid 84.

to later virtue ethicists, that while actions motivated by altruism are not morally obligatory, they may yet have moral value. He rejects the Kantian concern that acting to benefit a friend for the friend's own sake breaches the duty of acting with impartiality. Impartiality is enjoined only in certain institutional contexts. Nor is the altruism of friendship to be seen as simply a form of self-interest. This is because actions towards the friend are *motivated* by a genuine regard for the other's welfare. It will be true that acting in this way towards a friend *will also* reflect what is important to the actor, and in that sense is not a sacrifice of the actor's self-interest, but it is nevertheless an action fully for the sake of the good of the friend.[18]

FRIENDSHIP AND PUBLIC CONSTRAINTS

Pahl claims that 'the modern idea of friendship lies in its very freedom from public roles and obligations.'[19] We do not, as Ira Ellman, the noted American family lawyer, observed, 'have a law of close friends.'[20] CS Lewis refers to friendship's 'exquisite arbitrariness and irresponsibility': 'I have no duty to be anyone's Friend and no man in the world has a duty to be mine. No claims, no shadow of necessity.'[21] We noticed that Montaigne stressed the incompatibility between friendship and the bargains and ancillary constraints of marriage. It seems that the absence of externally imposed restraints is an important element in many people's conceptions of their intimate relationships today. The Personal Obligations research referred to earlier[22] found that people who were in close relationships had a strong sense that they should behave in certain ways towards their partner and their partner's close relatives. The source of such obligations varied greatly. For some, they were found in convention (eg, a marriage); for others, in distinct ethical principles (behaving well to those who

---

[18] LA Blum, *Friendship, Altruism and Morality* (Routledge & Kegan Paul, 1980) 10 and ch 4.

[19] Pahl, n 16, 37.

[20] IM Ellman, 'Why Making Family Law Is Hard' (2003) 35 *Arizona State Law Journal* 699, 700.

[21] Lewis, n 14, 67.

[22] Eekelaar and Maclean, 'Marriage and the Moral Bases of Personal Obligations', n 1.

behaved well to you); and for yet others, the obligations seemed to develop as the relationship developed (an 'evolutionary' approach). However, they often made the point that these were voluntarily accepted obligations; they did what they did because they wanted to, because they were that sort of person. It seems that the kernel of this type of relationship lies not in a sense of absence of *any* obligation, but in the belief that the obligation is *inherent, and not externally imposed.* It is voluntarily assumed. It seems to follow that such obligations are seen to be free of social coercion.

However, Aristotle does refer to external restraints on friendship, but only for utilitarian friendships, not full friendship. Where people are friends for some ulterior purpose, and do not receive the benefits they hoped for, conflict arises.

> In the same way as justice is divided into written and unwritten, so utilitarian friendship seems to carry with it a moral or a legal obligation. The consequence is that, if complaints arise, it is mainly at the time when the relative position of the friends is not the same at the end of their association as it was when the association was formed. If it was formed on certain fixed or stated terms, it has a legal character ... as for the moral type of utilitarian friendship, it is not expressed in set terms. The gift, or whatever it is that passes between the friends, is given as to a friend. Still, the giver expects to get back the equivalent or better ... and if he finds himself in a different position at the end of their friendly relations, he will cherish a grievance ... disputes might arise when an attempt is made to put a value on services rendered. Is the standard to be the advantage accruing to the recipient or the sacrifice made by the benefactor? And in the former case is the repayment of the service to be made in accordance with this standard? The recipient seeks to depreciate the value of the service rendered, arguing that it cost the man who gave it nothing worth mentioning and could have been had from somebody else. The giver insists that on the contrary it strained his resources, that no one else could have given it, that it was given in a time of danger or some such pressing occasion. Perhaps the best solution is to say that, where friendship has been formed for its utility, the service should be measured by its value to the beneficiary.[23]

Aristotle's tentative suggestion, that when utilitarian friendships end, repayment is to be measured by the value of the gift or the service to the beneficiary, rather than by the loss to the conferrer of the benefits,

---

[23] *Nichomachean Ethics*, n 9, Bk 8, ch 13.

is subtle and insightful. But why should this be confined to 'utilitarian' friendships? Aristotle thought it was appropriate only for utilitarian friendship because he assumed that problems caused by betrayal and loss simply could not arise in complete friendships. Full friendship, he said, exists only between the good, and goodness is enduring. But this is a fiction. Even such friendships can break down. So in what follows, references to 'friendship' are to 'full friendship' as described above.

MARRIAGE AND FRIENDSHIP COMPARED

When one considers the public face of marriage historically, it is not difficult to see why Montaigne considered that marriage, being a covenant, was for all practical purposes incompatible with full friendship. Think of the young Marie Antoinette, sent at the age of 15 to marry the French Dauphin, a clumsy youth with no interest in her, or possibly any woman, in order to fulfil the purposes of contemporary politicians.[24] The humiliations of surveillance of the bedchamber, of reporting back to her mother, Maria Teresa, about her menstrual cycle, are no doubt at the extreme, but they were mirrored in the myriad of ways in which marriage, through the concept of legitimacy, was central to the ordering of wealth and political power. As described in chapter 1, marriage was a powerful means for obliterating women's freedom of action. Of course there was another side to this. Marriage was the context in which something approaching the type of relationship described by Aristotle and others as full friendship might be experienced between a man and a woman, though we have seen that Montaigne felt this was a practical impossibility in the sixteenth century, and CS Lewis thought is was difficult in the twentieth.

But marriage is an institution, and this will encompass certain ideologies. Tony Honoré[25] distinguished three: the lifelong partnership model, according to which one partner could draw on the resources of the other even after divorce as if the marriage continued; an insurance model, where each spouse was committed to securing the needs of the other even after divorce; and the individualistic model that sees

---

[24] Antonia Fraser, *Marie Antoinette: The Journey* (Phoenix, 2002).
[25] T Honoré, *The Quest for Security: Employees, Tenants, Wives* (Stevens, 1982).

marriage as an arrangement which two persons enter for mutual benefits, but which may result in gains to one at the expense of the other. The first model has been rejected with the repeal of the 'minimal loss' principle in 1984;[26] the second, as we will see later,[27] has been maintained in an attenuated form, though the dominant model is probably the third.

The point here is that these are all models of an *institution*, whereas friendship describes a certain state of being. Hence, in some jurisdictions, being married attracts financial benefits. This is particularly evident in the United States.[28] Why should marriage attract such benefits? It is sometimes said that married people are happier, healthier, and wealthier than those who are not married, so people should be encouraged to marry. But even if that is true, it is difficult to know whether marriage has those consequences, or whether people blessed with those fortunes are more likely to marry than those who are not.[29] It is true that married people are less likely to separate than people who are living together unmarried, but again it may be that other factors, such as religiosity, economic security, and strength of the relationship dispose people to marry and to stay together rather than that marriage itself has that consequence. But whatever view is taken about that,[30] what interest does the state have in bribing friends, whether of the same or the opposite sex, whether married or unmarried, to continue their friendship if the friendship falls into difficulty? If they have been living together, some may say that the pressures on housing stocks caused by increasing numbers of single households could justify it. Perhaps this is true. Of course, if they are parents, the interests of the children may be used to justify creating incentives for their continued cohabitation, although the justification is likely to be defeated if they are in a state of conflict. But the important point is

---

[26] As described in chapter 2, p 44.   [27] See p 110.

[28] See D Solot and M Miller, 'Taking the Government Out of the Marriage Business: Families Would Benefit' in A Bernstein (ed), *Marriage Proposals: Questioning a Legal Status* (New York University Press, 2008) 71, who claim that marital status is a 'key determinant of eligibility for more than one thousand federal rights and obligations'.

[29] See LJ Waite and M Gallagher, *The Case for Marriage* (Broadway Books, 2000). These authors also often treat unmarried people who are living together as married people, so the benefits may arise from living together rather than singly, not from being married.

[30] For a full discussion, see J Eekelaar, 'Evaluating Legal Regulation of Family Behaviour' (2011) 1 *International Journal of Jurisprudence of the Family* 17.

that they are parents, not just friends. So the case for marriage incentives must rest on a view of the importance of sustaining the institution, not simply the underlying friendship.

If it is difficult to find a case for having financial incentives for people to remain friends, we will also have to say that there can be no legal (ie externally imposed, and enforced) duties on the friends to maintain the friendship, and to act for the well-being of one another. So, if we regard unmarried partners only as friends then it is appropriate that, while spouses may have a duty to maintain one another while they are living together arising from the institutional nature of marriage, unmarried partners should not. And, if that is so, why should entitlements arise if they part company? Again, the insurance model of marriage could generate some entitlement to provision for 'needs', but in the case of friends, are caring behaviour and financial support to be enforced only if they separate? Is property only then to be forcibly redistributed between them? It seems not. Of course, it is a feature of full friendship that the friends see their property as common. But this comprehends only common use during the friendship. How could such a friend, either through financial contributions or through any other form of participation in the friendship, be thought to be 'earning' a proprietary or other legal entitlement to the other's property, even if the entitlement is deferred to the moment of separation? That would contradict the central feature of friendship in the full sense.

Yet friendship involves trust, and with trust is always the possibility of betrayal, or, if not betrayal, failure.[31] So the erstwhile friend who inflicts deliberate damage on a former companion surely cannot expect immunity from redress. The legal immunities between spouses conferred by the old common law, particularly the non-applicability of the law of rape, had nothing to do with the ideals of friendship, and everything to do with male domination. That is why it is hard to accept Milton Regan's support for the rule against testimony between spouses, for how can it seriously be maintained that a person whose trust has been betrayed should keep loyal to the betrayer?[32] So friendship cannot confer immunity against deliberately harmful actions.

---

[31] For discussion of trust in married and unmarried relationships, see J Lewis, *The End of Marriage? Individualism and Intimate Relations* (Edward Elgar, 2001).

[32] M Regan Jr, *Law and the Meaning of Marriage* (Oxford University Press, 1999).

But what if the circumstances fall short of inflicting deliberate harm? The friendship has simply ceased to be. Perhaps one party dissembled or exploited the other, perhaps not; motivations are hard to unravel. Of course friends should be able to make gifts to one another, and these should not be recoverable. But when assets are treated as being for the friends' common use, the freedom and arbitrary nature of friendship surely do not imply that one party should walk away with all the other has made available for common use and enjoyment, or which they have built up together for those purposes, simply because he or she is stronger, or has acquired legal title. We would surely want to say that if friendship is betrayed or lost, each friend should, as far as possible, *have what they put into the commonality restored to them.* Indeed, this is a general principle of justice, applicable between any people, whether friends or not. The law has the means of bringing about restoration of benefits which it would be unjust to allow one party to take from the friendship should it end.[33]

This is straightforward where material contributions (in which might be included running a household) lead to material accumulations to wealth, though it may be necessary to impute intentions generously as to how the contributions are to be quantified.[34] But that assumes a material contribution to the assets. Suppose I advise my friend how to invest his money, or what horse to back, or I spend time producing information which he uses to write a book. While the friend might behave shabbily in giving no manifestation of gratitude for his success, I surely do not have, and should not have, an enforceable claim for a share in it. In those cases the very fact of friendship deprives the action of the requisite element of knowledge on the part of the beneficiary that the action was not offered gratuitously.[35]

But suppose a friend has given up much for the other and there are no acquests to which it can be said that person contributed. When the friendship finishes, should the other be required to compensate for those losses? If I give up something to help my friend, I do so on the basis of trust that the friend will repay in their own way. Perhaps

---

[33] See, for example, *Walker v Hall* [1984] FLR 126.

[34] See S Gardner, 'Problems in Family Property' (2013) 72 *Cambridge Law Journal* 301; *Jones v Kernott* [2011] UKSC 53.

[35] See P Birks, *An Introduction to the Law of Restitution* (Clarendon Press, 1985) 114; 281–3. The mere fact of free acceptance of the benefit seems insufficient: A Burrows, *The Law of Restitution* (Butterworths, 2002) 402–7.

continuing the friendship will be enough. To convert any such moral obligation to a legal obligation if the friendship fails destroys the notion of trust. If Mr Schmid, the refugee-lodger in the Personal Obligations research, should fortuitously come into money, and then fall out with my respondent, whatever we may think his moral obligations may be, to give her the right to claim recompense for her efforts over the years surely contradicts the virtue of her actions. Perhaps it would make such virtuous actions impossible. As will be explained shortly, longer-term financial provision (maintenance) can best be seen either as an insurance-type provision to relieve needs or as a form of compensation for the economic disparity between the couple on separation rather than restitution for contributions, so it seems to follow that there should be no entitlement to such compensation in the case of people who are friends, and nothing else.

FRIENDSHIP PLUS

But friendship can form part of a more complex relationship. We could have 'friendship plus', where the friends had arranged their mode of living and financial arrangements as a basis upon which they followed their common life together for the long term. This kind of joint 'life plan' (in the sense of a plan for organizing the way we live) could be described as a form of 'friendship plus', the additional element being not merely support of one by the other (or mutual support), but the investment of mutual resources (effort, money) in servicing a long-term project. This can be assumed if the friends marry, but that need not be necessary. This is surely what the New Zealand law is referring to when it states that 'the degree of mutual commitment to a shared life' and the 'degree of financial dependence and interdependence' are among the relevant criteria for deciding whether two unmarried people qualified as a 'couple' for the purposes of exercising jurisdiction over their property.[36] Gillian Douglas has argued that 'commitment' is an unsatisfactory basis for imposing obligations between former partners, since it may be lacking (especially in the absence of marriage),

---

[36] Property Relationships Amendment Act 2001, s 2D; *Scragg v Scott* [2006] NZFLR 1076.

particularly so when relationships breakdown.[37] However, a degree of commitment to 'care for' one another is likely to be an element in a 'life plan' involving a 'shared life', whether within the framework of marriage or outside it, though it is only one of the ingredients of such a relationship.[38]

There can of course be borderline cases. Some people have a personal relationship, and see themselves as a 'couple', but do not share a household. They are 'living apart together' (LAT).[39] Researchers at Uppsala University looking at evidence in Sweden and Norway found that some people chose such an arrangement although they would have preferred to live together, but commitments to others (children or elderly relatives) or work or education requirements prevented this. Others preferred it that way. But in most cases 'the couple already each have their own home and are used to paying for their own home expenses.'[40] A British study found a greater variety of relationships, but they were characterized by fluidity (people moved in and out of them fairly easily) and a desire on behalf of each person for a fairly marked element of independence.[41] It therefore seems difficult to see sufficient cohesion for a 'life plan' of the kind mentioned earlier in such cases. Such people are friends, entitled to recover material benefits acquired from one of them by the other for common use, but not to compensation if the friendship ends. But the possibility should be kept open for a former LAT partner to establish on direct evidence that such a project had indeed been set up.

What are the implications of 'friendship plus' on the claims the partners should have against one another? Craig Lind says that I 'seem to see unmarried people as 'friends' who should have no claims to the property of one another'.[42] But that ignores what I say about

---

[37] G Douglas, 'Towards an Understanding of the Basis of Obligation and Commitment in Family Law' (2016) 36 *Legal Studies* 1.

[38] See J Herring, *Caring and the Law* (Hart Publishing, 2013) 197, who proposes that 'caring' should be 'central to marriage'.

[39] In Sweden in 2001 it was estimated that some 14 per cent of people not married or living together unmarried were in such relationships: see I Levin, 'Living Apart Together: A New Family Form' (2004) 52 *Current Sociology* 223.

[40] Ibid 236–7.

[41] J Haskey and J Lewis, 'Living Apart Together in Britain: Context and Meaning' (2006) 2 *International Journal of Law in Context* 37. They estimated that in 2001–2002, 19 per cent of men and 21 per cent of women were in such relationships.

[42] C Lind, 'Power and the Taking of Responsibility: Shifting the Legal Family from Marriage to Friendship' in C Lind, H Keating, and J Bridgeman (eds), *Taking Responsibility, Law and the Changing Family* (Ashgate/Routledge, 2010) 77.

'friendship plus'. The idea that 'friendship plus' reflects a 'life plan' of the kind described earlier suggests something more deliberate than the experience of friendship itself. Therefore, while it is a characteristic of full friendship that it is founded on trust, and not on any form of agreement, it is plausible that parties might wish to determine the nature of their 'life plan'. For this reason, since marriage is one form of friendship plus, European systems are willing to allow couples to decide what is being put into the communality in advance of the formal inception of their relationship, and even to re-define this during their relationship. This is very different from specifying what financial and property arrangements should be made if their relationship ends, although of course what property constitutes the commonality affects the content of arrangements that can be made on breakdown, but not the principles applicable. So, while still subject to some regulation (eg, the need for notarial authentication), the couple are allowed more scope to agree the nature of the commonality, or alter it during the union, than to specify what is to happen on breakdown.[43] English law does not make these distinctions so sharply, and pre-marital agreements are usually directed at the point of breakdown of the relationship. In such circumstances, while it seems that the agreement will be regarded as a form of contract, the English courts may not enforce it if it is not 'fair'.[44] This suggests that there are considerations that arise when the relationship ends that can override the earlier agreement. What might these be?

It was suggested above that if friendship is betrayed or lost, each friend should, as far as possible, have restored to them what they put into the commonality: they had earned a share in such acquisitions. This applies of course also in the case of 'friendship plus'. If 'friendship plus' takes the form of marriage or civil partnership, civil law systems, including Scots law, assume that the character of the institution they have entered demands that they should be entitled to an equal share in such property (though there are some differences in the exact specification of the property covered).[45] While not formalized

---

[43] See JM Scherpe, 'Marital Agreements and Private Autonomy in Comparative Perspective' in JM Scherpe (ed), *Marital Agreements and Private Autonomy in Comparative Perspective* (Hart Publishing, 2012).

[44] *Radmacher v Granatino* [2010] UKSC 42.

[45] See Family Law (Scotland) Act 1985, s 10(1) and J Miles and JM Scherpe, 'The Legal Consequences of Dissolution: Property and Financial Support between Spouses'

in legislation, English law also tends towards presuming equal division of marital assets.[46] Any agreement to the contrary can properly be held to violate basic principles of fairness. But where the couple are not married or civil partners, it may not be so clear that they should not be able to specify some other basis for distribution, since they have not entered a legal institution.

However, there are other consequences which they should not be able to easily avoid in the case of 'friendship plus' *whether or not within marriage or civil partnership*. This is because, in addition to having what they put into the commonality restored (which follows from loss of friendship), compensation might be appropriate for the disadvantages suffered by one of the friends undergone as a result of the breakdown of the common project. However, it is important to be clear for what compensation is due.[47] The appropriate measure is the economic disparity between the couple at separation, since by entering a common project they should be taken to share the risks of its failure. However, this is not how compensation has been viewed.

In 2007 the English Law Commission recommended that financial or property orders might be made on the separation of unmarried cohabitants who had been living together with a child, or without a child for over two years, based on whether the respondent had a 'retained benefit' or the applicant had experienced an 'economic disadvantage' as a result of contributions made by the applicant to their shared lives or members of their families.[48] The reference to a 'retained benefit' covers the need to restore to the other what that other put into the commonality, but the reference to 'economic disadvantage'

in J Eekelaar and R George (eds), *Routledge Handbook of Family Law and Policy* (Routledge, 2014) ch 2.6, especially at 143.

[46] *White v White* [2001] AC 596; *Miller v Miller; McFarlane v McFarlane* [2006] UKHL 24. This may be modified for a short, childless marriage especially for assets that were 'unilaterally' acquired by each spouse: *Sharp v Sharp* [2017] EWCA Civ 408. The Divorce (Financial Provision) Bill 2016–7 would formalize this in the same way as is done in the Scottish legislation.

[47] In *Miller v Miller; McFarlane v McFarlane* [2006] UKHL 24 Lord Nicholls said compensation was for the 'way they conducted their marriage', and Baroness Hale called it compensation for 'relationship-generated' disadvantage. These expressions could be taken to refer to the relative positions of the parties at the point of separation, but have also been seen to refer to losses 'caused' by entering into the relationship.

[48] Law Commission, *Cohabitation: The Financial Consequences of Relationship Breakdown* (Law Com No 307, 2007) paras 3.91ff. The proposals have not been acted on.

contemplates compensation. Although the Commission stated that this was focused on the position at the point of separation,[49] it also said that this position was to be compared with the position at the start of the relationship.[50] But that would mean that a person whose economic position was improved by the relationship would receive nothing even if they were worse off than the other when the joint project ended. In Scotland, the Family Law (Scotland) Act 2006 provides that where a couple who have lived together 'as if' married or civil partners cease to do so, assets may be re-distributed based on the net economic advantage received by one from contributions by the applicant and the net economic disadvantages suffered by the applicant in the interests of the other.[51] The Supreme Court has decided that this does not simply seek to redress 'any clear and quantifiable imbalance that might have resulted from the cohabitation' but any deterioration in a person's economic position on entering the relationship: for example, by selling a house.[52] That treats forming the relationship as a potential misfortune in itself, when it cannot be known what such a person might have done had they not entered the relationship.

When in 2014 the Law Commission considered reforming the basis upon which financial provision might be made on *divorce*, it rejected the idea of 'compensation' in favour of the principle of meeting 'needs', which it called 'merger over time', to enable a transition to independence to the extent possible in light of the choices made within the marriage, the length of the marriage, the marital standard of living, the parties' expectation of a home, and continued shared responsibilities (importantly, childcare) in the future.[53] In rejecting a 'compensation' approach, the Commission treated the relevant loss as being that (if any) caused to the claimant 'by marrying'. They were right to reject 'compensation' on that basis. It wrongly treats marriage

---

[49] See ibid para 3.91 saying they wished to focus on 'the economic position of the parties at the point of separation'.

[50] Ibid para 3.96.

[51] Family Law (Scotland) Act 2006, ss 25, 28. There are further provisions covering circumstances where children are involved. For a comparison between the Scottish law and the Law Commission proposals, see J Miles, F Wasoff, and E Mordaunt, 'Cohabitation: Lessons from North of the Border' (2011) 23 *Child and Family Law Quarterly* 302.

[52] See *Gow v Grant* [2012] UKSC 29.

[53] Law Commission, *Matrimonial Property, Needs and Agreements* (Law Com No 343, 2014) para 3.16.

itself as if it were a personal injury. Quantifying such loss is largely speculative.[54] If the claimant had not entered this relationship, he or she may well have entered another, perhaps with even less favourable results. But a disparity of economic resources between the parties on breakdown *is* real and could be measured. This disparity brings about any *dependency* that exists at the time the relationship ends, and it is this disparity for which compensation may appropriately be made at the termination of friendship plus, whether the couple have been married or not.

The Scottish legislation on divorce and an English reforming Bill dealing with financial provision on termination of marriage and civil partnership both refer to this dependency.[55] It does not follow that the disparity needs to be redressed in its entirety in all circumstances. The primary guideline would be that a person would be entitled to compensation for the financial detriment *caused by the separation* to such extent and for such a time as is reasonable having regard to the duration of the relationship. This is the approach taken by the Canadian Spousal Support Guidelines. If no children are involved, the two major factors are the income difference between the parties at separation and the length of the marriage, and the Guidelines provide a basis for making the calculation.[56] Financial provision orders could be time-limited, though this should not be applied too rigidly, specially where the couple had been married or civilly partnered for a long period.[57] Since the award is compensatory, the opportunities open to an applicant to reduce the loss would need to be taken into

---

[54] This was how Mostyn J described the 'compensation' approach in *SA v PA (pre-marital agreement: compensation)* [2014] EWHC 392 (Fam), paras 28–37.

[55] Family Law (Scotland) Act 1985, s 9(1)(d): '[A] party who has been dependent to a substantial degree on the financial support of the other party should be awarded such financial provision as is reasonable to enable him to adjust, over a period of not more than three years from the date of the decree of divorce, to the loss of that support on divorce'. The provision is repeated in the English Divorce (Financial Provision) Bill 2016–7, cl 5(1)(c), but with an adjustment period of five years.

[56] See C Rogerson, 'Child support, Spousal Support and the Turn to Guidelines' in J Eekelaar and R George (eds), *Routledge Handbook of Family Law and Policy* (Routledge, 2014) 161. The Guidelines suggest an amount equivalent to 1.5 per cent to 2 per cent of the income difference for each year of the marriage, up to 50 per cent. A different calculation is made if childcare is an issue. The American Law Institute made a similar proposal: American Law Institute, *Principles of the Law of Family Dissolution: Analysis and Recommendations* (2002).

[57] See Family Law Scotland Act 1985, s 9(1)(e), allowing the three-year limitation in s 9(1)(d) to be overridden in cases of 'serious financial hardship'.

consideration. But all this must be subject to adjustment where necessary to make provision for needs arising from the care of children. When viewed in this way, the compensation approach begins to look very similar to the 'needs plus merger over time' principle favoured by the Law Commission in 2014.[58]

Furthermore, it is hard to see how it could be fair for a party to agree to forego some redress for this disadvantage occurring at the ending of a relationship which a party hoped would never happen. Yet in *Radmacher v Granatino*[59] the majority of the Supreme Court held that it was not unfair to uphold such an agreement. This was largely because the court thought the husband's disadvantage had not been incurred in the furtherance of the family's interests, but to allow him to seek an academic qualification. However, unless the behaviour is in some way unreasonable, it should not matter that the disadvantages were voluntarily incurred since the decision represented a choice that was perfectly consistent with the common project.

Although women will most often be beneficiaries of such awards, the view that such awards encourage female dependency is, it is suggested, difficult to demonstrate in a society where gender relations and roles are determined by many other things. The role of the law in this context should therefore be seen as seeking to uphold principles of justice given the prevailing social conditions.[60] It seems that, when courts do deal with these matters, they make some attempt to do this,[61] yet the evidence also shows how little this is achieved. It is clear that women who have dependent children when they divorce, and possibly even those who had children who are no longer dependent at that time, are in a worse financial position than men on separation, and for many years afterwards. In fact, the financial position of men frequently improves on and after divorce when the former partners' incomes are related to their household size (that is, 'equivalized').

[58] Law Commission, n 53.

[59] *Radmacher v Granatino*, n 44. The Divorce (Financial Provision) Bill 2016–7, cl 3, would remove this flexibility, effectively treating such agreements as commercial contracts.

[60] For a defence of the use of the matrimonial jurisdiction to redistribute economic wealth in this context, see S Thompson, 'In Defence of the "Gold-Digger"' (2016) 6 *Oñati Socio-Legal Series*, available at SSRN: https://ssrn.com/abstract=2887022 (accessed 13 June 2017).

[61] H Woodward, with M Sefton, *Pensions on Divorce: An Empirical Study* (Cardiff Law School, 2014).

It is this disparity which arises from the termination of 'friendship plus', including marriage and civil partnership, which it is reasonable to expect the better-off party to mitigate. In one study, three years after divorce only 2.2 per cent of women without dependent children reported receiving income from their ex-spouse, compared to 34 per cent of women with dependent children.[62] And evidence from Canada suggests that treating unmarried and married couples in a similar way has not resulted in a large number of new claims against former partners, but allowed a relatively small number of unmarried individuals to seek redress in circumstances similar to those in which married people do so.[63]

WHY CONSIDER FRIENDSHIP AT ALL?

To conclude, I should ask the question which should perhaps have been addressed at the beginning. It is all very well, it might be said, to identify a certain type of value (full friendship), set this up as a model, and use it as a template against which to evaluate some current legal provisions and policies. But this may not correspond to the real world. People may have no notion of such a relationship. All friendships may now be those which Aristotle described as utilitarian. If economic theory is to be believed, they will inevitably be such. On this view, our dealings with one another, even in the intimate sphere, should therefore be recorded as on a balance sheet, and provision made for redress from one to the other if either is economically disadvantaged by the experience.

To respond. I am not at all sure that the theoretical model of the modern 'pure relationship' popularized by Anthony Giddens as a

---

[62] H Fisher and H Low, 'Recovery from Divorce: Comparing High and Low Income Couples' (2016) 30 *International Journal of Law, Policy and the Family* 338. Very similar results were reported in J Eekelaar and M Maclean, *Maintenance after Divorce* (Oxford University Press, 1986). See also H Fisher and H Low, 'Who Wins, Who Loses and Who Recovers From Divorce?' in J Miles and R Probert (eds), *Sharing Lives, Dividing Assets* (Hart Publishing, 2009) ch 11; M Brewer and A Nandi, *Partnership Dissolution: How Does It Affect Income, Employment and Well-being?* (The Nuffield Foundation, 2014).

[63] See R Leckey, 'Cohabitation, Law Reform, and the Litigants' (2017) 31 *International Journal of Law, Policy and the Family* 131.

process of perpetual re-evaluation and re-negotiation to make its continuation worthwhile for each party[64] is fully supported by the evidence. The Personal Obligations research showed that many people felt bound to one another for the classical ethical reason known as the 'golden rule': you should behave to others as you would wish them to behave towards you. But the respondents found it difficult even to imagine circumstances in which they were separated, and hence what should be done then. So it is not always clear how people think others, or even they themselves, should behave. They may want something done in general terms. They may change after having gone through certain experiences. Holding up friendship, with the addition of friendship plus, allows us to explore some of the varied types of relationship that could exist, and the implications these could have for people's obligations, and the values at play. It can be seen that the reasons for responding in certain ways to breakdown of marriage lie in the fact that marriage is a form of 'friendship plus', and therefore could apply to such friendships outside marriage. Using friendship as the paradigm draws attention to a form of relationship that has been discussed since ancient times. It may not be easy to distinguish it from other relationships, of which it may form part, but it is surely worth trying.

---

[64] A Giddens, *The Transformation of Intimacy: Sexuality, Love and Eroticism in Modern Society* (Polity Press, 1992) 63. For similar doubts, see G Douglas, M Murch, C Miles, and L Scanlan, 'Enduring Love: Attitudes to Family and Inheritance Law in England and Wales' (2011) 38 *Journal of Law and Society* 245.

5

Responsibility

This chapter considers how the discussion of power, rights, and the values examined earlier might affect the concept of responsibility in personal law. We all like to think of ourselves as being 'responsible': or, at least, we surely do not like to think of ourselves as being 'irresponsible'. But what we mean by being 'responsible' cannot be so quickly answered. In 1991[1] I suggested that proponents of the expression 'parental responsibility' as it was employed in the discussions which preceded its enactment in the Children Act 1989 used it in two senses. One denoted the duties of care owed by parents to their children. It was put forward to qualify the idea that parents only had 'rights' regarding their children. The other expressed the idea that it was the role of parents rather than of the state to promote their children's interests. In this sense it has become a significant catchword in the process of disengagement by the welfare state in favour of 'empowerment' of parents. This has subsequently been seen as part of a wider political process, sometimes called 'neo-liberalism', involving diminution of state activity in favour of that by individuals.[2]

That was the simple part. Already Herbert Hart had distinguished between four senses of 'responsibility': role-responsibility, causal-responsibility, liability-responsibility, and capacity-responsibility.[3] My dichotomy seems to be merely two aspects of Role-Responsibility. It says nothing about the other three types. Peter Cane,[4] arguing that

---

[1] J Eekelaar, 'Parental Responsibility: State of Nature or the Nature of the State?' (1991) 13 *Journal of Social Welfare and Family Law* 37.

[2] For an extreme example of this analysis of family law in the United States, see AL Alstott, 'Neo-Liberalism in US Family Law: Negative Liberty and Laissez-Faire Markets in the Minimal State' (2014) 77(4) *Law and Contemporary Problems* 25.

[3] HLA Hart, *Punishment and Responsibility* (Oxford University Press, 1968) 212.

[4] P Cane, *Responsibility in Law and Morality* (Hart Publishing, 2002).

Family Law and Personal Life. Second edition. John Eekelaar. © John Eekelaar 2017.
Second edition published 2017 by Oxford University Press.

closer analysis of the idea of responsibility from the legal point of view will enrich its understanding even beyond legal contexts, contrasts 'historic responsibility' with 'prospective responsibility'. The former assesses past acts in terms of accountability, answerability, and liability. The latter imposes responsibility through certain roles either to promote what are believed to be good outcomes, or to avoid bad ones, whether by protecting against harms caused by actions or by preventing harms caused through failures. Cane is anxious to emphasize the pre-eminence of prospective responsibility over historical responsibility:

> [P]revention is better than cure, and fulfilment of prospective legal responsibilities is more to be desired than punishment of non-fulfilment, or repair of its consequences. A well-functioning and successful legal system is one in which non-compliance with prospective responsibilities, and hence occasions for the imposition of historical responsibility, are minimised. Historical responsibility … is subsidiary and parasitic.[5]

'Responsibility' has come to be a much-worked concept in personal law. It has been subjected to extensive analysis and application in two volumes published since the first edition of this book.[6] Alison Diduck suggested that family law is about 'determining responsibility for responsibilities'.[7] Its ascent to prominence in the late 1980s had been prefigured in a government Consultative Document in 1985 which stated that:

> The interests of the children are best served by their remaining with their families and the interests of their parents are best served by allowing them to undertake their natural and legal responsibility to care for their own children. Hence the focus of effort should be to enable and assist parents to discharge those responsibilities.[8]

This should be contrasted with the Committee on the Care of Children (Curtis Committee) of 1946,[9] which spoke throughout in

---

[5] Ibid 35.

[6] J Bridgeman, H Keating, and C Lind (eds), *Responsibility, Law and the Family* (Ashgate/Routledge 2008); C Lind, H Keating, and J Bridgeman (eds), *Taking Responsibility, Law and the Changing Family* (Ashgate/Routledge, 2010).

[7] A Diduck, 'What is Family Law For?' (2011) 64 *Current Legal Problems* 287.

[8] Consultative Document, *Review of Child Care Law: Report to Ministers of an Interdepartmental Working Party* (1985) para 2.8.

[9] Committee on the Care of Children (Curtis Committee), *Report of the Care of Children Committee (Training in Child Care)* (Cmd 6922, 1946).

terms of the responsibility of *social services* to assist children in their families. The new language talks of 'allowing' parents to 'undertake' *their* 'natural and legal responsibility' to care for their children. The state's role is now to be residual, confined to action only where the risks to the children are thought to be too great. The rhetoric of parental responsibility accelerated during the 1990s, especially in the context of the criminal law. In 2000 the courts were placed under a duty to 'bind over' parents of a convicted child or young person if satisfied that this 'would be desirable in the interests of preventing the commission by him of further offences'.[10] Parents may enter 'parenting contracts' and courts may make 'parenting orders' requiring a parent to attend counselling or guidance programmes,[11] and where the child is between 16 and 18, parents may be required to pay any fine or compensation where this is deemed a suitable penalty.[12] Many of these provisions were consolidated, refined, and in some respects widened in the Anti-social Behaviour, Crime and Policing Act 2014. This policy is heavily reliant on the assertion that parents have a responsibility to instil, or attempt to instil, patterns of behaviour in their children.

In my discussion, I will adopt Cane's distinction between historical and prospective responsibility. The interaction between the two is the location of many contested issues in personal law. But I will go further than Cane does in his description of prospective responsibility. Cane criticizes Hart for apparently associating prospective responsibility too closely to roles and tasks; for Cane it can be more open-ended.[13] However I am less sure about Cane's assertion that 'the law's ethic of responsibility is an ethic of obligation, not of aspiration' and that the law is concerned only with minimum standards.[14] Hart's more expansive view that 'a responsible person is one who is disposed to take his duties seriously; to think about them, and to make serious efforts to fulfil them'[15] may be closer to some aspects of the contemporary ethos in personal law and policy, as the discussions in the two volumes referred to earlier reveal.[16] But, as will be seen, even that might not go far enough.

---

[10] Powers of Criminal Courts (Sentencing) Act 2000, s 150.
[11] Crime and Disorder Act 1998, s 8; Anti-social Behaviour Act 2003, s 18.
[12] Powers of Criminal Courts (Sentencing) Act 2000, s 137.
[13] Cane, n 4, 33.   [14] Ibid 33–4.   [15] Hart, n 3, 213.   [16] N 6.

HISTORICAL RESPONSIBILITY

As described in chapter 1, the doctrine of the matrimonial offence was premised on the idea that divorce was a punishment against a person who had committed a wrong against the other spouse. Responsibility in this sense connoted blame for wrongdoing: the historical sense. In his dissenting opinion in the House of Lords in *Williams v Williams* in 1963, Lord Hodson, an experienced divorce court judge, was probably right when he said that, when introducing cruelty as a ground for divorce in 1937, 'Parliament must ... have recognised cruelty as connoting blameworthiness.'[17] But that was the older view. The majority of the Law Lords were prepared to hold that in that case, where one party to a marriage was suffering mental illness, the petitioner had suffered cruelty even though the respondent could not be blamed for his actions because of insanity. This was a significant step on the road to no-fault divorce because it was taken within a framework in which divorce was presumed to be a remedy against a wrongdoer,[18] and later cases were reluctant to follow its logic, reintroducing requirements of intention to harm and blameworthiness. It is now accepted that, after the reformed divorce law of 1971 replaced 'cruelty' with the ground that the 'respondent has behaved in such a way that the petitioner cannot reasonably be expected to live with the respondent',[19] blameworthiness is no longer a necessary ingredient in the conditions for granting a divorce in English law.

But does this mean that the law has abandoned the concept of responsibility in relation to divorce? In 1980, Jan Gorecki, surveying the growing international tendency to abandon the requirement that divorce could be obtained only on proof of a wrong done in favour of tests such as 'irretrievable breakdown', thought that it had.[20] He also noted that legal systems were abandoning the 'defence' of recrimination which would have allowed a person against whom divorce was

---

[17] [1963] 2 All ER 994 at 1017.

[18] There was a narrow exception when a respondent spouse had been treated for incurable mental illness for five years: Matrimonial Causes Act 1937, s 2; Divorce (Insanity and Desertion) Act 1958.

[19] Matrimonial Causes Act 1973, s 1(2)(b); see *Katz v Katz* [1972] 1 WLR 955.

[20] J Gorecki, 'Moral Premises of Contemporary Divorce Laws: Western and Eastern Europe and the United States' in JM Eekelaar and SN Katz (eds), *Marriage and Cohabitation in Contemporary Societies: Areas of Legal, Social and Ethical Change* (Butterworths, Toronto, 1980) ch 13.

being sought to defend the action on the ground that the person seeking the divorce was the 'guilty' party. He wrote:

> Those who are unilaterally guilty of disrupting their marriages, in particular if the amount of the guilt is great, should be punished, not rewarded, for what they did. Their punishment conveys a message to the general society: minimum of responsibility is anyone's family obligation, and so is an effort to avoid inflicting suffering on one's spouse and children, and wrecking their lives.

Here Gorecki explicitly expresses the idea of responsibility as being a duty to avoid blameworthy conduct. Although he spoke explicitly of punishment, he did not wish to introduce criminal penalties. If, however, the matter is one of civil law, as it is, then we are concerned with what Cane calls the 'civil law' paradigm for responsibility, under which the 'nature and quality of outcomes on their victim' are central to the determination of the agent's responsibilities.[21] Under the doctrine of recrimination, as supported by Gorecki, the remedy given is the denial of divorce to the person seeking it. This might, Gorecki claimed, help to redress the damage inflicted by the wrongs because 'if the other spouse wants to remarry, he will often pay any possible price for the freedom to do so.'[22] Apart from that, Gorecki offered no clear indication as to how denial of divorce may 'repair' (to use Cane's terminology) the interests of the victim. But Gorecki's solution, with its dubious overtones of encouraging a form of legal extortion, has become even less convincing than when he wrote. It is usually only on granting a divorce that the courts acquire their most extensive powers to make financial provision when a marriage breaks down; they can do little if the marriage continues. And with the decline in marriage, a wealthy husband (for simplicity I assume that the wrongdoer is the husband) is likely to prefer to live with a new partner without marrying her in order to avoid the risks of the divorce court. That is precisely why the proportion of wives who seek divorce is greater than husbands. But in any event the strategy would achieve nothing if the husband is lacking in sufficient resources to make it worthwhile for the wife to pursue it.

But that does not dispose of the issue. Gorecki in fact accepted that withholding divorce may not be a very good means of repairing the wrong done, but thought that alternatives, such as allowing

---

[21] Hart, n 3, 50.   [22] Gorecki, n 20, 128.

the wrongdoer to be punished through tort actions, property trans-
fers, or increased financial orders, are ineffective in practice. Let us,
however, suppose, for the sake of argument, that effective measures
could be devised to bring about significant reparation. Is 'blame' to
be a relevant factor in imposing them? Many believe that it should be.
One, who can be taken as speaking for that constituency, is Katherine
Spaht.[23] Spaht took issue with the assumption underlying the strategy
of the American Law Institute concerning compensatory payments
on divorce, discussed in chapter 4,[24] that issues connected with the
moral behaviour of the parties with respect to each other cannot be
assessed in the legal process and should not therefore be relevant to
the outcome in this matter.[25] Spaht saw this as expressing a 'psychological', and not a 'moral', view of relationships. She claimed that, if
fault is excluded as being a basis for making compensation, it is hard
to find any basis at all. The alternatives, breach of contract or unjust
enrichment, fail. The former fails because under no-fault divorce
there is no longer any implied term to remain married, so no one can
be in breach. Unjust enrichment fails because no reasons are given
why the compensated losses were unfair. Ultimately, Spaht considered
that the basis for the divorce jurisdiction reflects a view about marriage. The American Law Institute's view, Spaht claimed, is that marriage is a 'joint venture', terminable when no longer of benefit to either
party, and thus devoid of responsibilities. Spaht therefore advocated
the adoption of covenant marriage, under which responsibilities are
expressly articulated.[26]

The evidence of the retreat from punitive family law is of course
clear. The American Law Institute welcomed this because of the
difficulty of reaching sound moral conclusions through the legal

---

[23] See KS Spaht, 'Solidifying the "No-Fault" Revolution: Postmodern Marriage
as seen through the Lens of ALI's "Compensatory Payments"' in RF Wilson (ed),
*Reconstructing the Family: Critical Reflections on the American Law Institute's
Principles of the Law of Family Dissolution* (Cambridge University Press, 2006). See
also CE Schneider, 'Rethinking Alimony: Marital Decisions and Moral Discourse'
(1991) *Brigham Young University Law Review* 197. The view also surfaced in the
English Court of Appeal in *Miller v Miller* [2006] 1 FLR 151, but was roundly rejected
by the House of Lords: *Miller v Miller* [2006] UKHL 24.

[24] See p 111.

[25] See American Law Institute, *Principles of the Law of Family Dissolution: Analysis
and Recommendations* (2002).

[26] These have been introduced in a few US states as an optional alternative to
'standard' marriages.

process. Spaht was sceptical about this, remarking that the law is in fact increasingly willing to engage in moral evaluations in other areas, including contract law. But there are very good reasons why the law should respond differently in personal law to seemingly similar issues which arise in other contexts. One is that, unlike the area of commercial relations, family interactions cover a vast and diffuse area of activity, making moral evaluation through the legal process hazardous. Another reason is that exploring these matters in the legal process often violates the privileged sphere and inflicts further damage on the individuals concerned, including their children. But there is another reason for severely limiting moral evaluation through the legal process in these kinds of family matters. It is that, if people suffer punishment at the behest of others, even if those others hold judicial office, there must be reasonable confidence that those others are not themselves guilty of the offences for which they are imposing punishment. That is why judicial integrity is so highly valued. In most of the matters for which judges impose penalties, there can be reasonable confidence that they are not themselves contravenors. This most definitely cannot be said with regard to the matters which advocates of punitive family law would like to see reintroduced. The chances that judges would be acting with hypocrisy would be very high. The risk of damaging the legal system should not be contemplated.

PROSPECTIVE RESPONSIBILITY

Marriage

In any event, while it is true that the American Law Institute adopted the 'joint venture' view of marriage supported in chapter 4,[27] the fact that moral blame is removed from the assessment of compensation does not negate responsibility. As Cane observes, although punishment implies blame and fault, responsibility does not.[28] He makes the telling point that 'the restitutionary obligation of the passive recipient of a mistaken payment is not only strict, but arises regardless of whether any conduct of the recipient was causally related to the

---

[27] See p 108.   [28] Cane, n 4, 110.

transfer, however indirectly. In other words, both in law and outside it, an obligation to repair an undesirable outcome can arise independently not only of fault, but even of conduct'.[29] The responsibilities of marriage, whether expressly articulated, as in covenant marriages, or implicit, as in the standard case, can be seen as prospective responsibilities: guides as to what is expected in the relationship and what should be done if it ends. They need not be seen as articulating historical responsibility, breach of which requires a holding to account in a punitive manner.

Prospective responsibilities can be recognized by rewarding their fulfilment. This is what the American Law Institute's proposals do. They link both the amount and the duration of compensatory payments to time spent living together and caring for children, and allow for a partner to acquire an increasing share in the 'separate' property of the other (such as property owned by each before the marriage or acquired by inheritance after it) gradually during the course of the marriage, in the manner similar to that suggested as being appropriate in chapter 4.[30] Thus the entitlement is based on fulfilling a commitment to the marriage, and the responsibility is to reward the commitment fairly. The fact that the time spent making the relationship work and caring for children is rewarded shows that the discharge of those responsibilities is treated as significant. The individual who benefits by their discharge is under a duty to give recompense, in the same way as the passive recipient of a mistaken payment is. So it is not correct to talk as if this approach treats marriage as being devoid of responsibilities. The same reasoning applies if similar consequences are provided with respect to civil partnerships or informal unions, as also described in chapter 4.

Parenthood

In English law, a woman who gives birth will always be considered the parent.[31] If she is married to a man, her husband will be presumed to be the father of her naturally conceived child (and be entitled to be recorded as such on registration of the child's birth), as will a husband whose wife was inseminated by a donor using a licensed clinic unless

---

[29] Ibid 109–10.   [30] See pp 111–12.
[31] Human Fertilisation and Embryology Act (HFEA) 2008, s 33(1).

he did not consent to this, and also a man who has notified the clinic that he is willing to be regarded as the child's father when a woman is being treated by the clinic (and she agrees to this). Equivalent provisions apply if the mother is married to, or in civil partnership with, or simply in a relationship with, a woman, though that person will not be recorded as a 'mother', or even 'co-mother', but as a 'parent'.[32]

This is not just a matter of real or 'pretended' genetic relationships as these individuals will also be considered to be the 'legal' parents and have 'parental responsibility' which gives them rights and duties necessary for the care of the child without further assessment of their suitability for this role. A step-parent can acquire parental responsibility if those with such responsibility agree to this (or a court orders it).[33] This is not a bad working basis for indicating the people most likely to be committed to caring for the child. Adoption is, of course, subject to strict regulation. But, while 'parental responsibility' may extend beyond two individuals, 'legal' parenthood cannot.

Surrogacy raises special issues, for it involves a third adult who agrees, either altruistically or for reward, to bear a child for the commissioning parents. The child might be the surrogate's own (fertilized by one of the commissioning parents) or result from the implantation of an embryo from both commissioning parents. This raises reasonable concerns about surrogates, as well as over the risks for the welfare of children they bear. For this reason, some countries (such as France, Germany, and Sweden) prohibit the practice, and in others it is regulated in various ways. Yet it is a means of completing a family for some couples. In the case of male gay partners, it is the only one.

English law seeks a compromise. It tries to protect the surrogate mother by stating that any surrogacy agreement is unenforceable, so she is the child's legal mother, and can keep the child if she wants to, even if the child is not genetically hers. Here the intimacy of childbirth and the ensuing relationship can overcome genetics. This could be disturbed only through legal proceedings based on the child's best interests. To deter the 'sale' of children, payments (except for reasonable expenses) are illegal.[34] If the mother agrees, the court can make a 'parental order' which confers the status of parents on the

---

[32] HFEA 2008, ss 35, 37, 42–7. Marriage (Same Sex Couples) Act 2013, sch 7.

[33] Children Act 1989, s 2; Adoption and Children Act 2002, s 112, inserting s 4A into the Children Act 1989.

[34] HFEA 2008, s 54.

commissioning couple if one of them is genetically related to the child, and they are either married or in a civil partnership or 'enduring family relationship'.[35] It does not matter if they are of the same sex, male, or female. The child must be living with them and the order made before the child is six months old. These are laudable aims, though the requirement that such an order can only be made in favour of a couple and not one person alone has been held incompatible with the ECHR as being discriminatory.[36] But if the child has actually been transferred to the commissioning parents, courts have found it virtually impossible not to make a parental order in their favour even if the conditions have been breached and illegal payments made, especially where the child was born abroad. Even France has been censured by the European Court of Human Rights for refusing to recognize a child's new parental ties in such circumstances.[37]

So a parental order will normally achieve what the parties want if all proceeds as planned, and the court is satisfied that this is in the child's best interests.[38] But the view that the woman who bears the child using ART techniques should be treated as the mother, even as a 'starting point', is not widely accepted. It has been proposed that the proper criterion should be the genetic relationship, so where, for example, an embryo is implanted in a surrogate, the legal mother would be the genetic mother, not the surrogate.[39] But does this not place too much weight on the mere fact of a genetic link, with too little regard to all the circumstances, including the parties' intentions, and the role of the birth mother? And what of cases where the DNA from a donor is introduced in an egg to prevent certain birth defects and the result is an egg with mitochondrial DNA from a healthy donor and nuclear DNA from the mother? Of course, the genetic factor would be relevant as part of an assessment of the child's best interests if the issue were to be contested.

But should the parties' intentions perhaps determine the matter, a view widely held in the United States?[40] It is proper to ask whether

---

[35] Ibid.   [36] *Re Z (a child) (No 2)* [2016] EWHC 1191 (Fam).

[37] *Mennesson and Labassee v France* App No 65941/11, judgment 26 June 2014.

[38] *J v G* [2013] EWHC 1432 (Fam) para 24.

[39] See L Bender, 'Genes, Parents and Assisted Reproductive Technologies: ARTs, Mistakes, Sex, Race and Law' (2003) 12 *Columbia Journal of Gender and Law* 1.

[40] See *Johnson v Calvert* 5 Cal 4th 84, 851 P 2d 776 (1993); *Buzzanca v Buzzanca* 72 Cal Rptr 2d 280 (1998). RF Storrow, 'Parenthood by Pure Intention: Assisted Reproduction and the Functional Approach to Parentage' (2001–2) 53 *Hastings Law Journal* 597.

permitting surrogacy gives adults too much power to 'acquire' children according to their wishes, especially if they have the means to do this. The circumstances of women offering to act as surrogates certainly demand scrutiny, and, if the evidence were to point to this being a harmful practice for them and the children, it should indeed be circumscribed or even forbidden. Claire Fenton-Glynn[41] has suggested that these problems might be mitigated by requiring prior approval by a court or other agency of an intended surrogacy arrangement, although she concedes this would not completely prevent arrangements outside this framework. Intention may properly play some part in the allocation of responsibilities for children. Indeed it plays a role in the provisions of the HFEA 2008 discussed earlier, and 'parental orders' that transfer parenthood from a surrogate mother give formal effect to what the adults involved have agreed.[42] But it should not be the sole factor. It should not be forgotten that these arrangements reflect the exercise of power, in this case commercial power, over the mother and child, and therefore careful attention needs to be given to rights they have to protection of their well-being, including the child's identity.

In this regard it is also important to remember that the child's well-being may not necessarily require introduction into a 'traditional' family, at least according to the evidence as it currently stands. Families seem to function well, whether or not there is a genetic link between the child and one of the commissioning parents, and whether the commissioning parents are or are not of the same sex.[43] We do not, however, know how the children will fare in the long term. One could even imagine that such arrangements could result in a child having more than two (legal) parents, for example if a woman with her partner were to give birth to a child using the sperm of a known donor who by agreement remained involved with the child's life. However, this goes further than extending parental responsibilities, for legal parents have an enduring duty to support the child, there are reciprocal inheritance rights, and they form part of a 'lineage'. These

---

[41] C Fenton-Glynn, 'Outsourcing Ethical Dilemmas: Regulating International Surrogacy Arrangements' (2016) 24 *Medical Law Review* 59.

[42] See pp 123–4.

[43] S Golombok, *Modern Families: Parents and Children in New Family Forms* (Cambridge University Press, 2015) chs 2, 5, and 7.

matters have hitherto reflected actual or constructed biological relationships and it is not clear how easily they can be adapted to multiple parentage.[44]

As for unmarried fathers, when in 1982 the Law Commission
proposed to remove the status of illegitimacy, there was much
talk of meritorious and unmeritorious unmarried fathers. The
Commission expressed concern that to equalize the rights of married and unmarried fathers could put mothers at risk of harassment
and undue pressure by fathers to whom they were not married.[45]
Ultimately it came down to a perception that many unmarried
fathers were not in a position to bring up their children, and should
not therefore be readily given the legal powers to do so. Since then,
the growth of unmarried cohabitation has transformed the position,
and not much later the Commission recommended that an unmarried father should be able to acquire parental responsibility by
agreement with the mother,[46] and this was enacted in the Children
Act 1989.[47] Later, such a father could acquire parental responsibility if registered as the father on the child's birth certificate, an act
requiring the mother's consent.[48] In 2010, the draft Registration of
Births (Parents Not Married and Not Acting Together) Regulations
2010, made under the Welfare Reform Act 2009, went further and
would (subject to certain exemptions) *require* mothers to provide
information about the father, so he could register as the father and
thus acquire parental responsibility. The father could also register
himself against her wishes.

The government has hesitated to bring the 2010 regulations into
effect.[49] This is for good reasons. One lies in problems of implementation. The mother could obtain exemption simply by declar-
ing that she did not know who or where the father is, or that she

[44] But this is possible in British Columbia where more than two persons can be
parents with the agreement of the adult parties: Family Law Act 2011, s 30; Wills,
Estates and Succession Amendment Act 2011 s 23(2).

[45] Law Commission, *Family Law: Illegitimacy* (Law Com No 118, 1982) para 4.26.

[46] Law Commission, *Review of Child Law: Guardianship and Custody* (Law Com
No 172, 1988) paras 2.18–2.19.

[47] Section 4(1)(b).   [48] Adoption and Children Act 2002, s 111.

[49] See https://www.education.gov.uk/consultations/index.cfm?action=conResults
&external=no&consultationId=1666&menu=1 (accessed 13 June 2017). For a general
discussion, see J Herring, R Probert, and S Gilmore, *Great Debates in Family Law*
(Palgrave Macmillan, 2012) 38–45.

had reason to fear for her or the child's safety.[50] Another is that the mother may have good grounds for maintaining distance from the father, and the expectation that registration of the father in such circumstances will encourage more 'responsible' involvement by fathers with these children in such circumstances is likely to be misplaced.[51] It seems that it is only reasonable to expect a mother to act voluntarily in this matter. But just as importantly, the scheme could allow a person to initiate a relationship with a child for no reason other than the biological link, a risk detected by Jane Fortin in some cases where the courts seemed to think that a finding of paternity should invariably lead to a relationship between the father and the child.[52] The requirement that the mother should consent to the registration of a man as father of her child if she is not married to him seems a reasonable qualification to the genetic link alone for allowing involvement in the life of a child. If it is felt that this gives too much control to the mother over the recording of information, then at least her consent should be necessary for him to acquire parental responsibility. If she refuses, a court could grant a parental responsibility order in the father's favour if it thought this was in the child's interests.[53]

In some cases[54] the European Court of Human Rights has held that family life existed between a father and his non-marital child even though there was minimal contact between them. But much might depend on the circumstances of the conception and birth. It is unlikely that a man whose sperm is mistakenly used in IVF treatment resulting in the birth of a child he has not seen will have 'family life'

---

[50] Welfare Reform Act 2009, sch 6, inserting s 2B into the Births and Deaths Registration Act 1953.

[51] See, for further objections, J Wallbank, ' "Bodies in the Shadows": Joint Birth Registration, Parental Responsibility and Social Class' (2009) 21 *Child and Family Law Quarterly* 267.

[52] See J Fortin, 'Children's Right To Know Their Origins: Too Far, Too Fast?' (2009) 21 *Child and Family Law Quarterly* 336.

[53] This position is consistent with the view of the European Court of Human Rights in *Zaunegger v Germany* App No 22028/04, judgment 3 December 2009. Jens Scherpe, however, takes a different view: JM Scherpe, *The Present and Future of European Family Law* (Edward Elgar, 2016) 106–7.

[54] *Keegan v Ireland* (1994) 18 EHRR 342; *Boughanemi v France* App No 22070/93, judgment 24 April 1996; *Söderback v Sweden* App No 113/1997/897/1109, judgment 28 October 1998.

with the child.[55] In *Evans v Amicus Health Care*[56] the use of frozen embryos was considered to be part of the 'private life' of the persons whose gametes created them. But the protection of private life should not in itself give the right to *establish the relationship* with a child, with the responsibilities that entails, in such circumstances: a frozen embryo is not to be equated with a child.

It cannot be plausibly claimed that a parent needs to know his or her child in order to form a fuller picture of the parent's identity, as it could be claimed for a child regarding its parent. So while (absent agreements to the contrary) a genetic father may have a good case for obtaining information about his child based on the genetic link alone, that link by itself cannot be enough to establish a right to a relationship with the child. Of course, if a parent has engaged with the child, there will be an interest to maintain the engagement which may amount to 'family life' which requires respect under the European Convention.[57] Furthermore, if the genetic link is created within a context in which the child's carers have been agreed, as where sperm has been donated on the understanding that the donor will play a part in the child's upbringing, this understanding or agreement can be seen as an element in the donor's 'private' life that demands respect. This could happen if a donor has in practice been allowed some interrelationship with the child. In these cases, while the man's interests therefore deserve 'respect', and his views and position considered, any involvement by him with the child should turn on an assessment of the child's interests. Indeed, it would be wrong not to assess whether such involvement might be in the child's interests.[58] This does not imply that the relationship should not be encouraged, at least if circumstances are

[55] *Leeds Hospital NHS Trust v A* [2003] 1 FLR 1091.

[56] [2005] Fam 1; upheld by the European Court of Human Rights: *Evans v United Kingdom* App No 6339/05, judgment 7 March 2006.

[57] The stipulations of the European Court of Human Rights in classic cases like *Hokkanen v Finland* (1995) 19 EHRR 139, *Ignaccolo-Zenide v Romania* (2001) 31 EHRR 7, and *Elsholz v Germany* (2002) 34 EHRR 58 that states have a duty to facilitate contact in furtherance of the father's right to respect for family life should be understood in the context where the father actually enjoyed a relationship with the child which was disrupted. Here the claim did not rest solely on the genetic relationship. But even here the court has been careful to put emphasis on proceeding by way of negotiation and agreement: see *Nuutinen v Finland* (2002) 34 EHRR 15.

[58] See especially *Anayo v Germany* App No 20578/07, [2010] ECHR 2083; *Re G (A Minor); Re Z (A Minor)* [2013] EWHC 134 (Fam).

auspicious. Who could object to the development of good personal relationships?

Separated parents

The exercise by parents of their increased right to divorce appeared to conflict with their responsibilities towards their children, because it seemed to be the case that divorce harmed children. A solution was seen in allowing divorce, but acting as if the relationship between both parents and the children remained unaffected. Irène Théry, drawing on experience in France, called this the 'logique de pérennité', reflecting the belief that marriage was just one stage in the continuum of a family's existence.[59] In 1986, the English Law Commission had demonstrated the same belief. It criticized the way in which the courts often granted 'custody' (which seemed to mean all parental rights) of children to one divorcing parent, leaving the other only with vague 'reasonable access'.[60] The Commission proposed that both married parents should have equal 'parental responsibility' (comprising rights and duties respecting the child), which would survive the dissolution of the marriage intact. If necessary, courts could make orders for practical arrangements, such as where the children should live ('residence'), and how they should maintain a relationship with the 'non-resident' parent ('contact'). These proposals were enacted by the Children Act 1989. These orders were replaced by 'child arrangement orders' in the Children and Families Act 2014, but they deal with the same matters.[61]

In America, Elizabeth Scott went even further and put forward the proposition that after divorce a child's time should be allocated between its parents in proportions as closely approximate to the way it was allocated before the separation.[62] This was adopted as a model by the American Law Institute.[63] These proposals can be seen as attempts to

---

[59] I Théry, *Le Démariage* (Editions Odile Jacob, 1993) 154–6. See also R van Krieken, 'The "Best Interests of the Child" and Parental Separation: On the "Civilizing of Parents"' (2005) 68 *Modern Law Review* 25.

[60] Law Commission, *Family Law: Review of Child Law: Custody* (Working Paper No 96, 1986).

[61] Children and Families Act 2014, s 12.

[62] ES Scott, 'Pluralism, Parental Preferences and Child Custody' (1992) 80 *California Law Review* 615. See also R Mnookin, 'Child Custody Revisited' (2014) 77 *Law and Contemporary Problems* 249.

[63] American Law Institute, n 25, section 2.08.

reconcile the parental right to divorce with a sense that the responsibility of each parent towards one another, and also towards the children, demanded that the substance of the social unit should survive its legal breakdown.

In fact it seems that most parents have been sensitive to the spirit of this perception of their responsibilities. Consistently with other studies, Mavis Maclean and I found that in the mid-1990s contact of some kind between children and a separated parent was maintained in nearly three-quarters of cases where the parents had been married, and that the most significant predictor that contact would continue was the length of time the non-resident parent had lived with the child before the separation. Furthermore, the longer the contact persisted, the better the relationship between the parents became.[64] Nevertheless this still meant that contact between a child and a parent (usually the father) was lost or severely disrupted in over a quarter of cases, a proportion found in later studies as well.[65] An impetus therefore developed towards finding measures which would propel parents towards acting together in regard to their children even though the marriage was over. One example is the view that parents should be legally obliged to consult together over important decisions concerning the children. Neither the Law Commission nor the Children Act 1989 had gone this far, but the judiciary favour the idea.[66] While an order for consultation over specific issues may be a suitable way to resolve some conflicts, there are serious objections against making consultation a general legal obligation. It gives too many opportunities for aggravating conflict. What amounts to consultation? What matters are important enough to require it? How much effort needs to be made to communicate? What if communication would inflame conflict or upset the children?

[64] M Maclean and J Eekelaar, *The Parental Obligation: A Study of Parenthood Across Households* (Hart Publishing, 1997). Contact was less frequent where the parents had not been married (45 per cent) or had never lived together (35 per cent). This seems to be a consequence of the fact that the non-resident parent lived with the child for shorter periods (or not at all) in those cases.

[65] D Lader, *Non-Resident Parental Contact 2007/8* (Office for National Statistics, 2008); V Peacey and J Hunt, *I'm Not Saying It Was Easy ... Contact Problems in Separated Families* (Gingerbread, 2009).

[66] See J Eekelaar, 'Do Parents Have a Duty to Consult?' (1998) 114 *Law Quarterly Review* 337. Andrew Bainham takes a different view: see A Bainham, 'The Privatisation of the Public Interest in Children' (1990) 55 *Modern Law Review* 206.

More recent developments have gone further and strongly promoted the idea that post-separation parenting should be shared, or
at least that shared parenting should be presumed to be beneficial for
children.[67] Australia has enacted a presumption that equal parental
responsibility (requiring consultation between parents) is in a child
interests, and this triggers a requirement to consider whether it is further in the child's interests to spend equal or significant time with both
parents.[68] England and Wales now has a presumption that 'involvement' by each parent in the life of the child concerned will 'further the
child's welfare'. It is expressly stated that involvement means involvement of 'some kind, either direct or indirect, but not any particular
division of a child's time'.[69]

It is easy to assume that sharing parenting roles between separated parents must benefit children, but everything turns on the
circumstances. British Columbia, in contrast, expressly excludes presumptions of equal parental responsibility and time-sharing.[70] The
empirical evidence does not support the idea that *the mere fact that* a
child maintains contact with a parent who is not living in the home,
or that the child spends equal time with both parents after they have
separated, is beneficial for the child.[71] Having presumptions echoes
an approach which sees a particular social structure as in itself good
for the individuals concerned rather than a willingness to assess the
impact of the particular circumstances on the child in question. The
need is to respond to an evolving scenario, in which past events are
relevant, but should not dominate. I recall the argument made earlier[72] that, where a decision is directly about a child's upbringing, the
'best interests' principle, properly applied, demands that attention be

---

[67] See H Rhoades and SB Boyd, 'Reforming Custody Laws: A Comparative Study'
(2004) 18 *International Journal of Law, Policy and the Family* 119.
[68] Family Law (Shared Parental Responsibility) Act 2006.
[69] Children and Families Act 2014, s 11.
[70] Family Law Act (SBC 2011), s 40(4).
[71] For comprehensive reviews of the evidence, see B Fehlberg, B Smyth, M
Maclean, and C Roberts, 'Legislating for Shared Time Parenting after Separation: A
Research Review' (2011) 25 *International Journal of Law, Policy and the Family* 318; B
Fehlberg and B Smyth, 'Parenting Issues after Separation in Common Law Countries';
T Picontó-Novales, 'Parenting Issues after Separation in Spain and Southern Europe';
and A Singer, 'Parenting Issues after Separation: A Scandinavian Perspective' in
J Eekelaar and R George (eds), *Routledge Handbook of Family Law and Policy*
(Routledge, 2014) chs 3.3–5.
[72] See chapter 2, p 59.

paid holistically to the circumstances of the particular case and a reasoned justification made for the decision in terms of its impact on the
child's capability of realizing the goals that are valuable to the child
(the 'capability' approach).

The duty to support

Under the present English law, while a mother acquires a duty to support a child through giving birth, a father acquires the duty merely
through the genetic link. This responsibility is, however, under threat
in the United Kingdom where the parental obligation to pay child
support has begun to be treated as a matter of bargaining between
the parents, and related to the 'benefits' a parent enjoys from having
a relationship with the child.[73] Ironically, this is a consequence of the
failure of an administrative scheme, established in 1993,[74] designed
to make the enforcement of this obligation more effective. A Child
Support Agency (CSA), with connections to the Department for
Social Security, had been established which virtually replaced the jurisdiction of the courts to make orders for child support (except with
consent of the parties), though courts retained an important function
in regard to overall financial and property settlement on divorce. A
mother seeking certain welfare payments would be required to seek
a child support order, and therefore name the father (unless a CSA
officer considered this created unacceptable risks to her or the children), and there was no 'disregard', so that unless the support payments exceeded the totality of the welfare benefits, they would all be
diverted to the state. Discretion was to be minimized by the use of a
formula which was designed to extract as much from the liable parent as was feasible in order to meet the welfare 'bill' without destroy-
ing the incentive to work. There was a complex series of enforcement
measures, of which imprisonment for up to six weeks was to be the
ultimate step.

However, many mistakes were made. They include approaching
(and being perceived as approaching) the task as a taxing rather than a
child support measure; excessive severity of extraction rate; inclusion

---

[73] See C Skinner, 'Child Maintenance Reforms: Understanding Fathers' Expressive
Agency and the Power of Reciprocity' (2013) 27 *International Journal of Law, Policy
and the Family* 242.

[74] Child Support Act 1991.

of an element for the mother; a highly complex system of exemptions (eg for housing costs and the mother's income) and lack of flexibility, such as failure to take sufficient account of the debtor's newly acquired family responsibilities; retrospective operation; failure to integrate with the court system; failure to appreciate that procedures designed for paying benefits were unsuited to extracting payments; and serious administrative and processing shortcomings. Despite desperate attempts in 2003 to simplify the calculation of the amount owed, and the introduction of a computerized system, by July 2006 the CSA had a backlog of 300,000 cases and it was calculated that it cost 70p for every £1 collected (compared to 1.4p for every £1 collected in tax).[75]

The result has been a complete reversal of policy. First, the requirement that welfare claimants seek a child support order against the absent parent (which had in fact been strengthened in 2008 by treating any claim for welfare benefits as automatically an application for child support[76]) was abandoned for new applicants after July 2008; and it follows that the absence of any 'disregard' (which had been relaxed in 2003) was also reversed so that from April 2010 there has been a full disregard, meaning that welfare claimants can keep both the welfare benefit and the child support payments in full.[77] The state has effectively given up the policy dating back to the poor laws of trying to recoup its benefit payments from 'non-resident' parents. In 2012 a new Child Maintenance Service (CMS) was established within the Department for Work and Pensions which encourages parties to reach a 'Family Based Arrangement' using an online calculator showing the percentages that would be used if enforcement proceedings are taken.

If that fails, for a fee of £20 (with some exceptions), the CMS can calculate the amount owed for the parties by accessing their tax information, but would not be involved in ensuring payment (Direct Pay). It does however have power to collect payments by making orders deducting the amount owed from the debtor's earnings, or bank account (Collect and Pay), and to apply for court orders to seize property or suspend a driving licence or for committal to prison for up to six weeks. But using this power requires a further application and the recipient and payer must pay the CMS sums equivalent to 4 per cent

---

[75] See A King and I Crewe, *Blunders of Our Governments* (Oneworld, 2014) ch 6, 93.
[76] Child Support, Pensions and Social Security Act 2000, s 3.
[77] Child Maintenance and Other Payments Act 2008.

of the maintenance received and 20 per cent of the maintenance due respectively. From June 2014 to February 2016, Collect and Pay was used in only some 30 per cent of its cases.[78] The extent of compliance in the remaining (Direct Pay) cases is unknown, as is whether Family Based Arrangements follow any norms. So it could be argued that we have reverted to the earlier view that this responsibility is primarily a moral responsibility which the state will do what it can to encourage but is reluctant to enforce as a direct legal obligation.

Does this responsibility to support go further than supplying the means to provide for the child and extend to the physical care of the child? If so, such a duty must carry with it the entitlement to perform it. But, whatever certain legal formulations may take, it seems that the obligation should be seen as one to provide (usually financial) support rather than to provide care. That is because it is both difficult and undesirable to enforce a duty to provide care if the person concerned is hostile to giving it. Even Andrew Bainham, who believes that there should be a duty to provide care, concedes that such a duty is likely to be unenforceable.[79] And a parent surely does no legal wrong if they allow their child to be brought up by the other parent and a step-parent, provided they provide appropriate financial support. The primary legal duty must therefore be to provide financial support, not actual care.

Of course, the duty to support may be discharged in whole or in part by providing care, and usually is. This is the standard case of child-rearing in most societies. But does this mean that where parents are not living together there is a right to substitute financial support with actual care? If there was such an entitlement, the other parent and the child would be under a duty to allow it. The law now recognizes that relationships should not be forced on adults against their will. Why should it do this in the case of a child who is already being cared for? Similarly, the duty of the parent with care is to promote the best interests of the child. Any arrangements which involve the child having such a relationship must therefore be based on a pragmatic assessment of the child's day-to-day welfare, not a legal duty.

---

[78] *Child Maintenance Service 2012 Scheme Experimental Statistics August 2013–February 2016* (Department for Work and Pensions, April 2016). See also *House of Commons Work and Pensions Committee, Child Maintenance Service: Fourteenth Report of Session 2016–2017.*

[79] A Bainham, 'Contact as a Right and Obligation' in A Bainham, B Lindley, M Richards, and L Trinder (eds), *Children and Their Families: Contact, Rights and Welfare* (Hart Publishing, 2003) 61, 79.

It is open to debate whether a parent's prospective financial responsibility towards a child should be accompanied by similar responsibility towards the other parent if that parent is caring for the child. Responsibility towards the other parent could be characterized as an element of the responsibility towards the child, for the child needs care as much as clothes and food. American child support guidelines have tended to calculate the obligation by reference to the marginal costs which children impose on a family budget, rather than to the overall economic position for each parent.[80] The result is that the amount of the payments declines as a percentage of the debtor's total income as that income rises. The American Law Institute has recommended that a supplement be added to such payments as a means of redressing disparities between the financial position of the parent paying the support and the household receiving it.[81]

This would mean that the payments would benefit the child's carer financially as well. The formula which was first used when the United Kingdom introduced a child support scheme run by an administrative agency also included an element designed to benefit the child's carer.[82] This proved to be politically sensitive, and was not repeated when a simplified formula was later introduced.[83] Many fathers are reluctant that their child support payments should benefit, or even be controlled by, the mother, but there is evidence that some think it is acceptable[84] and that the public generally thinks that the legally calculated amounts are insufficient.[85] The problem is that non-residential

---

[80] See M Garrison, 'The Goals and Limits of Child Support Policy' in JT Oldham and MS Melli, *Child Support: The Next Frontier* (University of Michigan Press, 2000) 16. IM Ellman, 'Fudging Failure: The Economic Analysis Used to Construct Child Support Guidelines' (2004) *University of Chicago Legal Forum* 162; D Allen and M Brinig, 'Child Support Guidelines: The Good, the Bad, the Ugly' (2011) 45 *Family Law Quarterly* 135; IM Ellman and SL Braver, 'The Future of Child Support' in J Eekelaar (ed), *Family Law in Britain and America in the Twenty-first Century: Essays in Honor of Sanford N Katz* (Brill, 2016), ch 5.

[81] American Law Institute, n 25, section 3.05.

[82] M Maclean and J Eekelaar, 'Child Support: The British Solution' (1993) 7 *International Journal of Law and the Family* 205, 206–7.

[83] Child Support, Pensions and Social Security Act 2000. This too has now been abandoned: Child Maintenance and Other Payments Act 2008.

[84] J Bradshaw, C Stimson, C Skinner, and J Williams, *Absent Fathers?* (Routledge, 1999) 152–3, 192–4.

[85] IM Ellman and S Braver, 'Lay Intuitions about Child Support and Marital Status' (2011) 23 *Child and Family Law Quarterly* 465; IM Ellman, S McKay, J Miles, and C Bryson, 'Child Support Judgments: Comparing Public Policy to the Public's Policy', (2014) 28 *International Journal of Law, Policy, and the Family* 274.

parents will be inclined to see their obligation towards the other parent in terms of historical responsibility, which raises issues of blame, rather than of role, which they are more willing to accept as a basis of their responsibility to their children. Yet it seems inescapable that any duty to support a child must include some contribution to sustaining the environment in which the child lives. In any event, it appears that, in England at any rate, the amounts paid in child support are very small. However, they benefit single parents with very low incomes, lifting over half of the recipients out of poverty.[86] This clearly benefits the mother as well as the child.

Parental responsibilities and justice

These responsibilities are of course legal duties. But failures to fulfil them do not necessarily involve blame, in the way it applies for historical responsibility. So there can be cases where the responsibility is removed if a parent is unable to fulfil it, even if not to blame, as can often happen under child protection law. It might seem unjust that a parent who loves his or her child is unable to have a relationship with the child if this would harm the child, even if this is not the parent's fault, just as it might seem unfair that an unmarried father who does not have parental responsibility may still have some responsibility to provide financial support for the child. But these situations reflect the child's interests and a concept of social responsibility. As was so maliciously suggested to Malvolio about greatness,[87] some are born to responsibility, some achieve responsibility, and some have responsibility thrust on them. It may be that the political world of executive monarchy has passed, but we do not find the idea that a king's son inherited responsibilities to be an odd idea about responsibility,[88]

---

[86] C Bryson, A Skipp, J Allbeson, E Poole, E Ireland, and V Marsh, *Kids Aren't Free: The Child Maintenance Arrangements of Single Parents on Benefits in 2012* (The Nuffield Foundation, nd); Gingerbread, *Missing Maintenance* (June 2016). In a 2012 survey of single parents receiving welfare benefits, 12 per cent of their total median income was made up of maintenance. The consequence was that 57 per cent of those receiving maintenance would have been below the 'poverty' line without it; 38 per cent were below it even with maintenance.

[87] Shakespeare, *Twelfth Night*, Act 2, scene 5.

[88] As illustrated once again by Shakespeare's portrait of the future Henry V in *Henry IV*, Parts One and Two.

or that some people who try to fulfil their responsibilities have them removed if they are unable to do this adequately. Someone who could save a child from harm without risk to themselves has responsibility for the outcome thrust on them, and it probably does not go too far to suggest that we all have some responsibility for our environment simply by being born.

These responsibilities may be defeasible (eg if someone else has taken over care of the child). But their initial imposition has nothing to do with blame, as Scott Altman has suggested.[89] Cane, writing about tort liability, points out that 'once we take account of the interests of the victim, it seems less clear that victim-focused obligations of repair should always depend on fault.'[90] If we substitute children, or elderly people, for 'victims', and consider obligations to support them, rather than of 'repairing' a wrong it may also seem that those obligations need not always depend on fault either, nor even intention (although this can sometimes be important), nor, as Gillian Douglas has pointed out, on 'commitment'.[91] There does, of course, need to be a rational ground for imposing such responsibilities. Random selection would not do. But there are good reasons to choose a genetic parent, or a child, as the first source of responsibility in these cases rather than, say, a neighbour, or even the community. The parent has brought the child into existence; the child owes its existence to the parent. The duty is likely to reflect the predispositions of each in most contexts. A society may indeed prefer a different mode of allocation of responsibility. But such decisions are contingent on context-specific factors, whether cultural or economic. The United Kingdom, for example, dropped the legal obligation on grandparents to support their grandchildren, and children to support their parents, in 1948.[92] It was presumably felt that these duties should primarily fall on the community and voluntarily accepted obligations by the individuals

---

[89] S Altman, 'A Theory of Child Support' (2003) 17 *International Journal of Law, Policy and the Family* 173, argues that the support duty can be explained as a punishment for failing to love one's child, or to act as if one did.

[90] Cane, n 4, 107.

[91] G Douglas, 'Towards an Understanding of the Basis of Obligation and Commitment in Family Law' (2016) 36 *Legal Studies* 1.

[92] National Assistance Act 1948, s 42(1). For consideration of whether adult children should have a legal obligation to support their parents, see J Herring, 'Together Forever? The Rights and Responsibilities of Adult Children and Their Parents' in J Bridgeman, H Keating, and J Lind (eds), n 6, 163.

concerned. But this could change. There is nothing intrinsic in the nature of responsibility which would prevent this.

It will follow that in some cases fixing an adult with responsibility will result in the adult bearing some of the burdens of parenthood without the benefits. But entering sexual relationships, and begetting children, carries inherent risks. They can bring the adult's immense happiness; or a good-enough life; or great heartache. There can be no guarantees. Some people will suffer great misfortune, and of course friends and the community should work to mitigate this. But as Tony Honoré has written: 'To bear the risk of bad luck is inseparable from being a choosing person.'[93] If that misfortune cannot be corrected without harming the innocent, it is something which a truly responsible person must accept, even if it seems unjust. They might take comfort in Ronald Dworkin's bold suggestion[94] that there is not a clash of values in such cases because, properly interpreted, all values are integrated and mutually supporting: so perhaps the apparent 'sacrifice', which might seem unjust, that a person makes in favour of an innocent child is actually a way of respecting the apparently wronged person's interest to live a good life.

A FULLER CONCEPT OF RESPONSIBILITY

The cases of historical and prospective responsibility discussed above are all cases where the responsibility had been encapsulated into a legal obligation of some kind. States do this when behaviour perceived as dysfunctional is considered a social threat. For example, the English poor law 'legalized' a father's formerly merely moral obligation to support his children when the social turbulence of the sixteenth century disturbed the expectation that this would normally occur. Indeed, it could be said that, in regard to legal enforcement of support duties within the family, the strength of legal involvement in enforcement of family solidarity is directly related to the extent to

---

[93] AM Honoré, 'Responsibility and Luck' (1988) 104 *Law Quarterly Review* 530, 553.

[94] R Dworkin, *Justice for Hedgehogs* (The Belknap Press of Harvard University Press, 2011).

which the family system is failing to fulfil its role as resource distributor within the community.

People act responsibly if they comply with these obligations, even if they do so mainly because the law requires it, for it is usually responsible to uphold the law. But, as Craig Lind, Heather Keating, and Jo Bridgeman have written, 'whilst family responsibility includes obligations and duties, it is more than the sum of these.'[95] What constitutes this 'fuller' sense of responsibility? Helen Reece argued that 'post-liberal' responsibility is to be found in a way of thinking rather than in actions.[96] As long as we can understand what we do, or make a serious attempt to do so, we are acting responsibly. There is certainly a substantial literature which supports this position. But it is not so clear whether the concept of responsibility it describes does not exist more in the books than in people's perceptions. A mother who opposes contact for what a court considers to be no good reason, or a father who resorts to vexatious litigation to acquire contact, will be considered to be irresponsible because of what they do, however seriously they may have pondered their actions.

On the other hand, like Cane and Hart's views about the exercise of responsibility, Joseph Raz's sentiment that '[s]urely what counts, from the point of view of the person in authority, is not what the subject thinks but how he acts. I do all that the law requires of me if my actions comply with it' may be too narrow. Perhaps John Gardner, thinking possibly more of historical than prospective responsibility, captures the middle ground well when he states that responsibility 'in the basic sense' is the ability to give an account of oneself as a rational being.[97] This means that it is not sufficient simply that people think about their actions; or indeed, that they only comply with the law. They must be able to account for themselves rationally, which means engaging with others in an evaluative dialogue.

---

[95] Craig, Keating, and Bridgeman, n 6, 13. They may have misunderstood me. It is this fuller concept of responsibility, not responsibility as such, that would be lost if it were legally enforced.

[96] H Reece, *Divorcing Responsibly* (Hart Publishing, 2003) ch 6.

[97] J Gardner, 'The Mark of Responsibility' (2003) 23 *Oxford Journal of Legal Studies* 157, 161.

It is suggested that when we think of responsibility in this sense, we signal an expectation[98] that agents should demonstrate an appreciation of the effects of their actions, or inactions, on other people by modifying their behaviour accordingly even if this means not pressing all their legal entitlements, or taking on duties they are not legally bound to accept, sometimes even not doing what they are legally bound to do. It is a manifestation of recognition of 'the other' and of acceptance of community. It is the counterpoise to the engine that drives the language of rights. Its absence is seen in the action of the mother in Brecht's *Caucasian Chalk Circle* (whose insistence on asserting her right to have her child back by pulling him from the circle lost him to the maid, Grusha, who let him go for fear of injuring him) as much as its presence was demonstrated in the behaviour of both men in the *Leeds Hospital* case,[99] one by accepting duties he was not legally obliged to accept, the other by foregoing claims he might legally have made.

This is hardly new. A 'responsible' utility will not enforce payment of debts owed by customers suffering emotional or sometimes even financial crises. Responsible people will exercise restraint within their legal rights, and sometimes forego them. They will also act beyond their legal duties. A child who keeps in regular touch with her parents when she leaves home, especially in times of crisis, has no legal duty to do this, but will surely be regarded as acting more responsibly than one who rarely takes this trouble. Responsible parents will try to ensure that their children behave with consideration to others, and will surely wish to nurture them beyond the extent that they are legally obliged to. If relationships sadly fall apart, willingness to make accommodations responding to the interests of all other persons involved is a feature of responsible behaviour. So while we can say that a responsible person normally acts according to legal norms, responsibility does not stop there.

What are, perhaps, new are attempts by government to exert pressure on people on how to exercise this responsibility regarding their families without converting it into express legal obligations. Doing this narrows the scope for freely exercised responsible behaviour

---

[98] For a discussion of the relationship between responsibility and expectations in this context, see R George, *Ideas and Debates in Family Law* (Hart Publishing, 2012) ch 2.

[99] See p 128.

because acting under pressure reduces the extent to which the actions are based on moral responsibility. But it may, sadly, be necessary, just as it may sometimes be necessary to persuade someone to hold back from enforcing a debt. The question arises how far should the law go? In chapter 1,[100] reference was made to the failed attempt by the UK Parliament in the Family Law Act 1996 to introduce a divorce process which would influence parties contemplating divorce to choose goals which the state believed to be in their interests, or those of the community. The goal of the scheme was to establish greater freedom to divorce, but to convince people to exercise this entitlement in a responsible way. This surely goes beyond compliance with the minimal standards mentioned by Cane. It is closer to the one used by Hart when he talked about a responsible person as 'one who is disposed to take his duties seriously; to think about them, and to make serious efforts to fulfil them'.[101] But even this is probably too narrow. What seems to be sought is nothing less than a person who thinks not just of the legal rights of other family members, but of their general well-being, and is willing to forego, or abridge, his or her own rights to achieve this. This is to be done through the provision of information and persuasion.

It may, however, prove difficult to achieve this. The attempt to make people more responsible through persuasion at information meetings seemed to fail. But the quest for getting people to exercise responsible behaviour is nowhere more apparent than in the area of parenthood. It is particularly evident in relation to resolving difficulties that often arise when parents separate. One strategy has been to try to *persuade* parents to cooperate with one another.[102] In the United States and Canada separated parents are often compelled to attend 'parenting skills' classes. Schemes which aim to enhance sensitivity to the children's interests through information,[103] or achieving resolution through mediation, could be seen as trying to make parents behave responsibly. Felicity Kaganas and Alison Diduck

---

[100] See p 21.   [101] Hart, n 3, 213.

[102] *Making Contact Work* (Lord Chancellor's Department, 2002). Adoption and Children Act 2006.

[103] Such as the Family Resolutions Project: see (2004) 34 *Family Law* 919. For a full discussion, see H Reece, 'From Parental Responsibility to Parenting Responsibly' in M Freeman (ed), *Law and Sociology: Current Legal Issues 2005*, vol 8 (Oxford University Press, 2006) ch 26, 472–81.

detect attempts even to persuade children that they should cooperate in this endeavour.[104]

While most parents view such schemes favourably, there is little hard evidence on their effectiveness.[105] The value of imparting skills on how to handle significant family change and be responsive to the needs of other participants is clear. But there is also a danger that these efforts will create expectations that specific outcomes should be attained, such as living arrangements similar to the circumstances which prevailed prior to separation, for these may be disappointed. There is also a danger of encouraging a degree of self-deception that things can go on as if the separation between the parents had not happened. The research evidence is overwhelming that to act as a parent after separation often requires considerable adjustment, which is highly context-sensitive, and which many parents find extraordinarily difficult to make.[106] It may be better to accept that parental separation often requires a complete renegotiation of the family dynamics, focused on the circumstances of each family, rather than to aim at an idealized state of affairs which may not suit the individuals or their particular circumstances. But in the settlement process the line between protecting individual interests and encouraging individuals to be responsive to the interests of others who are involved is very difficult to draw. Concerns about this in the context of mediation will be considered in chapter 7.[107]

The apparent failure of parents to have prevented misbehaviour by their children might previously have been considered irresponsible: but it would have fallen outside the scope of official intervention. So how should the law treat the parents of children who misbehave? The prevention of such wrongdoing could be seen as simply one of the duties of parenthood for which they are responsible. The problem is that it mixes historic and prospective responsibility: the child

---

[104] F Kaganas and A Diduck, 'Changing Images of Post-Separation Children' (2004) 67 *Modern Law Review* 959.

[105] J Hunt and C Roberts, *Intervening in Litigated Contact: Ideas from Other Jurisdictions* (Family Policy Briefing 4, University of Oxford Department of Social Policy and Social Work, 2005); A Sigal, I Sandler, S Wolchik, and S Braver, 'Do Parent Education Programs Promote Healthy Post-divorce Parenting? Critical Distinctions and a Review of the Evidence' (2011) 49 *Family Court Review* 120.

[106] See GB Wilson, 'The Non-Resident Parental Role for Separated Fathers: A Review' (2006) 20 *International Journal of Law, Policy and the Family* 286.

[107] See p 108.

is liable on the principles of blame, the parent on the basis of role. A parent might have role responsibility to pay compensation for damage caused by a child, and also to meet fines incurred by a child who has no resources. But if the measure is a fine or other form of punishment, it should not be imposed on a parent unless the parent too has been guilty of wrongdoing.

Such measures may be viewed more as threats mainly designed to influence parental behaviour. The actions which comprise anti-social behaviour are necessarily broad and indeterminate[108] and even more indeterminate is the parental behaviour thought to be necessary to prevent it. There will be differing interpretations about what kinds of parental actions are appropriate in the multitude of micro-situations which arise in family relationships, and severe problems of monitoring what actions are actually taken within the home. It is difficult to know what could be achieved by using criminal penalties or their threat to modify the way parents seek to make their children behave better, and it could reduce the scope for parents themselves to assume responsibility for this. Children's behaviour could be affected more by events outside the parents' control than in the home. Perhaps we are all responsible, as politicians, educators, writers, employers, entertainers—just as citizens—for the behaviour of our society's children.

---

[108] For example, 'conduct capable of causing housing-related nuisance or annoyance to any person': Anti-social Behaviour, Crime and Policing Act 2014, s 2(1)(c).

6

Truth

Chapter 5 examined the nature of responsibility in various contexts in which personal law operates, and the basis of its allocation. This chapter looks at a particular feature of such legal provisions, namely the extent to which they are grounded in, or reflect, what I will call 'physical' truth, as distinct from legally constructed truths. The distinction between the two can be illustrated in a 1969 Ordinance of the Northwest Territories of Canada that required the Registrar-General of Births, on receiving a copy of an adoption order, to substitute the names of the adopting parents on the register of the adopted person's birth for those of the natural parents. The genuine registration was to be kept on a 'special register', which could be disclosed only on the order of a judge.[1] In 1970, Newfoundland allowed a judge to order that the place of birth of an adopted child which appears in the Adopted Children Register should be a place 'other than the actual place of birth of the adopted child.'[2]

What occurs in all such cases is a representation of physical actions and events which was not the case with regard to those actions and events. The representation does not correspond with 'physical truth': that is, what is or was the case regarding physical events and actions. No matter, one might say: a new reality has been constructed. We know that legal processes can create 'legal truth'. Gunther Teubner[3] described the way in which legal discourse 'reconstructs'

---

[1] An Ordinance to amend the Vital Statistics Ordinance, ch 11 of 1969 (Third Session).

[2] Adoption of Children Act, RSN 1970 ch 5, s 12(4). Such secrecy in adoption has not been uncommon in the past.

[3] G Teubner, *Law as an Autopoietic System* (Blackwell, 1993). Michael King has been prominent in arguing that this feature of the law makes it unsuitable for application in the context, especially, of child welfare issues: M King and C Piper, *How the Law Thinks about Children* (Gower, 1990).

Family Law and Personal Life. Second edition. John Eekelaar. © John Eekelaar 2017. Second edition published 2017 by Oxford University Press.

the activities of the world, by forcing them into classifications which are either approved or disapproved by the law. Jack Balkin has made a similar point, pointing out how strongly legal classifications, such as between trespassers and licensees, or legal findings, such as that behaviour amounts to sexual harassment, 'shape people's beliefs and understandings'.[4] It is indeed remarkable how legal findings can be transformed into apparently infallible proclamations of fact in public perception, as when an 'alleged' offender becomes an undoubted criminal when found guilty, or when an alleged defamation is found proved. Legal truth is important. How else could someone claim to have 'cleared his name'? How could we punish people with an easy conscience if we did not feel that legal truth corresponded to physical actions and events? Perhaps that is why a judge cannot refrain from making a finding of fact if this is relevant to his decision: he cannot say he thinks that Tom may have injured Sarah, but since he's not sure, he will award only partial damages; or that George may have injured Alice, but he has doubts, so he will knock some days off his sentence. He must proceed on an assumption of the truth, or not at all. And society seems to go along with this. Yet even then, the public, through the media, can sometimes be resistant to accepting verdicts, especially where, as in the case of the quasi-judicial 'Hutton' inquiry in the United Kingdom in 2003,[5] the evidence on which the findings were made was widely publicized.

There are three levels at which statements about legal truth operate. One is at the level of physical events and actions. A court makes a finding of 'fact', or applies a presumption, and proceeds on the basis that the fact is true. Both these types of legal 'truth' may or may not be defeasible. A presumption can usually be rebutted, a legal finding can sometimes be overturned with new evidence. Until those events happen, the legal truth holds good. But sometimes the legal truth cannot be challenged. Fresh evidence may not be admissible. A presumed fact, the paternity of a husband, for example, may be placed beyond question. A fictitious entry of birth may be irremovable. In those circumstances, the legal truth replaces physical truth. A second level refers to legal categories: for example, whether a certain

---

[4] JM Balkin, 'The Proliferation of Legal Truth' (2003) 26 *Harvard Journal of Law and Public Policy* 5.

[5] This inquiry, prompted by the death of an intelligence officer, investigated the intelligence upon which the decision to go to war in Iraq in March 2003 was based.

combination of agreed 'facts' constitutes a legal wrong, or, of more relevance here, whether a person is a 'legal' parent as defined by law. The third level concerns predictions about future physical events. The question whether Henry is Mary's father operates at the first two levels of legal truth: does he fall within a presumption identifying him as Mary's father (which may go unchallenged), or does he fall within the legal category establishing him as Mary's father? Whether any of these results will be in Mary's interests is the third level. This 'truth' is nothing more than prediction. Courts sometimes have to act on predictions, especially in cases involving children's welfare. But in such cases they have to be very careful when identifying the case before them with the case characteristics upon which predictions are based. They must act on evidence specific to the facts before them. It would be a mistake, for example, to conclude that a husband whose wife complains that he regularly assaults her is unlikely to kill her from information that most husbands do not kill their wives. These questions can have enormous importance for the individuals concerned, and for others too.

TRUTH, KINSHIP, AND MANIPULATION

The anthropologist Robin Fox wrote:

> Kinship and marriage are about the basic facts of life. They are about 'birth, and copulation, and death', the eternal round that seemed to depress the poet but which excites, amongst others, the anthropologist.[6]

Family law also revolves around these 'basic facts of life'. Humans need a way to ensure wealth and power pass from one generation on its demise to the newly born. It may be a bioevolutionary imperative that men should seek to keep their wealth and power within their gene-pool by ensuring that the children borne by the women whose reproductive and nurturing capacities they have conscripted are their own genetic offspring. But humans have not always followed that genetic route. Matrilineal societies demonstrate cases where the father's genes are appropriated for the benefit of the wife's blood family. Nor is it

---

[6] R Fox, *Kinship and Marriage* (Penguin Books, 1967) 27.

always the case that the apparent father is the genetic father. Adoption has been widely practised historically, usually for very specific reasons, such as the lack of an heir. It became commonly used to produce a successor to an Emperor during the Roman Empire.[7] In such cases, the participants knew what they were doing. They were not under any illusion as to the biological processes. But kinship rules created a new (legal) truth, and the departure from the need for a definite biological link between the transmitter of wealth and power and the receiver avoids serious truth problems which can arise where such a link is required, or assumed.

Nevertheless, since children succeed to what the adults leave behind, and carry on this legacy, it is very important for the adults to have a clear way of identifying *which* children will come into this inheritance. In patrilineal societies, the assumption is that the children who succeed have been begotten by their male ancestors. How are we to be sure that a particular child is the true heir? Medieval records show attempts from trial by ordeal (a genetically related son was one who could hold 'glowing metal') to demonstrations of male potency (or impotency) before witnesses.[8] Such uncertainties are reduced by requiring the birth to be within marriage, and assuming *pater is est quem nuptiae demonstrant* (the father is he whom marriage demonstrates to be such). The rule created a legal truth regarding physical events, whether or not it corresponded with the actual physical truth. At a time before science could demonstrate the physical truths, parental relationships were necessarily based on such legal truths. These legal truths were designed to serve social or political ends, and this has occurred throughout the history of kinship relations.

When truth is manipulated in this way, it is always important to try to understand whose interests are being served by the manipulation. This is often a complex issue. For example, prior to the Gender Recognition Act 2004, a person could not, legally, be treated as having the gender they later assumed if this differed from that recorded at their birth. The Act now made this possible by allowing a new birth certificate to be issued showing the person whose birth is recorded as the sex to which the person has been re-assigned; the fact that this is different from the sex with which the person was attributed in the

---

[7] See Mary Beard, *SPQR: A History of Ancient Rome* (Profile Books, 2015) 418–20.
[8] K Albrecht and D Schultheiss, 'Proof of Paternity: Historical Reflections on an Andrological Forensic Challenge' (2004) 36 *Andrologia* 31.

original certificate will not be revealed,[9] thus significantly enhancing their ability to enjoy rights they claimed. In doing this, the legislators were concerned with the interests, and possibly rights claimed by, transgender persons.

But the situation of children is more difficult. Of course children need adults to sustain them, and the primary allocation of this role to those who as a matter of physical truth have given them life has sense, as is the creation of replacement legal truths when the physical truth is unknown or for some reason cannot or should not be used. Yet, as discussed in chapter 1, institutional norms have, until very recently, been premised on the instrumental value that children have for adults.[10] So the 'truth' of parenthood, whether biological or fictive, has often been, and still is, used to give adults power over children. Marie-Thérèse Meulders-Klein has expressed it thus, saying of 'traditional' societies:

> In general, the prevailing impression is that the child is recognised *through* the interest of the group or of adults, that they are a source of labour, of wealth or of new alliances, that they are the means of perpetuating a race, a family or a cult, or just an individual who goes on after our death.[11]

Actions which serve the interests of parents may of course also benefit children, or at least certain children. When a man adopts a child to take forward his family lineage, he benefits not only the lineage, but usually also the child. Nevertheless, it remains possible to perceive the overall weighting of interests. In the adoption example, it is clear that the Roman institution was designed to enhance the interests of family groups, and was very different from the modern institution, which is primarily concerned with enhancing the interests of children in a world dominated by adults. Yet even when doing that, replacing physical truth (the true facts of birth) with a legally constructed relationship could, and did, violate children's interests by constructing false identities for them.

The period of the French revolution illustrated vividly, within a few tumultuous years, the way in which the truths of kinship can swing between serving the interests of the adult generation to a failed

---

[9] Gender Recognition Act 2004, s 10, sch 3.   [10] See p 10.
[11] M-T Meulders-Klein, *La Personne, La Famille & le Droit* (Bruylant, 1999) 164 (my translation).

attempt to serve the interests of children. The main lines of the pre-revolutionary system were clear, although there were variations of detail throughout the different regions of France. It was centred on marriage. Wealth and power passed only through legitimate children, and primarily to males. Sisters had fewer succession rights than their brothers, and non-marital children were completely excluded. Fathers controlled the way the succeeding generation used the inheritance they left behind through arranged marriages and preferred legacies. The legal family, constituted by marriage, and limited in the way described, not the biological family, determined the flow of wealth. The early years of the revolution tore this apart. Laws of October and November 1793 and January 1794 greatly reduced freedom of testation, and imposed egalitarian succession (brothers and sisters alike), including to non-marital children recognized by their fathers.[12] Here we see a decisive shift from a system which sees the successor generation defined in such a way as to be a means for perpetuating the will of its predecessor to one where the biological successors have claims in their own right against their forebears.

This does not mean that the interests of children had been entirely neglected under the *ancien régime*. Suzanne Desan's brilliant study of regional court proceedings during the revolutionary period[13] describes how paternity suits were successfully brought by many unwed mothers during the eighteenth century. The mothers and children might not expect the social and property benefits of marriage and legitimacy, but men might be required to pay a degree of compensation for the costs their actions had incurred (though this was partly by way of compensation to the *fathers* of the women they had seduced, for damaging *their* interests in the value of their daughters). When the revolutionaries swept away the distinctions between legitimate and illegitimate children for succession purposes, they were without doubt moved by egalitarian principles. However, they also embraced the ideals of freedom of personal relations, and, just as marriage was now to be freed from family tyranny, so parenthood outside marriage was to be undertaken freely. Women did this, the revolutionaries believed, by giving birth. Men did this, they believed, by voluntarily accepting their responsibilities. Hence revolutionary

---

[12] S Desan, *The Family on Trial in Revolutionary France* (University of California Press, 2004), ch 4.
[13] Ibid.

laws at first restricted, and eventually abolished, paternity suits. Conversely, freely acknowledged non-marital children had full legal status regarding their father. But it all depended on the man's willingness to accept that he was the father.

There is a terrible contradiction here. How is one to reconcile the revolutionary prioritization of the interests of children, marital and non-marital equally, over the claims of legally constructed lineage and property with this remarkable absolution of men from the consequences of their actions? Two factors may account for it. First, the reformers saw the act of recognition by fathers as being an acceptance of *responsibilities*, which they believed men would naturally accept.[14] But they were also suspicious of false claims of paternity, which might lead men to forced acknowledgements in order to fend off damaging paternity suits. This could threaten the stability of families. Thus the revolutionary lawyers were less willing than their earlier counterparts to accept confirmation of the truth of paternity by circumstantial evidence.[15] Desan concludes that few non-marital children gained by the opportunities for recognition, especially as their claims to inheritance arose only when the alleged father died. Many were harmed by the stifling of paternity actions.[16]

The promotion of equal status among children provoked reaction. 'Three groups', writes Desan, 'were especially perceived as threats to the family line: overly independent married women, illegitimate offspring, and adult children who defied marital and succession plans'.[17] The eventual solution incorporated in the *Code Civil* 1804 was to recentre power on to the married father. *Puissance paternelle* was reestablished, going as far as to allow fathers to imprison their children. The abolition of paternity suits was formalized, and non-marital children formally recognized by their fathers could no longer become heirs on the same basis as legitimate children. Adulterine illegitimate children could not be recognized at all. To underline the re-emphasis on the role of legally constructed kinship as a means of securing order, particularly with regard to property, the Code introduced a new form of adoption, confined to married couples who were over 50 and childless, and the adopted child was over 25.[18] Meulders-Klein summarized the position:

[14] Ibid especially 234.   [15] Ibid especially 208, 239.
[16] Ibid especially 222.   [17] Ibid 263.   [18] Ibid ch 8.

[B]iological truth was not admitted to the system of the Civil Code because it did not conform to the logic, or more exactly, the policy of the system: order and harmony of families and protection of their patrimonies.[19]

French law is still strongly oriented towards aligning the truth of parenthood with a conception of the 'natural' family: that is, that the child has been conceived within a two-parent family. Surrogacy is therefore banned as representing the idea that it treats the human body as a commercial instrument and the child as the object of a contract, and permitted medically assisted reproduction confined to circumstances which mimic natural reproduction within such a family (hence is unavailable to single women, same-sex couples, or post-menopausal women, and donor anonymity is guaranteed). In such cases the physical truth (of medically assisted procreation, or surreptitious surrogate birth) will be more easily concealed beneath the legal truths displayed on official documentation.[20] This could of course occur whenever parenthood is a creation of the law, as in the circumstances of donation for IVF conception described in chapter 5.[21] But the law there is concerned with identifying people with primary responsibility for the child's welfare, and also perhaps integrating the child into a lineage for inheritance purposes, and, as was observed, is prepared to do that even when it will be clear that the relationships cannot be biological. But where they could be biological, the question arises whether the truth should be always observable. This is discussed shortly.

TRUTH AND IDENTITY

Knowledge of parentage

Such issues have acquired a significant added dimension in recent years. The modern quest for authenticity is associated with openness

---

[19] Meulders-Klein, n 11, 167 (my translation).

[20] See LF Terminal, 'The Changing Concept of "Family" and Challenges of Family Law in France' in JM Scherpe (ed), *European Family Law*, vol II (Edward Elgar, 2016) ch 3, 52–7; K Parizer-Krief, 'Gender Equality in Legislation on Medically Assisted Procreation in France' (2015) 29 *International Journal of Law, Policy and the Family* 205.

[21] See pp 122–3.

about the physical facts of one's birth rather than constructed legal truths. Movements for open adoption have become important since the 1970s,[22] and, while not necessarily reflected in adoption legislation, openness has become widespread in practice.[23] In 1989 the UNCRC proclaimed the child's right to 'know and be cared for by his or her parents' and 'preserve his or her identity, including nationality, name and family relations'.[24] In England and Wales, the Adoption and Children Act 2002 provided a mechanism by which adult adopted children may access their birth certificate. In the same year, the child's right to an identity was fully acknowledged by the European Court of Human Rights in *Mikulić v Croatia*.[25] A man constantly evaded court proceedings by a mother and child who were alleging his paternity. The child complained that the courts' inefficiency amounted to a violation of her private and family life contrary to Article 8 of the Convention by prolonging uncertainty over her identity. The court held that there was no 'family tie' between the child and the alleged father. However, it went on to decide that the child's 'private' life:

> includes a person's physical and psychological integrity, and can sometimes embrace aspects of an individual's physical and social identity. Respect for 'private life' must also comprise to a certain degree the right to establish relationships with other human beings.[26]

The court therefore held that the facts fell within Article 8, and that the procedural deficiencies constituted a violation. It may go rather far to speak of a 'right to establish relationships', although only 'to a certain degree', and be preferable to characterize the right as to 'an opportunity' to establish a relationship. This recognition of a right to identity, however expressed, nevertheless constitutes a significant claim by the successor generation on its predecessor. The British government accepted this when on 21 January 2004 it announced that the system of sperm donor anonymity would be changed so that children

---

[22] See SN Katz, 'Dual Systems of Adoption in the United States' and N Lowe, 'English Adoption Law: Past, Present and Future' in SN Katz, J Eekelaar, and M Maclean (eds), *Cross Currents: Family Law and Policy in the United States and England* (Oxford University Press, 2000) 290–3, 326–7.
[23] See S Goedeke and KR Daniels, 'Embryo Donation or Embryo Adoption? Practice and Policy in New Zealand' (2017) 31 *International Journal of Law, Policy and the Family* 1.
[24] UNCRC, Arts 7 and 8.
[25] App No 53176/99, judgment 7 February 2002.   [26] Para 53.

born as a result of donations after April 2005 have a right of access to the identity of the donor once they reach eighteen.[27] Objections, usually voiced by the medical profession, that removal of anonymity would result in a reduction of donors, even if true,[28] are clearly entirely anchored in the interests of the adult generation. Children can now choose whether to seek identifying information, and if they do so, should be told the truth.

Of course this assumes that the children know the nature of their conception, which is currently a matter for the parents, most of whom do not disclose this fact, but it seems that more are doing so, or at least are intending to do so.[29] But should the state take steps to ensure this information reaches the children, for example by annotating a birth certificate? Mhairi Cowden argues that children should be informed if they have been conceived through donation, as a consequence of their right to respect.[30] In chapter 3 I suggested that 'respect for something or someone lies in acknowledging that a feature of that entity has value in and of itself, the value usually not being assessable in monetary terms.'[31] I have also indicated that attributing rights implies adopting the rightholder's viewpoint of the interest claimed.[32] We could supplement those principles by asserting, as Aristotle does regarding friendship,[33] that it is hard to believe that anyone would choose to live their life under a false understanding of their genetic origin. Therefore to enable this to happen fails to give them sufficient respect. This provides a powerful basis for concluding that the state should ensure that such information should always reach children whose procreation it has assisted.

However, Carol Smart[34] gives accounts from research of cases where family members strongly believed disclosure to children of

---

[27] Human Fertilisation and Embryology Authority (Disclosure of Donor Information) Regulations 2004. See also *Rose v Secretary of State for Health* [2002] 2 FLR 962.

[28] Donation has actually increased after the removal of anonymity in some countries: M Cowden, ' "No Harm, No Foul": A Child's Right To Know Their Genetic Parent' (2012) 26 *International Journal of Law, Policy and the Family* 102.

[29] See S Golombok, *Modern Families: Parents and Children in New Family Forms* (Cambridge University Press, 2015) 98–102.

[30] Cowden, n 28. See also A Bainham, 'Arguments about Parentage' (2008) 67 *Cambridge Law Journal* 322, 348.

[31] See p 66.   [32] See p 36.   [33] See p 98.

[34] C Smart, 'Law and the Regulation of Family Secrets' (2010) 24 *International Journal of Law, Policy and the Family* 397.

their genetic origins would harm the children and create significant family disruption. Some children themselves opposed it. These
accounts suggest that the timing and manner in which such information becomes known can have important consequences for family
relationships, and sometimes harm children. Would a better solution
therefore be to leave the choice whether to inform the child to the
parents? They could receive encouragement, and counselling, but
ultimately it would be a judgement in the exercise of what is described
in chapter 6 as a 'fuller' concept of responsibility.

The difficulty with this is that it still leaves the decision in adults'
hands. Even Smart, who suggests that the pursuit of genetic truth pays
too little regard to the complexities of family life, writes that 'secrets
fold themselves into complex power plays between generations and
kin.'[35] In these power plays, the interests and viewpoint of the child
concerned can be easily forgotten or subsumed into adult concerns.
It could therefore be argued that these secrets and power plays could
be minimized in the case of children conceived through artificial technology with the help of state agencies if it were understood that part
of the process included a procedure that would reveal this fact to the
child. Language could be important. It is of course true that the terms
'mother' and 'father' can be used in everyday life, and even legally, to
denote a social rather than legal relationship. Nevertheless, there is still
a dominant association with a biological relationship, and this is suggested by recording a man as a child's 'father', thus implying a biological
connection which does not exist. Perhaps the male partner of a woman
who conceives through IVF by donation should be recorded officially
as a 'parent', rather than a 'father', in the same way as a female partner is
recorded as a 'parent' rather than a 'mother' or 'co-mother' on the child's
birth certificate. This would not prevent the people concerned calling
them something different if they preferred. The child would therefore
be very likely to grow up with this knowledge, in the same way as a
half-sibling grows up with the knowledge of the nature of his or her
relationship with the other half-sibling. A UK study has shown that
mothers who had not disclosed their children's origins displayed higher
levels of emotional distress than those who had disclosed them.[36] This
might be a consequence of guilt associated with keeping the nature of

---

[35] Ibid 404.
[36] Golombok, n 29, 107. For further discussion, see Goedeke and Daniels, n 23.

the conception secret. A leading researcher concludes that evidence is emerging from longitudinal research of more positive functioning in families in which parents have disclosed the child's donor conception, although it cannot necessarily be assumed that the more positive functioning is a direct result of the disclosure; disclosing families may show more open communication generally. Taking these findings together, openness with children in the preschool years seems to be optimal in terms of the emotional well-being of donor offspring.[37]

Where conception has occurred naturally, the position is more complicated. When a child is born, while a mother is required to register the birth of her child, the father's name will not be recorded unless he is married to the mother or the mother agrees. It has been suggested that a child has a right that the name be recorded.[38] This right should be viewed from the child's perspective. If the issue is just one of providing information, it is hard to see why the child would not want this. But it may also involve complicated personal relationships which would necessitate disclosure of intimate behaviour by the mother which should not be extracted by state actions. As strong as a child's right to identifying information is, it can never be absolute.[39]

This limitation was recognized by the European Court of Human Rights in *Odièvre v France*[40] which upheld the French system allowing mothers to give birth anonymously: *accouchement sous X*. Introduced as a humane measure in the seventeenth century to protect women and children from the deprivation and ostracism which would accompany extra-marital birth, the measure is relatively little used today (about 600 cases occur each year) and has led to intense controversy in France. The justification given is that this provides a way

[37] Golombok, n 29, 115–16.

[38] A Bainham, 'What is the Point of Birth Registration?' (2008) 20 *Child and Family Law Quarterly* 449, 460. Department of Work and Pensions and Department of Children, Schools and Families, *Joint Birth Registration: Recording Responsibility* (Cm 7293, 2008).

[39] See generally J Marshall, 'Concealed Births, Adoption and Human Rights Law: Being Wary of Seeking To Open Windows into People's Souls' (2012) 71 *Cambridge Law Journal* 325.

[40] (2004) 38 EHRR 43. See N Lefaucheur, 'The French "Tradition" of Anonymous Birth: the Lines of Argument' (2004) 18 *International Journal of Law, Policy and the Family* 322 and S Besson, 'Enforcing the Child's Rights To Know Her Origins: Contrasting Approaches under the Convention on the Rights of the Child and the European Convention on Human Rights' (2007) 21 *International Journal of Law, Policy and the Family* 137.

of assisting distressed women who might otherwise have abortions, or even kill their newborn children. Recent modifications allow non-identifying information about the natural family to be provided to the children, and for the mother to waive her confidentiality should she later so choose. But it remains in the mother's power to veto disclosure. Such an exemption from registration of the mother has not been thought necessary in England. But it has been found to have reduced cases of neonatal infanticide in Austria, so is possibly a result of social hardship and guilt associated with non-marital conception.[41] Any scheme for disclosure must clearly take these matters into account, though the solution should be found in overcoming such obstacles rather than neglecting the position of the child.

In cases of dispute, English judges approach this issue through the 'best interests' principle, and courts are increasingly taking the view that the best interests of the child are achieved through clearing up uncertainty about the child's true genetic origins through scientific means. The child's interests may justify a 'cover-up', but it is hard to see circumstances where this will happen when a judge says: 'If, as she should, this mother is to bring up her children to believe in, and act by, the maxim, which it is her duty to teach them at her knee, that honesty is the best policy, then she should not sabotage that ... by living a lie.'[42] So where the issue is in the 'public domain', or even where uncertainties have been raised within the family, the judges are likely to say that it is better for the child that the doubts are resolved by scientific means. So if a man raises such doubts, he is likely to have the 'truth' established.[43]

Names

Genetic truth is not sought only for providing information which children may want. Parents have continued to assert claims over their

[41] See 'BJOG study finds unique "anonymous delivery" law effective in decreasing rates of neonaticide in Austria': https://www.rcog.org.uk/en/news/bjog-release-new-study-finds-unique-anonymous-delivery-law-effective-in-decreasing-rates-of-neonaticide-in-austria/ (accessed 13 June 2017).

[42] *Re H (paternity: blood tests)* [1996] 4 All ER 28, 44. See also *Re H & A* [2002] 1 FLR 1145. Technically, the matter is not governed by s 1 of the Children Act 1989, which makes the child's welfare paramount (*S v S; W v Official Solicitor* [1972] AC 24), but in practice the child's interests will dominate the decision: *Re P (a child)* [2008] EWCA Civ 499, para 12.

[43] See, for example, *Re T (paternity: ordering blood tests)* [2001] 2 FLR 1190.

genetic offspring. These have taken a different form from those made during the era of patriarchy described earlier. Passing on social status and family wealth are now less important. But for some men, passing on their name assumes similar significance. Surnames are legally controlled in European countries, and Carolus van Nijnatten has provided an argument for fixing the child with the father's surname. He says that this gives the child a source of identity beyond the mother–child dyad, and in this way links the child to the entire social order.[44] This argument appeals to the child's interests, as many patriarchal arguments do, but is founded on the maintenance of the existing social order, it being held that identification with the father is necessary for the child to be integrated with it. Less grandiloquently, fathers who are living apart from their children often see the attachment of their name as a final link to a child with whom they have otherwise lost a relationship.[45] In *Dawson v Wearmouth*[46] Lord Jauncey said that he understood an unmarried father's wish that his son should bear his surname rather than that of the mother's (estranged) former husband (Wearmouth). 'The child has after all not a drop of Wearmouth blood in his veins', he said. For Lord Jauncey, a surname is 'a biological label which tells the world at large that the blood of the name flows in [the] veins'. This pathetic hangover from the patriarchal era did not impress Lady Justice Hale, who said that 'it is a poor sort of parent whose interest in and commitment to his child depends upon that child bearing his name. After all, it is a privilege not enjoyed by many mothers, even if they are living with the child. They have to depend upon other more substantial things.'[47]

Sex and gender

Is someone's sex a 'fact'? While there may be more indeterminacy in the matter than is sometimes thought,[48] and there is certainly an

---

[44] C van Nijnatten, 'In the Name of the Father: Changing the Law on Naming Children in the Netherlands' (1996) 10 *International Journal of Law, Policy and the Family* 221.

[45] See *Re B (Change of surname)* [1996] 1 FLR 791, where the court refused to allow the formal change of surname of three teenagers who had long abandoned their father's name and had no wish to re-use it.

[46] [1999] 2 AC 308.   [47] *Re R (a child)* [2002] 1 FCR 170 para 13.

[48] See the excellent discussion by P-L Chau and J Herring, 'Defining, Assigning and Designing Sex' (2002) 16 *International Journal of Law, Policy and the Family* 327.

identifiable condition of 'inter-sex', it is nevertheless the case that the vast majority of people can be classed either as 'male' or 'female' from birth. But that apparent 'physical' truth does not conclude the matter. We have seen that it is possible to change that attribution,[49] thus allowing a 'legal' truth to override, and conceal, an apparent 'physical' truth (the sex to which the person was assigned at birth). Of course, it may be said that the original assignment was incorrect, and that the person always possessed the subsequently acquired gender. One could go further and say that gender is always a matter for self-identification.

Could this problem be resolved by distinguishing between sex and gender? The former refers to physical characteristics, the latter to social roles. Since social roles can be changed, and chosen, gender is not physically determined. If it is always possible to change a gender role, whatever physical sexual characteristics a person may have, it could be concluded that physical characteristics are an irrelevance, and that the law should only respond to a person's gender, understood in this way. But are gender roles so easily identifiable as 'male' and 'female', given differences between cultures and classes and changes of fashion? This is a very controversial area, which extends far beyond the issue of concern here, which is whether a person's apparent physical sex (if identifiable) should be legally recorded at birth, and thereafter used as an identifier from which legal consequences can flow.

The surprising conclusion may be that, at least in societies where legal equality and sex-neutrality prevail, not much turns on this in principle. Much of family law could now be expressed in gender-neutral terms. 'Wife' and 'husband' can be replaced by 'spouse' and 'mother' and 'father' could be replaced by 'parent'. Even sexual reassignment by one person to a heterosexual marriage has no effect on the marriage, since marriage is possible between people of the same sex.[50] People could simply assume whichever gender role they wished and conform to the current social practice regarding that role. However, it does not seem to be realistic to completely abandon the use of such a prevalent characteristic as physical sex as at least an initial identifier at birth (inter-sex cases excepted[51]). Without it,

---

[49] Gender Recognition Act 2004, above pp 147–8.
[50] Gender Recognition Act 2004, s 11A.
[51] Germany and Australia allow a passport recording the holder's gender as 'X' on the basis of official documentation establishing gender re-assignment or inter-sex status.

opportunities for fraud ('biological' men and women assuming the opposite roles for nefarious purposes) and invasions of accepted gender segregated spaces would abound. It also provides useful demographic information, including about fertility.

This should not prevent genuine cases of people departing from that identification and adopting a different social role. The original biological allocation of sex is seldom relevant in daily life.[52] What matters is how a person is currently perceived. This does not mean, however, that it may not be so for some people in some contexts. For example, it has been provided that a person who marries someone who had changed gender but not disclosed this may have the marriage annulled. Alex Sharpe[53] complains that this not only fails to recognize the change in gender effected by the Gender Recognition Act 2004, but treats intimate contact with a transgender person as harmful and is discriminatory against transgender people. But the provision does not require the transgender person to disclose. It simply gives the option to the other partner to terminate the marriage by nullity rather than divorce proceedings should they find they cannot live with the transgender person in the rather unlikely event that they had not realised this when they married. This is arguably a more considerate approach than assigning the parties to the divorce law, with its association with fault, as would happen in the comparative cases (such as the undetected homosexuality of the other person) referred to by Sharpe.

TRUTH AND JUSTICE

I have presented the material about truth from two opposing standpoints: those of the older and its successor generation. Yet, it may be said, these interests need not be opposed. A very significant impetus in the movement for reform of adoption laws like those of Newfoundland mentioned at the beginning of this chapter has come

---

[52] Despite attempts to make it so, for example, by laws ascribing the use of public toilet facilities according to people's biological sex. These make little sense. But determining eligibility to participate in sports divided on a gender basis is more difficult.

[53] A Sharpe, 'Transgender Marriage and the Legal Obligation to Disclose Gender' (2012) 75 *Modern Law Review* 33.

not only from adopted children themselves,[54] but also from mothers seeking to trace their children. The beneficiaries of the 2003 Adoption Act in Newfoundland and Labrador have been adopted children who, on reaching 19, have access to their adoption records (subject still, however, to a veto entered by the mother). But parents will characteristically frame their claims as being beneficial to the children. How could they not? So requiring unwilling teenagers to keep their father's surname at least for official purposes, while they used a different one in everyday life, has been justified as retaining a potentially beneficial link.[55] Allowing a non-residential father to keep contact is standardly justified as furthering the interests of the children concerned.

Of course there must be a convergence of interests. The family itself is premised on the assumption that it is in the interests of both the adult members and the children that the adults provide care and nurture for the children. This is why such interests are often described as being 'relational'. But we cannot assume, in our complex society, that there will always be such a coincidence of interests. We must remember that adults are capable of articulating, and taking steps to actualize, their interests. It is much more difficult for children to do this. This should require strict scrutiny of adult assertions about children's interests. We must remember, too, that adults create the social structures into which children are introduced, and the interests of children are often measured against these structures. Where, for example, arranged marriage is the norm, there is no scope for a child to actualize an interest which does not comply with the norm. The child has to take what is on offer, however unwilling they may be to conform to it. Yet Ronald Dworkin has said that a daughter who lives in an 'associative' community which genuinely believes that depriving her of freedom to marry is in her interests, and who marries against her father's wishes, 'has something to regret. She owes him at least an accounting, and perhaps an apology.'[56] Such is the extent to which even one of liberalism's foremost exponents allows the present generation to impose its will on its successors.

Physical truth plays an important part in the interaction between the generations. We should remember that adults can create legal

---

[54] See, for example, the Green Ribbon Campaign for Open Record in the United States.

[55] *Re B (Change of surname)* [1996] 1 FLR 791.

[56] R Dworkin, *Law's Empire* (Fontana, 1986) 205.

truths which are at odds with physical truth. They may deliberately disguise physical truths. When they do that, you can be sure that it is normally in order to project the social order constructed by the adults into the future. This may or may not be for the benefit of the children. Access to 'physical truth', then, is an important way in which the new generation can challenge these adult powers. Physical truth provides the raw material of the world into which the new member is introduced. A child may live their life in the belief of the 'truth' of their parentage which is in fact false. For some, this may be of no consequence, and matters of genetic origins of little concern. But for others it may be, so we cannot assume that by withholding the truth we are not undermining an important part of a person's understanding of their place in the world, even though they may not know it. Informed of the physical truth, the child can say: 'My conception occurred in such-and-such a way. Given these circumstances, what are *my* needs and wants? What should these people be doing for *me*? What should *I* be doing for them? What other relationships might be open to me?' Of course, young children will not be able to answer these questions immediately, but they will some day form an opinion about them. So this knowledge, or its prospective availability, allows the individual to confront the world as it is *on his own terms*, and influence solutions according to his perception of his interests given the physical truth. But with physical truth forever obscured, society's new members are doomed to manipulation.

TRUTH AND SHAME

It is possible for a woman to conceal from the child, and indeed from her partner, her child's true paternity. The soap opera staple, where a woman conceals from her partner that the child she is carrying is fathered by another, may or may not reflect widespread reality. Estimates, based on very unreliable data, vary wildly (from 3 per cent to 30 per cent) as to the extent to which men are mistaken about the paternity of their partner's children.[57] So mothers are able to rely on the legal truths generated by registration or presumptions to

[57] See Cowden, n 28, 119.

conceal the physical truths of their children's paternity. They may be
mistaken, but also may do so for many reasons, such as avoiding the
shame that would be thrown on them, or the complications to their
relationships, by the revelation of their unsuspected sexual actions.
These of course concern their own interests rather than those of the
children, for the degree of importance which knowledge of genetic
identity holds for an individual can be judged only by that individual,
not by someone else. The state, too, may have an interest in exposing
the mother's concealment, for it may lose the opportunity to claim
reimbursement from the father for supporting his child. But there
are limits to the extent to which state agencies can intrude into private affairs which have not been brought into dispute, or where state
assistance has not already been invoked. Compulsory DNA testing of
all children would be too great an intrusion into private life. So these
mothers have to weigh the moral issues for themselves, and exercise
the 'fuller' type of responsibility referred to in chapter 5.[58]

My argument has been that the interests that children have in know-
ing the physical truth are always stronger than those of the adults,
because for children they give rise to claims in justice, whereas for
adults they form the basis for attempts at exercising power, sometimes
beyond the grave. These claims may indeed be beneficial to children,
but care has to be taken about when they arise, and they may need to
be monitored. In addition to these interests, there is another which
speaks for physical truth. Its concealment has usually been associated with shame over departures from conventional norms. This still
seems to be the basis for systems of anonymous birth. It certainly was
the basis for the concealment of the births, and deaths, of illegitimate children in Mother and Baby homes in Ireland, which is subject
to a Commission of Investigation established by the Irish government in 2015. But these departures have not always been dishonour-
able. Conception outside marriage has reflected the strong currents
of human sexuality which conventional norms have frequently
oppressed. Maintaining secrecy of illegitimate birth supports those
oppressive norms by sustaining the stigma and shame of illegitimate conception. Maintaining secrecy in cases of parenthood by donor
insemination sustains a perception of the shame of infertility, and the
deviant nature of artificial reproduction. Even concealing the fact of

gender re-assignment through altered birth certificates feeds the climate of discrimination and harassment it seeks to avoid. If society provides the means of gender re-assignment and artificial reproduction it presumably believes they are morally acceptable practices. Let it then shout it from the rooftops. I do not say there can be no exceptions. But in general it is better to confront the world as we have made it than pretend it is otherwise.

7

Community

We all live in communities, but the nature of the relationship between individuals and the community around them is complex and controversial. This is of concern for family law, for families (even if only of two people) are a kind of community: many say they are the primary form of community. Since the 1970s, social and political theorists have been particularly troubled about the relationship, their concern aggravated by the rise in the 1980s of neo-liberal social and economic thought in the Anglo-American world under the stewardship of President Ronald Reagan and Prime Minister Margaret Thatcher, and which remains in the ascendancy. This was thought to have fostered individual greed at the expense of the responsibilities that should exist between people and within social groups. For example, David Cameron complained that 'the recent growth of the state has promoted not social solidarity, but selfishness and individualism',[1] although it is hard to see why this should be attributed to the growth of the state rather than to its contraction and replacement by private enterprise. Some of such concerns may have been tempered by countervailing concerns about the influence of cultural groups in promoting religious fundamentalism.

THE FEAR OF INDIVIDUALISM

The contemporary intellectual movement reflecting these discontents was significantly influenced by the frontal assault on the fundamentals

---

[1] http://www.theguardian.com/commentisfree/2009/nov/10/big-society-government-poverty-inequality (accessed 10 November 2009).

Family Law and Personal Life. Second edition. John Eekelaar. © John Eekelaar 2017. Second edition published 2017 by Oxford University Press.

of liberal moral thought by Alasdair MacIntyre in 1981.[2] This included a rejection of the possibility of rational justifications for moral positions which are independent of social context, the claim that enlightenment philosophers centred morality on the individual,[3] and that individuals without a role within a communal context can have no moral bearings.[4] While MacIntyre traced the origins of what he saw as our present dire condition to the breach from Aristotelian and Thomistic thought wrought by enlightenment philosophers such as Kant and Hume, Peter Singer's similarly trenchant critique of liberal individualism attributed its origins primarily to Calvin and Adam Smith.[5] I leave assessment of these historical claims aside, save for one comment. Even if it were true that there is a line of development from those earlier thinkers to a dominant ideology of the contemporary western world, it had to survive two hundred years of significantly illiberal political ideology and practice. I refer to nineteenth-century European nationalism and imperialism, which subordinated the role of individuals to the interests of their nations, and extolled the role of European nations as purveyors of civilization across the world with scant regard to its effects on the welfare of subject individuals,[6] and to twentieth-century totalitarianism, both communist and national socialist, which subsumed individual identity within the community of the state.

The core of this critique of individualism seems to be that unless individuals are viewed within a social context, there is no reference point by which their conduct can be evaluated. The generalized, a-contextual 'rules' of justice, as developed, for example, by Robert Nozick, John Rawls, and even Immanuel Kant, do not provide a basis for moral action, it is said, because (as in the case of Kant's categorical imperative) they do not point unequivocally to a particular action, or because they are mutually contradictory.[7] Since they fail, all that is left is the freedom to further one's own interest as far as possible.[8] This

---

[2] A MacIntyre, *After Virtue* (Duckworth, 1981; 2nd edn, 1985).

[3] Ibid 6 ('What was then invented was the *individual* ...') (original italics).

[4] A MacIntyre, *Dependent Rational Animals: Why Human Beings Need Virtues* (Open Books, 1999).

[5] P Singer, *How Are We to Live?* (Opus Books, 1993) chs 3 and 4.

[6] For a revealing account in the context of British imperialism, see AWB Simpson, *Human Rights and the End of Empire: Britain and the Genesis of the European Convention* (Oxford University Press, 2000).

[7] MacIntyre, n 2, ch 17 and 45–6.   [8] Singer, n 5, ch 4.

objection to liberal moral theory is similar to the starting point of the objection to liberal legal theory made by the American Critical Legal Studies movement in the 1980s. Writers of that persuasion characterized 'liberal law' as falsely claiming 'objective validity' when it was in fact the manifestation of power, and as being inherently indeterminate, thus permitting unrestrained subjective applications.[9]

These accounts share a vision of a system which has failed to provide standards that can constrain subjective decision-making. Of course law is a manifestation of power, but is it *only* that? Law in liberal societies *does* seem to apply, often predictably, and create constraints on that power. And the vast majority of people *do* seem to follow shared ways of relating towards one another in their day-to-day practices, even though they may no longer do so within the traditional institutional forms they used to. Researchers into people's attitudes to inheritance have concluded that 'enduring love, built on a sense of shared life, values and commitment, and a sense of obligation towards one's dependants, one's blood line, and heritage, are reflected in the range of beneficiaries that most people appear to contemplate as suitable for inheritance on their death'.[10] It is perhaps more remarkable that the alternative programmes offered by MacIntyre, Singer, and Unger differ so much between themselves. MacIntyre follows a form of conservative Catholicism; Singer proposes some type of 'green' agenda; and Unger a model of radical economic and civic de-centralization.

Feminist scholarship has often advanced similar critiques. In particular, as Elizabeth Frazer and Nicola Lacey have put it: 'Critical feminist politics has been strongly concerned to emphasise the facts of human connectedness and, flowing from this practical insight, to argue for the reassessment of values and practices which flow from ideals of reciprocity, sisterhood and solidarity'.[11] This has led to the view that individuals should always be seen in the context of their

---

[9] Roberto Unger saw this apparent failure of liberal law as an opportunity to subvert the whole liberal project: R Unger, *The Critical Legal Studies Movement* (Harvard University Press, 1986).

[10] G Douglas, H Woodward, A Humphrey, L Mills, and G Morrell, 'Enduring Love: Attitudes to Family and Inheritance Law in England and Wales' (2011) 38 *Journal of Law and Society* 245, 247.

[11] E Frazer and N Lacey, *The Politics of Community: A Feminist Critique of the Liberal-Communitarian Debate* (Harvester Wheatsheaf, 1993) 69.

relationships with others, particularly their family relationships, and their rights as being 'relational' incorporating reference to their responsibilities to others and their well-being as being promoted by fulfilling those responsibilities, and even going beyond that.[12]

No one, of course, could be unaware of the dependence of individual humans on one another, whether in reproduction and nurturing of human generations, or by providing collective security for the group. Hence assertion of individual rights implies recognition of similar rights for all individuals (described in chapter 2 as the 'social base' of claims to entitlement), and a corresponding duty to respect them. The rights of family members, carers, and others exist and demand respect in their own right, as it were, and are not derivatives of the rights or duties of others. Furthermore, it is the role of a society's 'background morality' to fashion the outlook that individual well-being, which is protected through the recognition of rights, is enhanced by care and concern for others. This can be reflected in social arrangements. The discussions of friendship in chapter 4 and of responsibility in chapter 5 referred to the way societies impose duties of responsibility on individuals towards other individuals simply by the fact of their relationships, particularly parent and child, but also between adults who have conducted their lives together in a certain way. It was even argued that these duties might extend beyond legally or socially imposed duties to moral behaviour in what was called a 'fuller' concept of responsibility. Although these duties might be supported on the basis of what I have called 'societal arguments',[13] namely those which find justification solely in the assertion of the virtue of particular social arrangements, they become valuable when they can also be supported as reflecting individual rights, and promoting individual well-being, understood in the manner of the 'capability' approach referred to in chapter 2.[14]

Could one however base these duties on an obligation to the community itself rather than to individual members of it? Statements suggesting that people should act first according to their responsibilities

---

[12] See, for example, M Minow and ML Shanley 'Relational Rights and Responsibilities: Revisioning the Family in Liberal Political Theory and Law' (1996) 11 *Hypatia* 4; J Herring, *Relational Autonomy and Family Law* (Springer, 2014); J Herring, 'Compassion, Ethics of Care and Legal Rights' (2017) 13 *International Journal of Law in Context* 158.
[13] See chapter 1, pp 7–9, 14, 18.   [14] See p 37.

rather than in response to the rights of others might suggest this.[15] Here it is necessary to be very cautious because relegating individual rights to a secondary place can give primacy to duties to the state. Holders of certain public offices (police, judiciary, government, military) can reasonably be held to be under legal duties primarily owed towards the state, but historically where such duties have been placed on people generally, it has often been done in order to advance sectional interests (think of patriarchal structures and forced marriage) or religious or political ideologies even of a populist nature. They should therefore be subject to particularly close scrutiny as to whether they do in fact instantiate individual rights and promote individual well-being. Group loyalty, patriotism, honour, and tradition can be fine things, but are so only if rendered voluntarily, not imposed as obligations.

COMMUNITIES, POWER, AND RIGHTS

It is unfortunate that discomfort with increasing economic competitive behaviour may have led to an almost romantic idealization of community. Amartya Sen has powerfully demonstrated the destructive consequences of supposing that most individuals have a single overarching identity, which binds them closely with particular communities, particularly religious communities.[16] This not only falsely confers all the attributes associated with a single community on individuals who may accept only some of them; it also allows communities to claim, and exercise, control over the identity which individuals might wish to develop for themselves. Ascribed roles within communities are not manifestations of acts of nature (although they are often presented as such): they represent the script for sanctioned behaviour. The question is: who writes the script?

Do communities have rights to exercise such forms of control? There has been much debate on whether such rights can exist and,

---

[15] See J Bridgeman, H Keating, and C Lind, (eds), *Responsibility, Law and the Family* (Ashgate/Routledge, 2010) 9.

[16] A Sen, *Identity and Violence: The Illusion of Destiny* (Allen Lane, 2006).

if they do, how they interact with individual rights.[17] Groups may be thought to have rights for (at least) four reasons. One is through institutions which represent a collectivity of individuals, whether of a public nature (such as legislatures or governments), or a private nature (such as corporations or unincorporated associations). Such institutions can have rights, even in the strong sense,[18] since there are institutional means by which their preferences may be expressed. They will not be further considered here. 'Informal collectives'[19] may *seem* to have rights because, as explained in chapter 2, it is a characteristic of all *individual* rights that a rights claimant identifies himself or herself with a 'social base' through which the entitlement derives.[20] The person claims the right, for example 'as a citizen', or 'as a [member of an ethnic community]', or 'as a disabled person' or 'as a student', or even, 'as a human being'. However, when such rights are socially recognized, they are not conferred on the group as such but on *all individual members of the group*.

A third reason why collectives may be thought to have rights is that rights usually presuppose the existence of social structures in order to be effective. But, as James Griffin has pointed out,[21] this applies to many individual rights (perhaps to all), but does not convert them into group rights. The fourth reason is found in the argument of Joseph Raz that a collective right can exist where the interests of individual members of a group in a public good can only be realized by the group as a group.[22] An example is the right to national self-determination. Each member of a nation has an interest in this good, but it can only be realized by the group collectively. It 'rests on the cumulative interests of many individuals'. Another example could be where certain individual rights, such as the right to practise one's religion, can only be fully exercised through identification with a group and group practice.

---

[17] See, for example, C Kukathas, 'Are there any Cultural Rights?' (1992) 20 *Political Theory* 105.

[18] See chapter 2, p 33.

[19] Y Tamir, 'Against Collective Rights' in LH Meyer, SL Paulson, and TW Pogge (eds), *Rights, Culture, and the Law: Themes from the Legal and Political Philosophy of Joseph Raz* (Oxford University Press, 2003) 190–1.

[20] See pp 38–9.

[21] J Griffin, 'Group Rights' in Meyer, Paulson, and Pogge (eds), n 19, at 167.

[22] J Raz, *The Morality of Freedom* (Clarendon Press, 1986) 208–9. See also 'National Self-Determination' in J Raz, *Ethics in the Public Domain: Essays in the Morality of Law and Politics* (Clarendon Press, 1994) ch 6.

We must be cautious about this last reason too. The fact that the expression of an individual claim to a right is conditional upon the concurrence of the same claim being made by other individuals does not mean that the claims are not to individual rights. An offer to buy shares subject to a condition of a minimum subscription by the offeree shareholders does not rob the rights of each shareholder of their individual character if the condition is met. This is, after all, the standard feature of majority decision-making, where an individual vote is only socially recognized if it is among the majority. What is gained by thinking of the majority as holding a 'group' right rather than of each individual having a right to the claim being recognized? Similarly, while it can indeed be true that an individual's religious practice may be enhanced, or even realized, through association with a group, the justification for any group right in that case depends upon the extent to which the practice of the group in fact secures the rights of its individual members. That is contingent on a variety of factors, and does not necessarily follow from affording rights to the group as a group.

Another reason why groups may appear to have rights is where people are (rightly) punished for discriminating against or attacking them in such a way as to undermine the security of their place within wider communities. But, as Jeremy Waldron remarks when discussing 'group libels' of this kind, 'the concern, in the end, is individualistic', that is, the harm to individual members of the group.[23] In such cases, while protection is ostensibly given to groups, this does not confer rights on the groups as a whole, but upon each of their members who are threatened by virtue of their identification with the group.

Granting rights to groups could be undesirable. Farrah Ahmed has discussed how granting group rights can lead to the construction of a false uniformity among members of the group, thus misrecognizing the self-identity of certain individuals and thereby restricting religious autonomy. She points out that the Indian 'personal law' system, which is applied by state courts:

> ignores the fact that the religious interpretations of many people within this group may well deviate from that of the state ... By bundling together a religious label – 'Hindu', 'Muslim', etc—with a certain interpretation of that religion, the personal law system misrecognizes or fails

---

[23] J Waldron, *The Harm in Hate Speech* (Harvard University Press, 2012) 56.

to appropriately recognize those who identify with that religion, but do not share the personal law system's interpretation of religious doctrine. Despite the fact that a person's understanding of their religion may be central to their identity and self-perception, it is not important enough (it may seem) for the state to take the trouble to do more than paint everyone in one personal law group with the same brush.[24]

Claims made on behalf of groups are usually made by sectional interests within those groups. This is often true even with regard to claims for political self-determination, as the history of many secessionist movements shows. While claims by groups for protection against outsiders could often be innocuous, or even beneficial, to those individuals by enhancing the force of their claims to be protected from attacks on their identity,[25] they may simultaneously be claims to exercise control over other sections of the group. Now it may be that those with power act in a way that they believe is in the interests of all members of the community, and even that some, or all, of the individuals in the community are willing to follow what the group, through its 'leaders' dictate, or proclaim is demanded by 'tradition'. As Fareda Banda has powerfully observed, this is also true of those who seek distinctive treatment on the basis of cultural identity.[26] Members of ultra-traditional or fundamentalist groups will think this way. They may even assert that it is their right to do this.

It is here where the 'background' morality referred to in chapter 2 becomes relevant. It must be asked whether there is an opportunity to make any evaluation of the rules and practices ordained in such a society. If not, any dialogue with such a community is foreclosed. But it is unlikely that such societies will always maintain that their mode of operation promotes no value other than conformity in itself. This provides a possibility to discuss such values, and in particular whether and how the practices support the well-being of individual

[24] F Ahmed, 'Remedying Personal Law Systems' (2016) 30 *International Journal of Law, Policy and the Family* 248, 254. See also F Ahmed, *Religious Freedom under the Personal Law System* (Oxford University Press, 2016) ch 4 ('group life') and 166–8 (the 'millet' system).
[25] W Kymlicka, *Multicultural Citizenship* (Clarendon Press, 1995) 37. See also M Pinto, 'What are Offences to Feelings Really About? A New Regulative Principle' (2010) 30 *Oxford Journal of Legal Studies* 695.
[26] F Banda, *Women, Law and Human Rights: An African Perspective* (Hart Publishing, 2005) 252, 260.

members.[27] The position put forward in this book is that well-being is enhanced through supporting individuals to achieve what they consider valuable in their lives, which includes recognizing this in others. How this is brought about in particular contexts is a matter for discussion, and consideration of the available evidence.

Similar issues can arise in the context of the upbringing of children. Must children of a particular ethnicity always be brought up within that ethnic group? Should children only be placed for adoption with adoptive parents of the same ethnicity as them? There are two 'rights' at issue here. One is an alleged 'group' right that the nature of the group be sustained into the future. The other is the child's 'right' to forge his or her own identity, as described in chapter 2 with reference to the case of the Zulu boy, where absorption into his ethnic group was mischaracterized as his 'right'.[28] Recognizing group rights of this kind confronts the problems considered earlier: who within the community determines its nature, and how is the group defined? But there is an even deeper problem. How can interference with *the child's* right be justified? It seems that children in diverse societies can develop a very fluid sense of identity, drawing on various elements of the cultures that surround them.[29] Of course it is important to most people to live within a cultural context, but that does not presuppose any particular culture, or foreclose on adapting the culture or movement between cultures.

The right to perpetuation of cultural practices must therefore be contingent on their effect on the well-being and autonomy of those affected by them, and should not be founded solely on the existence of the practice. This could lead to the modification or even abandonment of group practices, and has often done so. As Kwame Appiah has put it: '[I]f autonomy is the sponsoring concern, the diversity principle—the value of diversity *simpliciter*—cannot command our loyalty'.[30] Take the long view. People naturally wish to project the way they live into the future, but throughout history

---

[27] This is discussed further in J Eekelaar, 'Law, Culture, Values' in A Diduck, N Peleg, and H Reece (eds), *Law in Society: Reflections on Children, Family, Culture and Philosophy: Essays in Honour of Michael Freeman* (Brill, 2015) 31–44.

[28] See p 56.

[29] This is discussed in detail in J Eekelaar, 'Children between Cultures' (2004) 18 *International Journal of Law, Policy and the Family* 178; similar conclusions are reached by Y Ronen, 'Redefining the Child's Right to Identity' (2004) 18 *International Journal of Law, Policy and the Family* 147.

[30] KA Appiah, *The Ethics of Identity* (Princeton University Press, 2005) 153.

political communities, cultures, and religious ideas and practices have flourished, then faded, some for unacceptable reasons, many simply as a result of social evolution. This may be a cause for sadness or nostalgia, but successor generations are generally no worse off, and often better off. And, to cite Appiah again: 'It is far from clear that we can always honor ... preservationist claims while respecting the autonomy of future individuals'.[31] Open societies will embrace this process, while subjecting all changes to examination and debate.

PERSONAL LAW AND CULTURE

Individuals in families which are embedded within minority communities are enfolded by at least two levels of community within the third, wider, community: their own family and the community of their ethnic or religious group (though these may not be identical).

How family law responds to these circumstances has become increasingly debated from the beginning of this century, and the debate has become progressively more intense in the context of migration within Europe and concerns over religious fundamentalism. In England and Wales much of this has centred on the practices of Islamic (or shari'ah) Councils (sometimes called courts), to the extent that in 2011 a bill was introduced into the House of Lords which attempted to prohibit their use in family matters.[32] That initiative was unsuccessful but was followed by a later one which would not have forbidden their operation unless they claimed to act as a court or make binding arbitrations (which it seems they do not).[33] The government agreed to examine the question as part of its anti-extremism strategy.[34] In 2015 and 2016 two European authors published books purporting to reveal practices by these institutions

---

[31] Ibid 135.
[32] Discussed by J Eekelaar, 'Family Law: What Family Law?' in R Probert and C Barton (eds), *Fifty Years in Family Law: Essays for Stephen Cretney* (Intersentia, 2012)
[33] The Arbitration and Mediation Services (Equality) Bill 2016–17.
[34] On 26 May 2016 the Home Secretary announced the appointment of Professor Mona Siddiqui to examine the issue.

which oppressed women, attributing their development to 'multi-cultural' policies.[35]

Other more extensive research has shown a more complex picture. Sonia Shah-Kazemi mainly focused on the role of the Muslim Law Shariah Council (MLSC), to which many Muslim women turned when their marriages broke down. Although only the husband could pronounce divorce, the Council was able to dissolve the marriage contract if the husband refused to take that step. Shah-Kazemi explains how important it was to the women to be able to communicate with the Council.[36] Samia Bano observed how women would seek councils that were more sympathetic to women, some of which took an approach more favourable to them than their own community.[37] John Bowen thoroughly explored the workings of shari'ah councils over the period 2007 to 2013 and gives a comprehensive and historically informed description of institutions which draw on a variety of strands of Islamic tradition, combining different types of advisory function with processes resulting in certifications of divorce.[38] These are usually at the instance of wives in circumstances where the husband can be deemed to consent to the divorce (*khula*), but could in some circumstances be given against his will (*faskh*). Bowen describes the discussions among the scholars in the councils of the religious issues that can arise in this complex landscape, with the dominant objective seeming to be to find ways to meet the needs of these women in ways that are reconcilable with religious tradition. It is a process found in many religions.

How should the law respond to these community practices? One approach would allow the application of a range of 'personal' laws to adherents of various religions either in the state's courts themselves or by institutions of the communities recognized by the state as having authority to do this. Versions of such 'personal' law systems apply in a number of countries, notably in the Middle East, North Africa,

[35] M Zee, *Choosing Sharia? Multiculturalism, Islamic Fundamentalism and Sharia Councils* (Eleven Publishing, 2015); E Manea, *Women and Shari'a Law: The Impact of Legal Pluralism in the UK* (IB Tauris, 2016).

[36] S Shah-Kazemi, *Untying the Knot: Muslim Women, Divorce and the Shariah* (The Nuffield Foundation, 2001).

[37] S Bano, *Muslim Women and Shari'ah Councils: Transcending the Boundaries of Community and Law* (Palgrave Macmillan, 2012).

[38] J Bowen, *On British Islam: Religion, Law, and Everyday Practice in Shari'a Councils* (Princeton University Press, 2016).

and India. In 1998 Sebastian Poulter examined claims for Islamic law to be treated in this way in Britain.[39] Apart from practical difficulties, he considered that perhaps the 'most insuperable' difficulty lay in incompatibility with the United Kingdom's international human rights obligations. The concerns of Farrah Ahmed that such systems can restrict religious autonomy have been mentioned earlier[40] and similar problems arise if the state gives legal recognition to the determination of the family issues of their members by group institutions. It has even been maintained that to give state endorsement to community norms in this way 'strips [religious norms] of their divine authority and legitimacy, and turns them into ordinary enactments of the temporal political authority'.[41]

The opposite strategy would be to attempt to forbid the application of such norms by making it unlawful for any community's religious authorities to operate in the area of family law, as proposed by the 2011 bill referred to earlier.[42] But this would deprive members of these communities of the means to comply with many norms they consider essential according to their religion. Alternatively, a community's institutions could be allowed to operate, but their decisions given state recognition only if they apply state norms, as in Ontario.[43] Ayelet Shachar suggests a more nuanced approach: that the decisions of religious authorities should be recognized provided that the authorities are licensed by the state on receiving training, and apply basic equality norms.[44] The success of this form of 'regulated interaction' is

---

[39] S Poulter, *Ethnicity, Law and Human Rights: The English Experience* (Oxford University Press, 1998) 213–21.

[40] Ahmed, n 24.

[41] Y Sezgin, *Human Rights under State Enforced Religious Family Laws in Israel, Egypt and India* (Cambridge University Press, 2013) 44.

[42] The Arbitration and Mediation Services (Equality) Bill 2016–17.

[43] See A Shachar, 'Privatizing Diversity: A Cautionary Tale from Religious Arbitration in Family Law' (2008) 9 *Theoretical Inquiries in Law* 573.

[44] A Shachar, 'State, Religion and the Family: New Dilemmas of Multicultural Accommodation' in R Ahdar and N Aroney (eds), *Sharia in the West* (Oxford University Press, 2010) 127. See also JE Bond, 'Culture, Dissent, and the State: The Example of Commonwealth African Marriage Laws' (2011) 14 *Yale Human Rights and Development Journal*, Issue 1, Article 1. For other suggestions of a similar kind, see JA Nichols, 'Multi-tiered Marriage: Ideas and Influences from New York and Louisiana to the International Community' (2007) 40 *Vanderbilt Journal of Transnational Law* 135; LC McClain, 'Marriage Pluralism in the United States' in JA Nichols (ed), *Marriage and Divorce in a Multicultural Context: Multi-tiered Marriage and the Boundaries of Civil Law and Religion* (Cambridge University Press, 2013) 309–40.

dependent on the extent to which the communities feel it is important for their norms to receive state recognition. Yet another strategy
is what I have called 'cultural voluntarism', which allows groups to
pursue their practices in whatever diverse ways they choose, the state
giving legal effect to, or prohibiting, practices depending on facts and
context and only insofar as consistent with the principles of state law.[45]

English law presently does something like that. If you are an
Anglican, a Jew, or a Quaker, and you marry in accordance with the
requirements of your faith, the marriage will be recognized by English
law. If you are of any other faith, your religious marriage will be recognized by that law if specified preliminaries have occurred, and the
marriage has taken place in a registered building, conducted by an
authorized person and contains recitation of a specific form of words.
Anyone may marry according to an entirely civil procedure (but there
must be no religious element, not even any religious music),[46] and
take part in a separate religious ceremony of any kind. Same-sex marriages can only be formalized by the civil procedure, unless a religious
group 'opts-in' to the power to perform such marriages.[47] This has
resulted in a very complex system for contracting legally recognized
marriages in England and Wales, and many marriages following community practices are not legally recognized, for example because they
do not take place in a registered building. Many Muslim marriages
take place in private homes.[48]

This complexity could be avoided if a civil (register office) ceremony was required for every marriage. However, this could reduce
still further the number of legally recognized marriages by members of certain groups, which would affect their access to the matrimonial jurisdiction. It could also be maintained that there is value
in the state giving legal recognition to a form of marriage which is
important for the couple and seen by them as of particular significance, both out of respect for them and also as a demonstration of its
acceptance of a diverse society. This suggests a mixed system, which

---

[45] J Eekelaar, 'From Multiculturalism to Cultural Voluntarism: A Family-based
Approach' (2010) 81(3) *The Political Quarterly* 344, developed by M Malik, 'Family
Law in Diverse Societies' in J Eekelaar and R George (eds), *Routledge Handbook of
Family Law and Policy* (Routledge, 2014) ch 7.4.
[46] Marriage Act 1949; Marriage Act 1994.
[47] Marriage (Same Sex Couples) Act 2013, ss 2–4. The Church of England does not,
however, have the power to opt-in.
[48] See Bowen, n 38, 210–13.

provides both for civil marriages for those who prefer them but also recognizes marriages formalized according to the religious or other 'belief' (or lifestyle) system of the couple. Scotland has such a system, allowing marriages to be solemnized by an authorized officiant of a 'religious or belief body', the latter being defined as an 'organised group of people the principal object of which is to uphold or promote philosophical beliefs and which meets regularly for that purpose'.[49] There would need to be limits to such recognition, for example concerning monogamy, age, and free consent. These could be controlled through stipulating compulsory preliminaries (such as the grant of a licence) and subsequent registration by the authorized person. The Law Commission has put forward principles for reforming English marriage law which are consistent with this view.[50]

The marriages so recognized would only be legally dissolved in accordance with state law, and the legal consequences of the marriage and its dissolution would be those of that law, although the parties would be free also to dissolve or annul the marriage according to their religious system. However, under the approach of cultural voluntarism, any agreement reached through a mediation or arbitration process in a community institution could be given effect in the courts, but only if consistent with the law of the state. For example, in *AI v MT* [51] an English court gave effect to a decision of a Jewish tribunal on matters concerning the child and finances following divorce. However, the judge made it very clear that it only did so insofar as the decision was consistent with the principles of English law.

Those who fear that some community institutions could depart too drastically from the standards upheld by the state, for example by maintaining practices discriminatory against women, as some may do, may argue that they should not be permitted to operate, even outside the state system, as it may be difficult for women to exercise their right to resort to the state's institutions. That is a reasonable concern, but, outside extreme cases such as violence and forced marriage, there is little that the law can, or possibly even should, do about this. What is important is that the state's law should only give legal effect to

---

[49] Marriage and Civil Partnership (Scotland) Act 2014, s 12(4).
[50] Law Commission, *Getting Married: A Scoping Paper* (December 2015). See also K O'Sullivan and L Jackson, 'Muslim Marriage (Non) Recognition: Implications and Possible Solutions' (2017) 39 *Journal of Social Welfare and Family Law* 22.
[51] [2013] EWHC 100 (Fam).

arrangements that comply with its standards and be as widely available as possible. Complete uniformity cannot be expected in diverse societies, and community practices, like those of their institutions, or some aspects of them, can be expected to evolve slowly towards some form of convergence with those of the wider community.

CARING COMMUNITIES

It is often pointed out that communities represent the interconnectedness of people and demonstrate an ethic of care. Carol Gilligan[52] and Nel Noddings[53] have suggested that caring for the well-being of another is characteristic of women, in the sense that their ethical decisions will be strongly coloured by their impact on ability to care for others. But this may be more a question of the social roles ascribed to the genders than the nature of gender itself because there is evidence that both men and women will be inclined to emphasize the importance of caring as a determinant or modifier of ethical decisions when a caring role is capturing an important part of their life.[54] But whatever view is taken of that matter, the question may be raised: if community is associated with care and support, why should it be seen to be a problem? Is it not an unalloyed good? In particular, in our context, surely there can be no anxieties about encouraging the 'protection of families', as the UN Human Rights Committee re-asserted in 2014.[55]

In the first edition of this book I wrote: 'However, to exercise care is *also* to exercise power. True, it is to be hoped that it is a beneficent exercise of power, but it is power nonetheless.' Jonathan Herring has rightly pointed out that to exercise care does not *necessarily* involve the possession of power.[56] After all, a woman under control of a domineering man may still provide care for him; perhaps it is the price he exacts. It could be argued that this is the basis of patriarchal societies.

---

[52] C Gilligan, *In a Different Voice: Psychological Theory and Women's Development* (Harvard University Press, 1982). See also Frazer and Lacey, n 11, ch 5.

[53] N Noddings, *Caring: A Feminine Approach to Ethics and Moral Education* (UCLA Press, 1984).

[54] M Maclean and J Eekelaar, *The Parental Obligation: A Study of Parenthood across Households* (Hart Publishing, 1997) 141–2.

[55] Human Rights Committee, HRC/RES/26/11.

[56] J Herring, *Older People in Law and Society* (Oxford University Press, 2009) 128–9.

Yet many carers do have power: adults over small children, hospital staff over patients; teachers over students; providers in 'care' homes for children and the elderly. This demonstrates that the provision of care *occurs within societies' power structures* and can never displace the need for those structures to be balanced by individual rights as described in chapters 1 and 2.

When the power is used to marshal resources to support individuals, including of course individuals within families, it operates to further individual well-being.[57] But there are many examples where the role of caregiver, even if applied with good intentions, has adverse consequences. The welfarism thesis set out in chapter 1 argues, and, it is hoped, demonstrates, that this could occur beyond individual relationships, and extend to social policy. But the problem is deeper still than that. It centres on the question: what indeed *is* beneficial to the individual? Is the answer to be found only by reference to the opinion of the carer, or the caring community, often grounded in the assumption that certain social structures are beneficial in themselves? Or if the answer is, as it should be, that it is found in the opinion of the individual concerned, it becomes necessary to consider ways by which that opinion can be expressed, assessed, and protected. This raises all the issues of competence and autonomy considered in chapter 2 in connection with rights, especially in relation to children. But it raises much more. It requires the existence of secure institutions and processes in which and through which individuals can have their voice heard in contradistinction to that of the community and either safely exit from the community or start a process which may lead to the transformation or adaptation of the nature of the community to reflect the evolving identities of individuals. In short, they must have the opportunity to assert the rights they have.

ASSERTING RIGHTS

As argued in chapter 2, individual rights are an essential protection against these assertions of power. But it is all very well for the law

---

[57] As argued in M Eichner, *The Supportive State: Families, Government, and America's Political Ideals* (Oxford University Press, 2010).

to ascribe legal rights to people. For this to be effective, institutional mechanisms must exist through which they can be asserted. The primary mechanism is the legal system. But this requires ability to use it, which has been difficult, and even impossible, for many. In the past, reliance on the goodwill of lawyers to provide free services for the poor did little to remedy the problem. In 1914 a procedure had been introduced according to which Prescribed Officers of the High Court identified solicitors who would assess whether the client had a case and was financially eligible, and if the court granted a certificate, the Prescribed Officer would refer the case to a volunteer solicitor or barrister to conduct it without payment.[58] But this broke down with the shortage of lawyers and surge in divorces after the First World War. Solicitors especially found the work 'distasteful'. Colin Gibson reports that '[l]ess than a tenth of the 790 London solicitors undertaking divorce work in 1918 had handled a Poor Persons case'.[59]

To try to overcome this, appeals were made to the lawyers' conscience. The Second Lawrence Committee (1925) enunciated that there existed 'a moral obligation on the part of the profession in relation to the monopoly in the practice of the law which it enjoys to render gratuitous legal assistance, provided that no undue burden is thereby cast on any individual member of the profession'[60] and the Law Society reiterated the message.[61] In order to distribute the 'burden', the granting of certificates was removed from the High Court and transferred to local committees of the Law Society, populated solely by solicitors, who would decide whether an applicant qualified. Government funding was confined to administrative costs. But

---

[58] *Rules of the Supreme Court (Poor Persons) 1914.* For full accounts, see RI Morgan, 'The Introduction of Civil Legal Aid in England and Wales 1914–1949' (1994) 5 *Twentieth Century History* 38; T Goriely, 'Rushcliffe Fifty Years On: The Changing Role of Civil Legal Aid within the Welfare State' (1994) 21 *Journal of Law and Society* 545.

[59] C Gibson, *Dissolving Wedlock* (Routledge, 1994) 87.

[60] *Report of the Poor Persons Rules Committee* (Second Lawrence Committee) (1925) Cmd 2358, para 12.

[61] See 'Law Society Annual Report 1927', 30: 'Poor's work is one of the duties undertaken by the legal profession in return for its privileges . . . So long as the burden is equitably distributed we think that no real hardship is involved', cited in A Paterson, 'Professionalism and the Legal Services Market' (1996) 3 *International Journal of the Legal Profession* 137, n 29.

while provision was improved, difficulties in recruiting solicitors remained,[62] with the Welsh Law Society refusing to operate it at all after 1939.

The post-war legal aid system originated in the Report of the Rushcliffe Committee (1945),[63] published a month after the German surrender, and reflecting confidence in state institutions and a determination to build a fairer society after military victory. It envisaged a comprehensive network of area offices, with paid administrative staff, overseeing local offices serviced by full-time or part-time paid solicitors who would assess cases for eligibility, issue legal aid certificates, using the National Assistance Board to assess means, and assign appropriate cases to solicitors or barristers on a panel or volunteers. The eligibility levels were to be raised, with contributions to be paid on a graduated scale, extending the scheme beyond those 'normally classed as poor',[64] and no longer confined to the High Court. The 'charitable' nature of the provision of services would be abolished, with lawyers being entitled to remuneration at 85 per cent of their taxed costs. The scheme would be financed by a block grant from the Treasury, which would cover not only administrative costs, but also professional fees. A special Services Divorce Department, staffed by salaried lawyers, established during the war was extended.

The report was largely translated into law by the Legal Aid and Advice Act 1949, though only implemented in stages. As regards legal advice, the Rushcliffe Committee proposed that advice could be offered within its envisaged network of local and area offices by employed solicitors for payment of 2s 6d (if it could be afforded), but it did not extend to negotiation (though it might involve the solicitor writing a letter).[65] To obtain help for that, the applicant would need to apply for a legal aid certificate. The proposals were enacted in the 1949 Act, but advice was limited to oral advice, although a written note could be made of it.[66] However, the financial crisis of the late 1940s meant that the whole section on advice was put on ice as it would have involved substantial salaried staff. It was estimated

---

[62] Morgan, n 58, 51.

[63] *The Rushcliffe Committee on Legal Aid and Legal Advice in England and Wales: Report* (Cmd 6641, 1945).

[64] Ibid para 127(2).   [65] Morgan, n 58, 70.

[66] Legal Aid and Advice Act 1949, s 7.

that the salaried Services Divorce Department and advice provision would have consumed 44 per cent of the legal aid budget.[67] So when the advice scheme was implemented in 1959, the envisaged structure of local offices and paid employees was abandoned; instead lawyers would be paid on a case-by-case basis in their own offices. However, fearing the loss of clients, the profession forced down the eligibility levels. In 1961 the Services Divorce Department was closed.[68] But the scheme was still limited by the exclusion of further work unless it was covered by a legal aid certificate that contemplated litigation. This was remedied by the implementation, in April 1973, of the Green Form Scheme which allowed £25 worth of written advice and other assistance for eligible clients by the simple submission of a form and its acceptance by a solicitor (a certificate from the legal aid authorities was required for further work).[69]

Colin Gibson[70] has shown how closely the divorce rate was affected by the availability of legal aid after the Second World War. It is very unlikely that the developments in the law of matrimonial property so greatly influenced by Lord Denning in the 1950s and 1960s discussed in chapter 2 could have occurred without the greater access to the courts which legal aid provided at that time or that the divorce law would have been reformed in 1969 if it were not for the pressures these developments placed on the existing system. Hazel Genn's large study in the 1990s of individual responses to events perceived to 'raise legal issues' found that people who encountered what they believed to be such a problem within their family relationship (some 6 per cent of the sampled population) were more likely than people who experienced any other problem (eg concerning faulty goods, employment difficulties, accidents, or property issues) to seek advice.[71] They were also the least likely to do nothing ('lump it'). The advice was most often sought from a solicitor, and this was so across all income groups.[72] While later surveys found slightly lower proportions of people reporting such problems,[73] it was still true that those who

---

[67] Goriely, n 58, 548.   [68] Ibid 551–2.

[69] See HL Deb, 23 June 1972, vol 332, cols 502–31.

[70] C Gibson, 'The Association between Divorce and Social Class in England and Wales' (1974) 25 *British Journal of Sociology* 79.

[71] H Genn, *Paths to Justice* (Hart Publishing, 1999) 23–4.   [72] Ibid 86.

[73] *Report of the 2006–9 English and Welsh Civil and Social Justice Survey* (2010), Table 1 (6 per cent between 2004 and 2010); N Balmer, *The English and Welsh Civil and Social Justice Panel Survey, Wave 2* (Legal Services Commission, 2013), Table 1 (4.4

did were more likely than others to seek professional help. Citizens Advice states that in 2014/5 they 'helped' over 284,000 people with relationship issues, 38 per cent related to divorce and 34 per cent related to child maintenance or other issues concerning children.[74] So when such problems do occur, people very commonly feel the need to look to 'external' sources for advice.

What kind of assistance were people given? For those who used lawyers, in our observations of the practical work of 'family' solicitors in 1998 and 1999, Mavis Maclean and I saw many examples of the way solicitors provided support for clients. Of course they would give legal advice where appropriate. But it took other forms. One was to give 'reassurance'. This could be simply through listening to the client, supplying a chance to hear the voice: 'The very fact of listening sympathetically to a client might be counted as providing "emotional" support'.[75] This might take the form of calming the client down, and outlining the legal position. But the support often extended into advice on other practicalities, whether on how to go about seeking alternative accommodation, how to 'get a grip' on their financial situation and make ends meet—or where best to go to find advice on such things. Cases were observed where a solicitor acted as an intermediary through whom parties communicated with one another during a period of estrangement, after which they came together again;[76] and protected the interests of a vulnerable client who had suffered mental illness against pressures from the wider family.[77] They were also central to a process of negotiation with the 'other' party.

In the divided legal profession of England and Wales, barristers too have an important role in providing individuals with protection against the pressures of family or other communal institutions. Formulating legal arguments which are presented to the highest courts is only the most well-known. But there is a less visible side.

---

per cent and 4.6 per cent for the period 2009–11); Law Society and Ipsos Mori, *Legal Needs Survey* (2015), Table 4.1 (5 per cent); Ministry of Justice, *The Findings from the Legal Problem and Resolution Survey (LPRS) Survey* 2014–15 (2017) (1 per cent, plus up to 1 per cent divorce only). The differences may reflect the nature of the sample and the questions asked.

[74] Citizens Advice, *Standing Alone: Going to the Family Court without a Lawyer* (2016) 5.

[75] J Eekelaar, M Maclean, and S Beinart, *Family Lawyers: The Divorce Work of Solicitors* (Hart Publishing, 2000) 81–2.

[76] Ibid 104–5.   [77] Ibid 106–8.

Family conflicts which reach the stage of formal adjudication are invariably those where hostility is most deeply embedded, and the parties most angry and distressed. These are cases that simply will not settle through normal discussion or negotiation. So, on the day of the hearing, barristers can be the only source of guidance, support, and comfort to clients embarking on what is really the ultimate day of battle in court. Our observations showed that they could spend much more time trying to resolve the matter in the corridors outside the formal courtroom hearing than they might spend in the courtroom. This involves face-to-face discussions with the barrister for the other party, with court officials, and welfare personnel and even discussions with the judge.[78] These are by definition extreme events. It is difficult to see how people could manage them without professional assistance of the kind provided by a barrister. Barristers have even been observed assisting parties accessing health services, finding accommodation, providing money for lunch, and even cleaning their homes.[79]

Since clients in these situations often lack economic independence (and this makes them more vulnerable to the pressures of their immediate community, as they are also largely dependent on it) it was important that the lawyers obtained funding from the legal aid system. Yet from the late 1990s UK governments have progressively sought to cut back on legal aid expenditure, particularly in family-related work. This culminated in the Legal Aid, Sentencing and Punishment of Offenders (LASPO) Act 2012. From April 2013 legal aid is excluded entirely for most private family law cases, even when children are involved,[80] apart from narrowly defined areas (eg public law cases where state institutions are involved, or cases with an international element, or where there is evidence of violence or abuse). The justification given was that private family disputes arose from the 'private' decisions of individuals, and are therefore not the concern of the state.[81] As a consequence the types of services from

---

[78] M Maclean and J Eekelaar, *Family Law Advocacy: How Barristers Help the Victims of Family Failure* (Hart Publishing, 2009) 16–23. See also Citizens Advice, *Standing Alone* (n 74) on the need for support for people attempting to represent themselves in court.

[79] J Pearce, J Masson, and K Bader, *Just Following Instructions? The Representation of Parents in Care Proceedings* (ESRC and University of Bristol, 2011).

[80] There is some availability where mediation is used, discussed later.

[81] F Kaganas, 'Justifying the LASPO Act: Authenticity, Necessity, Suitability, Responsibility and Autonomy' (2017) 39 *Journal of Social Welfare and Family Law* 1.

legal professionals described earlier have been almost obliterated for those who cannot afford to pay professional fees.[82] The change in attitude from that which prevailed just after the war appears starkly in the government decision in August 2015 to increase the fee for obtaining a divorce decree (a process which is almost always virtually administrative only) from £410 to £550, well above the amount needed to cover administrative costs. So, although remissions can be obtained, from being a process which entailed considerable public expenditure, divorce is now openly used by the government to raise revenue: an estimated £12 million.[83] There could hardly be anything more unprincipled than to use a legal requirement to effect a change of status for people who undergo the misfortune of family breakdown for this purpose. Would one use the registration of births and deaths in this way?

This might be seen as an aspect of what has been called a 'neoliberal' political agenda, developed from the 1980s, which grounds policy in support for economic efficiency perceived to arise from free markets, the promotion of individual responsibility, and reductions in public expenditure and the role of the state,[84] though the wider reach of legal rights over this period would in any case have put pressure on the funding arrangements. Possible alternative sources for legal advice, such as community law centres, have also been affected

---

See generally, F Wilmot-Smith, 'Necessity or Ideology?' (2014) 36 *London Review of Books* 15.

[82] See M Maclean and J Eekelaar, *Lawyers and Mediators: The Brave New World of Services for Separating Families* (Hart Publishing, 2016).

[83] Ministry of Justice, *Court and Tribunal Fees: The Government Response to Consultation on Enhanced Fees for Divorce Proceedings, Possession Claims and General Applications in Civil Proceedings and Consultation on Further Fees Proposals* (August 2015). House of Commons, Justice Committee, *Courts and Tribunals Fees, 2nd report of Session 2016–2017*, paras 86–9.

[84] The literature on 'neo-liberalism' is extensive. For examples, see D Harvey, *A Brief History of Neoliberalism* (Oxford University Press, 2005); T Judt, *Ill Fares the Land* (Penguin Books, 2010); T Piketty, *Capital in the Twenty-first Century* (The Belknap Press of Harvard University Press, 2014); DS Grewal and J Purdy, 'Law and Neo-Liberalism' (2015) 77(4) *Law and Contemporary Problems* 1. For an account within the Canadian family law context, see R Treloar, 'The Neoliberal Context of Family Law Reform in British Columbia, Canada: Implications for Access to (Family) Justice' in M Maclean, J Eekelaar, and B Bastard (eds), *Delivering Family Justice in the 21st Century* (Hart Publishing, 2015) ch 1. For an Anglo-Australian perspective, see A Flynn and J Hodgson (eds), *Access to Justice & Legal Aid: Comparative Perspectives on Unmet Legal Need* (Hart Publishing, 2017).

by reductions in financial support from public sources. Their number fell from 63 to 45 (29 per cent) between 2005 and 2014[85] and in any case they do not offer services where legal aid is not available. With respect to court proceedings, the difficulties facing parties who have no legal representation have been commented on by judges[86] and researchers.[87]

With serious reductions in public funding of legal services, governments have been promoting the idea that the internet can be used as a means by which people can become informed of their legal rights. They also think this is much cheaper. So the UK government has constructed a web 'app', Sorting out Separation, and a more focused one, Child Maintenance Options, that seek to provide information, including links to helpful organizations, to people experiencing family breakdown. An online system (CourtNav) guides individuals in submitting divorce petitions. Solicitors' websites often provide similar information, and sometimes free telephone advice.

Such developments are common in many jurisdictions. These sources, if well designed, can undoubtedly be useful, especially if the parties are in agreement about what they want to achieve. Since, as described earlier, not all the assistance people require is necessarily 'legal', much could perhaps be supplied by non-legal actors. However, if someone is seeking to bring about action, especially by an unwilling party, information and support alone may not be enough. It is important therefore that the state must continue to play a significant, if not exclusive, role in assuring access to justice.

DIVERSION

It need not follow from the centrality of legal rights to the protection of individuals against those with power that efforts should not be made to avoid litigation. After all, it was argued in chapter 5 that a full concept of responsibility could involve a willingness to forego strict

---

[85] Law Centres Network, *Funding for Law Centres* (ICF International, 2014).

[86] See *Q v Q* [2014] EWFC 31; *Re D* [2014] EWFC 39; *K & H (Children)* [2015] EWCA Civ 543.

[87] L Trinder et al, *Litigants in Person in Private Family Law Cases* (Ministry of Justice, 2014).

entitlements. An example is provided in the Family Relationship Centres in Australia. In 2006, their role was described in this way:

> First and foremost, they are an early intervention initiative to help parents work out post-separation parenting arrangements in the aftermath of separation, managing the very difficult transition from parenting together to parenting apart. They will provide an educational, support and counselling role to parents going through separation, with the goal of helping parents to understand and focus upon children's needs, providing them with initial information about such matters as child support and welfare benefits, and negotiating workable agreements about partnering after separation. They will also be available to help ongoing conflicts and difficulties as circumstances change. They will not only be a resource for parents but for grandparents as well.
>
> The FRCs will not only have a role in helping parents after separation. They will also play a role in strengthening intact relationships by offering an accessible source for information and referral on marriage and parenting issues, providing a gateway to other government and nongovernment services to support families.[88]

To the extent that such mechanisms act in a neutral way, directing individuals to services which are most appropriate for their needs, they have the potential to provide invaluable short-term assistance to people who are in conflict with the communal dimension of their lives. Originally, lawyers were excluded from their services. However, it was found that 65 per cent of users also saw a lawyer, and in 2009 a Legal Assistance Partnership Programme to ensure that clients of Family Relationship Centres receive accurate legal advice was introduced.[89] But even accurate advice can be of limited value if there are limited means for implementing legal entitlements. The latest scheme for ensuring child maintenance payments in the United Kingdom is premised on voluntary payments. Those wishing to use state enforcement mechanisms must pay a fee, and even forego part of the payments, if made. In 2014/15, the service collected only 53 per cent of payments due.[90]

---

[88] P Parkinson, 'Keeping on Contact: The Role of Family Relationship Centres in Australia' (2006) 18 *Child and Family Law Quarterly* 157, 159.

[89] R Kaspiew, M Gray, R Weston, L Moloney, K Hand, and L Qu and the Family Law Evaluation Team, *Evaluation of the 2006 Family Law Reforms* (Australian Institute of Family Studies, 2009).

[90] Gingerbread, *Missing Maintenance* (June 2016) 13. See p 136.

Mediation can also be seen as a means of restraining access to legal mechanisms. UK government policy was initially attracted to mediation in family cases because of its perceived potential to save public expense associated with court procedures. This has been a persistent theme.[91] While the 2013 legal aid changes in England and Wales withdrew legal aid for the use of lawyers from most private law family issues (as described earlier), public funding was nevertheless retained to a limited degree (for persons satisfying the financial eligibility criteria) for those undertaking mediation.[92] The government also enacted that anyone wishing to make various applications in family matters must first attend a Mediation Information and Advice Meeting (MIAM).[93] This would explain about mediation and no doubt urge its use.

Worries about mediation in the family context have been expressed over many years. In the 1980s, Richard Abel highlighted fears that informal justice could be oppressive for those whose social or economic vulnerability made it difficult to challenge the powerful.[94] Swedish research suggests that parties to mediation tend to focus on the need to find settlement rather than on children's interests,[95] which would be the focus in a legal settlement governed by the 'best interests' principle. The risks of mediation to women in cases of domestic violence have long been recognized,[96] and this seems to be just an extreme case of the effects of removing, or reducing, legal entitlements designed to counteract de facto exercises of power.

---

[91] See the Consultation and White Papers, both entitled *Looking to the Future: Mediation and the Ground for Divorce* (Cm 2424, 1993) and (Cm 2799, 1995) discussed in Eekelaar, Maclean, and Beinart, n 75, ch 1.

[92] Legal Aid, Sentencing and Punishment of Offenders Act 2012, sch 1, Part 1, para 14.

[93] Children and Families Act 2014, s 10.

[94] RL Abel, *The Politics of Informal Justice* vols 1 and 2 (The Academic Press, 1982). See also CS Bruch, 'And How Are the Children? The Effects of Ideology and Mediation on Child Custody Law and Children's Well-being in the United States' (1988) 2 *International Journal of Law and the Family* 106, 119–20.

[95] E Ryrstedt, 'Mediation Regarding Children: Is the Result Always in the Best Interests of the Child: A View from Sweden' (2012) 26 *International Journal of Law, Policy and the Family* 220. See also Maclean and Eekelaar, n 81, 87–91.

[96] T Grillo, 'The Mediation Alternative: Process Dangers for Women' (1991) *Yale Law Journal* 1545; L Trinder, A Firth, and C Jenks, ' "So Presumably Things Have Moved On Since Then?" The Management of Risk Allegations in Child Contact Dispute Resolution' (2009) 24 *International Journal of Law, Policy and the Family* 29.

A different aspect of mediation has been emphasized by Robert Dingwall. This is that mediation creates possibilities for individual values of mediators to influence outcomes. While this is true for adjudication as well, judges' decisions are (at least in theory) held up to the standards of the law (and may be subject to appeal), and are therefore more accountable and transparent than the actions of mediators.[97] This has also been emphasized in recent studies in Scotland and in England. In the former, the researchers concluded:

> For solicitors, the approach to option appraisal is a transparent process of outlining, on the basis of their knowledge and experience, the pros and cons of different approaches. In the mediation context the process is both transparent and opaque. The transparency of the process lies in the appearance of information sharing, the identification of aims, objectives and issues, and the joint discussion of possible options. The opacity of the process emerges from the way in which practitioners, also drawing on their expertise and experience appear, from their accounts, to subtly lead people in particular directions. This strategy is more indirect than is evident from solicitors' accounts. While a sophisticated approach it may be at odds with the rhetoric of mediation which suggests neutrality, impartiality and couple control.[98]

The English study, also involving observations of mediations conducted by lawyers and non-lawyers, showed that, contrary to theory and official codes of practice, mediators often sought to steer participants towards or away from certain outcomes, and that the distinction drawn between giving information (which is allowed) and giving advice (which is not) was unsustainable. If this is so, and legal advice is sometimes given under the guise of information, this undercuts the government's intention that legal aid moneys should not be given for such advice, but the overall practice is unclear. Take-up of mediation after the legal aid cutbacks has in fact been low, partly, perhaps, because fewer people are seeing lawyers who would refer them to mediation, but also because both parties need to want it, not just one, and also because many people may not be in dispute (which is a condition for receipt of public funding), but simply want advice. And

---

[97] D Greatbatch and R Dingwall, 'Selective Facilitation: Some Preliminary Observations on a Strategy Used by Divorce Mediators' (1989) 23 *Law and Society Review* 613.

[98] F Myers and F Wasoff, *Meeting in the Middle: A Study of Solicitors' and Mediators' Divorce Practice* (The Scottish Executive, Central Research Unit, 2011) 5.

mediators are not supposed to provide advice.[99] Mavis Maclean and I have therefore suggested that lawyers should be permitted to advise both parties together whose relationship is in difficulty in the same circumstances where it would be appropriate for the lawyer to act as mediator (for example, there should be no violence or undue imbalance of power). That would allow the lawyer to assist the parties to reach agreement, provide advice and draw up a draft consent order all in the same process, rather than splitting the process as presently required, thus saving money and expanding the choice of procedures available.[100]

Arbitration is another way in which court may be avoided. It is promoted by the Institute of Family Law Arbitrators (initially in financial cases, and later for child arrangements too) as superior to the court process in terms of confidentiality, costs, speed, and flexibility. But it can be expensive, and, although the arbitral award is often represented as being 'binding on the parties' (apart from limited grounds for challenge, mostly of a procedural nature, set out in the Arbitration Act 1996) it is usually necessary to incorporate the terms of the award in a court order for enforcement purposes. Although the parties must have agreed to seek such an order, it is unlikely that this will prevent either party from seeking a different order should they disagree with the award. This is because it is a fundamental principle that the jurisdiction of the courts to make financial and property orders under s 25 of the Matrimonial Causes Act cannot be ousted by the parties' agreement, and courts are bound by s 1 of the Children Act 1989 to treat the welfare of the children as paramount. Baker J has said that an agreement that an arbitral award 'shall be binding and enforceable upon the parties in the courts of Ontario and worldwide' would be unlawful.[101] Of course the parties may be content with the arbitrated outcome, as might be the case for religious arbitrations discussed earlier.[102]

---

[99] See Maclean and Eekelaar, n 82, especially 17–18, 98–100.

[100] Ibid 128–37. We call the proposed procedure 'legally assisted family mediation'.

[101] *AI v MT* [2013] EWHC 100 (Fam) para 27. The courts will of course place much weight on the arbitral award.

[102] See the full discussion by L Ferguson, 'Arbitration in Financial Dispute Resolution: The Final Step in Reconstructing the Default(s) and Exception(s)?' (2013) 35 *Journal of Social Welfare and Family Law* 115. For a comparative study of arbitration in family matters generally, see W Kennett, 'It's Arbitration, but Not as We Know It: Reflections on Family Law Dispute Resolution' (2016) 30 *International Journal of Law, Policy and the Family* 1.

CHILDREN

One of the most important provisions in the UNCRC is Article 12 which states that 'States Parties shall assure to the child who is capable of forming his or her own views the right to express those views freely in all matters affecting the child, the views of the child being given due weight in accordance with the age and maturity of the child' and that '[f]or this purpose, the child shall in particular be provided the opportunity to be heard in any judicial and administrative proceedings affecting the child, either directly, or through a representative or an appropriate body, in a manner consistent with the procedural rules of national law'. This underlines the importance of the child's perspective when thinking of what rights they have.

The scope of the article is enormous: 'all matters affecting the child'. Needless to say, it is a difficult provision to implement, but a range of actions have developed, most notably, the establishment in a number of jurisdictions of 'Children's Commissioners'.[103] Representation of children in court raises particularly difficult problems. Is it desirable for children to appear in court, especially where their parents are in dispute? Should they be represented by lawyers or social work professionals, and should their representatives merely represent the child's expressed views, or make an assessment of the child's capacity to form them independently of other participants, or even give their own view of the child's interests? Should they be put in a position to pass judgement on their parents? How would they feel if they express a view which is disregarded?[104]

These problems are, however, not dissimilar to those that inevitably arise when dealing with competence issues respecting children. That they are difficult is not a good ground for ignoring the child's perspective.

---

[103] See the UN Committee on the Rights of the Child, General Comment No 12, CRC/C/GC/12 1 July 2009.

[104] See F Bell, 'Barriers to Empowering Children in Private Family Law Proceedings' (2016) 30 *International Journal of Law, Policy and the Family* 225; T Morag, 'Child Participation in the Family Courts' (2012) 26 *International Journal of Law, Policy and the Family* 1; A James, 'Responsibility, Children and Childhood' in J Bridgeman, H Keating, and C Lind, *Responsibility, Law and the Family* (Ashgate/Routledge, 2008), ch 8; G Douglas, M Murch, C Miles, and L Scanlan, *Research into the Operation of Rule 9.5 of the Family Proceedings Rules 1991* (Department of Constitutional Affairs, 2006).

INTERNATIONAL ISSUES

Theresa May's aphorism shortly after the UK's referendum on EU membership that 'if you believe you are a citizen of the world, you are a citizen of nowhere' was a different manifestation of a belief in the significance of community, in this case, the national state. Yet, as argued earlier, people can identify with different aspects of a variety of communities, both within and outside individual states. Most strikingly, as argued in chapter 2, the basis for human rights claims lies in identification with all humans on a specific issue. This can, of course, create difficulty when it implies conflict between norm systems. In the case of human rights, the normative consequences are handled by international human rights instruments with which specific nation states commit themselves to comply. A method of reconciling such conflicts when they arise within a single state system was suggested in the section on personal law and culture earlier in the chapter.

But when people have personal connections with different states, the normative consequences of such overlapping allegiances raise particularly sensitive issues in personal law because of the close identification between the relevant norms and local practices. They are dealt with primarily through systems of private international law which are designed to settle which system can properly deal with an issue, and promote mutual recognition of legal acts between jurisdictions.[105] This has been particularly developed within the European Union, where overlapping identities are very common, and the efficient operation of movement between national jurisdictions requires such measures. However, goals such as the common recognition of civil status documents, pursued by the International Commission on Civil Status, and even the harmonization of family law, pursued by the European Commission on Family Law, go further, perhaps towards the realization of a common European citizenship. It may be difficult, however, to find sufficient common ground to achieve that objective. While it has been maintained earlier that diversity should not be viewed as a goal in itself, in this case allowing different traditions and systems to coexist seems at present to be a strong contingent benefit.[106]

---

[105] See R George, *Ideas and Debates in Family Law* (Hart Publishing, 2012), ch 3.
[106] See J Eekelaar, 'A Utopian Dream? A Review of European Family Law, vols I–IV, edited by Jens Scherpe' (2017) 31 *International Journal of Law, Policy and the Family* 114.

COMMUNITIES, OBLIGATIONS, AND LAW

Law has a role in enforcing obligations people owe to a community. But it should be the secondary, not the primary, means for discharging them. There are many reasons. The main one is that the very virtue of community lies in its social nature. Communal activity involves positive interaction between people. This, happily, is normally achieved through a combination of social forces and psychological disposition (to put it simply, natural love and community spirit). These should of course be celebrated and promoted. In complex societies legal structures are needed to provide efficient ways in which people can give effect to these values. Tax, safety, health, and environmental laws are examples.[107]

But this should be a restrained and secondary role. Most people should not require threats and coercion to comply with these obligations. It is in protecting individuals *against the power that people can exert within communities* (including families) where law, or legal-type institutions are essential. The great international lawyer Hersch Lauterpacht believed that 'the well-being of an individual is the ultimate object of all law'.[108] This may include providing a means by which individuals can achieve a modification of community norms or practice, but in other cases, find the path of escape from them. In the case of families, they might range from the creation of norms for, and enforcement of, fair settlements on divorce, to police protection against violence and honour killing and straightforward legal advice and representation in high conflict cases. For this, people may need help from the community. This was well expressed in a report on disputes concerning children in English courts:

Many of the parents in our cases were trying to recover from episodes of serious mental ill health while fighting court cases about where the children should live. Yet mental ill health is unlikely to be seen as constituting an exceptional circumstance for the purposes of legal aid … Accurate legal advice was important. Many of the parents led chaotic lives, which made them prone to missing directions hearings or documentation deadlines. Granting them a legal aid solicitor not only

---

[107] See T Honoré, 'The Dependence of Morality on Law' (1993) 13 *Oxford Journal of Legal Studies* 1.

[108] Quoted in P Sands, *East West Street: On the Origins of Genocide and Crimes against Humanity* (Weidenfeld & Nicolson, 2016) 85–6.

ensured that their rights, and their children's rights, were adequately protected, but also made cases run more smoothly.[109]

Yet it may not be a coincidence that the withdrawal of state support for protecting legal entitlements given by family law to individuals has occurred when family law no longer seeks primarily to enforce individual compliance with social structures, as described in chapter 1, or develop countervailing remedies to empower individuals, as described in chapter 2, but is now largely involved in matters of justice between individuals. Yet the UK state seems little concerned about the power imbalances that may occur between individuals unless this carries serious risks to physical well-being. Yet it is *only* legal or kindred institutions that can counterbalance the power of communities or individuals, and often that is difficult enough. The exercise of power by communities and people within them may have changed their form, and become more complex. It has not gone away. The need for the protective role of the law may be greater now than ever.

---

[109] M Harding and A Newnham, *How do County Courts Share the Care of Children between Parents?* (The Nuffield Foundation, 2015) 129.

Bibliography

Abel, Richard L, *The Politics of Informal Justice* vols 1 and 2 (The Academic Press, 1982).

Ahdar, Rex and James Allen, 'Taking Smacking Seriously: The Case for Retaining the Legality of Parental Smacking in New Zealand' [2001] *New Zealand Law Review* 1.

Ahmed, Farrah, 'Remedying Personal Law Systems' (2016) 30 *International Journal of Law, Policy and the Family* 248.

Ahmed, Farrah, *Religious Freedom under the Personal Law System* (Oxford University Press, 2016).

Albrecht, K and D Schultheiss, 'Proof of Paternity: Historical Reflections on an Andrological Forensic Challenge' (2004) 36 *Andrologia* 31.

Allen, Douglas W, 'The Impact of Legal Reforms on Marriage and Divorce' in AW Dnes and R Rowthorn (eds), *The Law and Economics of Marriage and Divorce* (Cambridge University Press, 2002) ch 11.

Allen, Douglas and Margaret Brinig, 'Child Support Guidelines: The Good, the Bad, the Ugly' (2011) 45 *Family Law Quarterly* 135.

Alstott, Anne L, 'Neo-Liberalism in US Family Law: Negative Liberty and Laissez-faire Markets in the Minimal State' (2014) 77 *Law and Contemporary Problems* 25.

Altman, Scott, 'A Theory of Child Support' (2003) 17 *International Journal of Law, Policy and the Family* 173.

American Law Institute, *Principles of the Law of Family Dissolution: Analysis and Recommendations* (2002).

Anderson, Michael, *Approaches to the History of the Western Family* (Macmillan, 1980).

Anderson, Michael, 'What Is New about the Modern Family?', OPCS Occasional Paper, *The Family*, 31 (1983), reprinted in M Drake (ed), *Time, Family and Community: Perspectives on Family and Community History* (Blackwell, 1994).

Appiah, Kwame, *The Ethics of Identity* (Princeton University Press, 2005).

Archard, David, *Children: Rights & Childhood* (Routledge, 1993).

Archard, David, 'Wrongful Life' (2004) 79 *Philosophy* 403.

Aristotle, *Nichomachean Ethics* (trs JAK Thomson) (Penguin Classics, 2004).

Bainham, Andrew, 'The Privatisation of the Public Interest in Children' (1990) 55 *Modern Law Review* 206.

Bainham, Andrew, 'Contact as a Right and Obligation' in A Bainham, B Lindley, M Richards, and L Trinder (eds), *Children and Their Families: Contact, Rights and Welfare* (Hart Publishing, 2003).

Bainham, Andrew, 'Arguments about Parentage' (2008) 67 *Cambridge Law Journal* 322.

Bainham, Andrew, 'What is the Point of Birth Registration?' (2008) 20 *Child and Family Law Quarterly* 449.

Balkin, Jack M, 'The Proliferation of Legal Truth' (2003) 26 *Harvard Journal of Law and Public Policy* 5.

Bamforth, Nicholas, 'Same-sex Partnerships and Arguments of Justice' in R Wintemute and M Andenaes (eds), *Legal Recognition of Same-sex Partnerships: A Study of National, European and International Law* (Hart Publishing, 2001).

Banda, Fareda, *Women, Law and Human Rights: An African Perspective* (Hart Publishing, 2005).

Bano, Samia, *Muslim Women and Shari'ah Councils: Transcending the Boundaries of Community and Law* (Palgrave Macmillan, 2012).

Beard, Mary, *SPQR: A History of Ancient Rome* (Profile Books, 2015).

Beaujouan, Éva and Máire Ní Bhrolcháin, 'Cohabitation and Marriage in Britain since the 1970s' (2011) 145 *Population Trends* 2.

Beaumont, Paul, Katarina Trimmings, Lara Walker, and Jayne Holliday, 'Child Abduction: Recent Jurisprudence of the European Court of Human Rights' (2015) 64 *International and Comparative Law Quarterly* 39.

Beck, Ulrich and Elisabeth Beck-Gernsheim, *Individualization* (Sage, 2001).

Bell, Felicity, 'Barriers to Empowering Children in Private Family Law Proceedings' (2016) 30 *International Journal of Law, Policy and the Family* 225.

Bellah, Robert N, Richard Madsen, William M Sullivan, Ann Swider, and Steven M Tipton, *Habits of the Heart: Individualism and Commitment in American Life* (University of California Press, 1985 and 1996).

Bellamy, Richard, *A Republican Defence of the Constitutionality of Democracy* (Cambridge University Press, 2007).

Bender, Leslie, 'Genes, Parents and Assisted Reproductive Technologies: ARTs, Mistakes, Sex, Race and Law' (2003) 12 *Columbia Journal of Gender and Law* 1.

Besson, Samantha, 'Enforcing the Child's Rights to Know Her Origins: Contrasting Approaches under the Convention on the Rights of the Child and the European Convention on Human Rights' (2007) 21 *International Journal of Law, Policy and the Family* 137.

Bird, Colin, 'Status, Identity, Respect' (2004) 32 *Political Theory* 207.

Birks, Peter, *An Introduction to the Law of Restitution* (Clarendon Press, 1985).

Blackstone's *Commentaries on the Laws of England* (ed HW Ballantine) (Blackstone Institute, 1915) 310

Blum, Lawrence, *Friendship, Altruism and Morality* (Routledge & Kegan Paul, 1980).

Blyth, Eric, 'To Be or Not To Be? A Critical Appraisal of the Welfare of Children Conceived through New Reproductive Technologies' (2008) 16 *International Journal of Children's Rights* 505.

Boele-Woelki, Katharina, 'The Impact of the Commission on European Family Law (CEFL) on European Family Law' in JM Scherpe (ed), *European Family Law*, vol 1 (Edward Elgar, 2016) ch 4.

Bond, Johanna E, 'Culture, Dissent, and the State: The Example of Commonwealth African Marriage Laws' (2011) 14 *Yale Human Rights and Development Journal*, Issue 1, Article 1.

Bowen, John, *On British Islam: Religion, Law, and Everyday Practice in Shari'a Councils* (Princeton University Press, 2016).

Bowlby, John, *Child Care and the Growth of Love* (Pelican Books, 1953).

Boyle, Robert J and Julian Savulescu, 'Ethics of Using Preimplantation Genetic Diagnosis to Select a Stem Cell Donor for an Existing Person' (2001) 323 *British Medical Journal* 1240.

Bradshaw, Jonathan, Carol Stimson, Christine Skinner, and Julie Williams, *Absent Fathers?* (Routledge, 1999).

Brewer, Mike and Alita Nandi, *Partnership Dissolution: How Does It Affect Income, Employment and Well-being?* (Nuffield Foundation, 2014).

Bridgeman, Jo, Heather Keating, and Craig Lind (eds), *Responsibility, Law and the Family* (Ashgate/Routledge 2008).

Broadhurst, Karen and Claire Mason, 'Birth Parents and the Collateral Consequences of Court-ordered Child Removal: Towards a Comprehensive Framework' (2017) 31 *International Journal of Law, Policy and the Family* 41.

Bruch, Carol S, 'And How Are the Children? The Effects of Ideology and Mediation on Child Custody Law and Children's Well-being in the United States' (1988) 2 *International Journal of Law and the Family* 106.

Brundage, James, *Medieval Canon Law* (Longman, 1995) ch 3.

Bryson, Caroline, Amy Skipp, Janet Allbeson, Eloise Poole, Eleanor Ireland, and Vicky Marsh, *Kids Aren't Free; The Child Maintenance Arrangements of Single Parents on Benefits in 2012* (The Nuffield Foundation, 2012).

Burrows, Andrew, *The Law of Restitution* (Butterworths, 2002).

Butler-Sloss, Judge Elizabeth, *Report of the Inquiry into Child Abuse in Cleveland 1987*, Cm 412 (HM Stationery Office, 1988).

Cane, Peter, *Responsibility in Law and Morality* (Hart Publishing, 2002).

Cassidy, Eoin, 'Classical and Christian Perspectives on the Limits of Friendship' in J Haseldine (ed), *Friendship in Medieval Europe* (Sutton Publishing, 1999) ch 2.

Cave, Emma and Julie Wallbank, 'Minors' Capacity to Refuse Treatment: A Reply to Gilmore and Herring' (2012) 20 *Medical Law Review* 423.

Chau, P-L and Jonathan Herring, 'Defining, Assigning and Designing Sex' (2002) 16 *International Journal of Law, Policy and the Family* 327.

Cherkassky, Lisa, 'The Wrong Harvest: The Law on Saviour Siblings' (2015) 29 *International Journal of Law, Policy and the Family* 36.

Choudhury, Shazia and Jonathan Herring, 'Righting Domestic Violence' (2006) 20 *International Journal of Law, Policy and the Family* 95.

Citizens Advice, *Standing Alone: Going to the Family Court Without a Lawyer* (2016).

Cowden, Mhairi, '"No Harm, No Foul": A Child's Right To Know Their Genetic Parent' (2012) 26 *International Journal of Law, Policy and the Family* 102.

Cranor, Carl, 'Toward a Theory of Respect for Persons' (1975) 12 *American Philosophical Quarterly* 303.

Cretney, Stephen, *Family Law in the Twentieth Century: A History* (Oxford University Press, 2003).

Cretney, Stephen, *Same Sex Relationships: From 'Odious Crime' to 'Gay Marriage'* (Oxford University Press, 2006).

Curry-Sumner, Ian, 'Same-sex Relationships in a European Perspective' in JM Scherpe (ed), *European Family Law,* vol III (Edward Elgar, 2016).

Darwall, Stephen, 'Two Kinds of Respect' (1977) 88 *Ethics* 36.

d'Avray, David, *Medieval Marriage: Symbolism and Society* (Oxford University Press, 2005).

Deech, Ruth, 'The Principles of Maintenance' (1977) 7 *Family Law* 230.

Deech, Ruth, 'The Case against the Legal Recognition of Cohabitation' in J Eekelaar and SN Katz (eds), *Marriage and Cohabitation in Contemporary Societies: Areas of Legal, Social and Ethical Change* (Butterworths, 1980) ch 30.

de Mause, Lloyd, *The History of Childhood* (Souvenir Press, 1976).

Department of Work and Pensions and Department of Children, Schools and Families, *Joint Birth Registration: Recording Responsibility* (Cm 7293, 2008).

Desan, Suzanne, *The Family on Trial in Revolutionary France* (University of California Press, 2004)

Devlin, Patrick, *The Enforcement of Morals* (Oxford University Press, 1965) ch IV.

Dewar, John, 'The Normal Chaos of Family Law' (1998) 61 *Modern Law Review* 467.

Dicey, Albert Venn, *Law and Public Opinion in England during the Nineteenth Century* (Macmillan, 1963 edition).

Diduck, Alison, 'What is Family Law for?' (2011) 64 *Current Legal Problems* 287.

Dingwall, Robert, John Eekelaar, and Topsy Murray, *The Protection of Children: State Intervention and Family Life* (Basil Blackwell, 1983).

Dingwall, Robert, 'The Jasmine Beckford Affair' (1986) 49 *Modern Law Review* 489.

Dixon, Rosalind, 'Weak-form Judicial Review and American Exceptionalism' (2012) 32 *Oxford Journal of Legal Studies* 487.

Donzelot, Jacques, *The Policing of Families* (Hutchinson, 1980).

Donnelly, Jack, *Universal Human Rights in Law and Practice* (Cornell University Press, 1989).

Douglas, Gillian, Mervyn Murch, Claire Miles, and Lesley Scanlan, *Research into the Operation of Rule 9.5 of the Family Proceedings Rules 1991* (Department of Constitutional Affairs, 2006).

Douglas, Gillian, Hilary Woodward, Alun Humphrey, Lisa Mills, and Gareth Morrell, 'Enduring Love: Attitudes to Family and Inheritance Law in England and Wales' (2011) 38 *Journal of Law and Society* 245.

Douglas, Gillian, 'Towards an Understanding of the Basis of Obligation and Commitment in Family Law' (2016) 36 *Legal Studies* 1.

Dworkin, Ronald, *Taking Rights Seriously* (Duckworth, 1977).

Dworkin, Ronald, 'Do We Have a Right to Pornography?' (1981) 1 *Oxford Journal of Legal Studies* 177.

Dworkin, Ronald, *Law's Empire* (Fontana, 1986).

Dworkin, Ronald, *A Matter of Principle* (Clarendon Press, 1986).

Dworkin, Ronald, *Sovereign Virtue: The Theory and Practice of Equality* (Harvard University Press, 2000).

Dworkin, Ronald, *Justice for Hedgehogs* (The Belknap Press of Harvard University Press, 2011).

Dwyer, James G, *The Relationship Rights of Children* (Cambridge University Press, 2006).

Eekelaar, John, 'Parental Responsibility: State of Nature or the Nature of the State?' (1991) 13 *Journal of Social Welfare and Family Law* 37.

Eekelaar, John, 'The Importance of Thinking that Children have Rights' (1992) 6 *International Journal of Law and the Family* 221.

Eekelaar, John, 'The Interests of the Child and the Child's Wishes: the Role of Dynamic Self-Determinism' in P Alston (ed), *The Best Interests of the Child: Reconciling Culture and Human Rights* (Oxford University Press, 1994).

Eekelaar, John, '"The Chief Glory": The Export of Children from the United Kingdom' (1994) 21 *Journal of Law and Society* 487.

Eekelaar, John, 'Do Parents Have a Duty To Consult?' (1998) 114 *Law Quarterly Review* 337.

Eekelaar, John, 'Child Endangerment and Child Protection in England and Wales' in MK Rosenheim, FE Zimring, DS Tanenhaus, and B Dohrn (eds), *A Century of Juvenile Justice* (Chicago University Press, 2002) ch 14.

Eekelaar, John, 'The End of an Era?' (2003) 28 *Journal of Family History* 108.

Eekelaar, John, 'Children between Cultures' (2004) 18 *International Journal of Law, Policy and the Family* 178.

Eekelaar, John, 'Invoking Human Rights' in T Endicott, J Getzler, and E Peel (eds), *Properties of Law: Essays in Honour of Jim Harris* (Oxford University Press, 2006) ch 16.

Eekelaar, John, 'From Multiculturalism to Cultural Voluntarism: A Family-based Approach' (2010) 81 *The Political Quarterly* 344.

Eekelaar, John, 'Naturalism or Pragmatism? Towards an Expansive View of Human Rights' (2011) 10 *Journal of Human Rights* 230.

Eekelaar, John, 'Evaluating Legal Regulation of Family Behaviour' (2011) 1 *International Journal of Jurisprudence of the Family* 17.

Eekelaar, John, ' "Not of the Highest Importance": Family Justice under Threat' (2011) 33 *Journal of Social Welfare and Family Law* 311.

Eekelaar, John, 'Family Law: What Family Law?' in R Probert and C Barton (eds), *Fifty Years in Family Law: Essays for Stephen Cretney* (Intersentia, 2012).

Eekelaar, John, 'Then and Now: Family Law's Direction of Travel' (2013) 35 *Journal of Social Welfare and Family Law* 415.

Eekelaar, John, 'Perceptions of Equality: The Road to Same-sex Marriage in England' (2014) 28 *International Journal of Law, Policy and the Family* 1.

Eekelaar, John, 'Law, Culture, Values' in A Diduck, N Peleg, and H Reece (eds), *Law in Society: Reflections on Children, Family, Culture and Philosophy: Essays in Honour of Michael Freeman* (Brill, 2015) ch 2.

Eekelaar, John, 'Two Dimensions of the Best Interests Principle: Decisions about Children and Decisions Affecting Children' in EE Sutherland and L-AB Macfarlane (eds), *Implementing Article 3 of the United Nations Convention on the Rights of the Child: Best Interests, Welfare and Well-being* (Cambridge University Press, 2016).

Eekelaar, John, 'Family Law and Love' (2016) 28 *Child and Family Law Quarterly* 289.

Eekelaar, John (ed), *Family Rights and Religion* (Routledge, 2017).

Eekelaar, John, 'A Utopian Dream? A Review of European Family Law, vols I–IV, edited by Jens Scherpe' (2017) 31 *International Journal of Law, Policy and the Family* 114.

Eekelaar, John, Robert Dingwall, and Topsy Murray, 'Victims or Threats? Children in Care Proceedings' (1982) 3 *Journal of Social Welfare Law* 68.

Eekelaar, John and Mavis Maclean, *Maintenance after Divorce* (Oxford University Press, 1986).

Eekelaar, John and Mavis Maclean, 'Marriage and the Moral Bases of Personal Relationships' (2004) 31 *Journal of Law and Society* 510.

Eekelaar, John, Mavis Maclean, and Sarah Beinart, *Family Lawyers: The Divorce Work of Solicitors* (Hart Publishing, 2000).

Eekelaar, John and Mavis Maclean, *Family Justice: The Work of Family Judges in Uncertain Times* (Hart Publishing, 2013).

Eichner, Maxine, *The Supportive State: Families, Government and America's Political Ideals* (Oxford University Press, 2010).

Ellman, Ira M, 'Why Making Family Law Is Hard' (2003) 35 *Arizona State Law Journal* 699.

Ellman, Ira M, 'Fudging Failure: The Economic Analysis Used To Construct Child Support Guidelines' (2004) *University of Chicago Legal Forum* 162.

Ellman, Ira M and Sanford Braver, 'Lay Intuitions about Child Support and Marital Status' (2011) 23 *Child and Family Law Quarterly* 465.

Ellman, Ira M, Stephen McKay, Joanna Miles, and Caroline Bryson, 'Child Support Judgments: Comparing Public Policy to the Public's Policy' (2014) 28 *International Journal of Law, Policy and the Family* 274.

Ellman, Ira M and Sanford L Braver, 'The Future of Child Support' in J Eekelaar (ed), *Family Law in Britain and America in the Twenty-First Century: Essays in Honor of Sanford N Katz* (Brill, 2016) ch 5.

Fahey, Tony, 'Divorce Trends and Patterns: An Overview' in J Eekelaar and R George (eds), *Routledge Handbook of Family Law and Policy* (2014) ch 2.2.

Fehlberg, Belinda, Bruce Smyth, Mavis Maclean, and Ceridwen Roberts, 'Legislating for Shared Time Parenting after Separation: A Research Review' (2011) 25 *International Journal of Law, Policy and the Family* 318.

Fehlberg, Belinda and Bruce Smyth, 'Parenting Issues after Separation in Common Law Countries' in J Eekelaar and R George (eds), *Routledge Handbook of Family Law and Policy* (Routledge, 2014) ch 3.3.

Feinberg, Joel, *Rights, Justice and the Bounds of Liberty: Essays in Social Philosophy* (University of Princeton Press, 1980).

Feinberg, Joel, 'The Nature and Value of Rights' in J Feinberg (ed), *Rights, Justice and the Bounds of Liberty: Essays in Social Philosophy* (Princeton University Press, 1980).

Feinberg, Joel, 'Wrongful Life and the Counterfactual Element of Harming' (1987) 4 *Social Philosophy and Policy* 164.

Fenton-Glynn, Claire, 'Outsourcing Ethical Dilemmas: Regulating International Surrogacy Arrangements' (2016) 24 *Medical Law Review* 59.

Ferguson, Lucinda, 'Arbitration in Financial Dispute Resolution: The Final Step in Reconstructing the Default(s) and Exception(s)?' (2013) 35 *Journal of Social Welfare and Family Law* 115.

Ferguson, Lucinda, 'The Jurisprudence of Making Decisions Affecting Children: An Argument To Prefer Duty to Children's Rights and Welfare' in A Diduck, N Peleg, and H Reece (eds), *Law in Society: Reflections on Children, Family, Culture and Philosophy: Essays in Honour of Michael Freeman* (Brill, 2015).

Finch, Janet, *Family Obligations and Social Change* (Polity Press, 1989).

Fineman, Martha, 'The Meaning of Marriage' in A Bernstein (ed), *Marriage Proposals: Questioning a Legal Status* (New York University Press, 2006) ch 1.

Finnis, John, 'Law, Morality and Sexual Orientation' (1994) 69 *Notre Dame Law Review* 1049.

Fisher, Hayley and Hamish Low, 'Who Wins, Who Loses and Who Recovers from Divorce?' in J Miles and R Probert (eds), *Sharing Lives, Dividing Assets* (Hart Publishing, 2009) ch 11.

Fisher, Hayley and Hamish Low, 'Recovery from Divorce: Comparing High and Low Income Couples' (2016) 30 *International Journal of Law, Policy and the Family* 338.

Flynn, Asher and Jacqueline Hodgson (eds), *Access to Justice & Legal Aid: Comparative Perspectives on Unmet Legal Need* (Hart Publishing, 2017).

Fortin, Jane, 'Children's Right To Know Their Origins: Too Far, Too Fast?' (2009) 21 *Child and Family Law Quarterly* 336.

Foucault, Michel, *Discipline and Punish: The Birth of the Prison* (Penguin Books, 1991).

Fox, Robin, *Kinship and Marriage* (Penguin Books, 1967).

Fraser, Antonia, *Marie Antoinette: The Journey* (Phoenix, 2002).

Frazer, Elizabeth and Nicola Lacey, *The Politics of Community: A Feminist Critique of the Liberal-Communitarian Debate* (Harvester Wheatsheaf, 1993).

Fredman, Sandra, 'Foreign Fads or Fashions: The Role of Comparativism in Human Rights Law' (2015) 64 *International and Comparative Law Quarterly* 631.

Freeman, Michael, *The Rights and Wrongs of Children* (Frances Pinter, 1983).

Freeman, Michael, 'Human Rights, Children's Rights and Judgment: Some Thoughts on Reconciling Universality and Pluralism' (2002) 10 *International Journal of Children's Rights* 345.

Freeman, Michael, 'Re-thinking *Gillick*' (2005) 13 *International Journal of Children's Rights* 201.

Fukuyama, Francis, *The Great Disruption* (Profile Books, 1999).

Gal, Tali and Benedetta Duramy (eds), *International Perspectives and Empirical Findings on Child Participation* (Oxford University Press, 2015).

Gallie, Walter B, 'Essentially Contested Concepts' (1955–6) 56 *Proceedings of the Aristotelian Society* 167.

Gardbaum, Stephen, *The New Commonwealth Model of Constitutionalism: Theory and Practice* (Cambridge University Press, 2013).

Gardner, John, 'The Mark of Responsibility' (2003) 23 *Oxford Journal of Legal Studies* 157.

Gardner, Simon, 'Problems in Family Property' (2013) 72 *Cambridge Law Journal* 301.

Garrison, Marsha, 'The Goals and Limits of Child Support Policy' in JT Oldham and MS Melli, *Child Support: The Next Frontier* (University of Michigan Press, 2000).

Geldof, Bob, 'The Real Love That Dare Not Speak Its Name' in A Bainham, B Lindley, M Richards, and L Trinder (eds), *Children and Their Families: Contact, Rights and Welfare* (Hart Publishing, 2003).

Genn, Hazel, *Paths to Justice* (Hart Publishing, 1999).

George, Rob, *Ideas and Debates in Family Law* (Hart Publishing, 2012).

George, Rob, *Relocation Disputes: Law and Practice in England and New Zealand* (Hart Publishing, 2014).

Gibson, Colin, 'Changing Family Patterns in England and Wales over the last Fifty Years' in SN Katz, J Eekelaar, and M Maclean (eds), *Cross Currents: Family Law and Policy in the US and England* (Oxford University Press, 2000) ch 2.

Giddens, Anthony, *The Constitution of Society* (Polity Press, 1984).

Giddens, Anthony, *The Transformation of Intimacy: Sexuality, Love and Eroticism in Modern Society* (Polity Press, 1992).

Gilbert, Neil (ed), *Combating Child Abuse: International Perspectives and Trends* (Oxford University Press, 1997).

Gilligan, Carol, *In a Different Voice: Psychological Theory and Women's Development* (Harvard University Press, 1982).

Gilmore, Stephen and Jonathan Herring, ' "No" Is the Hardest Word: Consent and Children's Autonomy' (2011) 23 *Child and Family Law Quarterly* 3.

Gibson, Colin, 'The Association between Divorce and Social Class in England and Wales' (1974) 25 *British Journal of Sociology* 79.

Gibson, Colin, *Dissolving Wedlock* (Routledge, 1994).

Gingerbread, *Missing Maintenance* (June 2016).

Glendon, Mary Ann, *Rights Talk: The Impoverishment of Political Discourse* (The Free Press, 1991).

Goedeke, Sonja and Ken Daniels, 'Embryo Donation, or Embryo Adoption? Practice and Policy in the New Zealand Context' (2017) 31 *International Journal of Law, Policy and the Family* 1.

Golombok, Susan, *Modern Families: Parents and Children in New Family Forms* (Cambridge University Press, 2015).

Goodin Robert E and Diane Gibson, 'Rights, Young and Old' (1997) 17 *Oxford Journal of Legal Studies* 15.

Goody, Jack, *The Development of the Family and Marriage in Europe* (Cambridge University Press, 1983).

Gorecki, Jan, 'Moral Premises of Contemporary Divorce Laws: Western and Eastern Europe and the United States' in JM Eekelaar and SN Katz (eds), *Marriage and Cohabitation in Contemporary Societies: Areas of Legal, Social and Ethical Change* (Butterworths, Toronto, 1980) ch 13.

Goriely, Tamara, 'Rushcliffe Fifty Years On: The Changing Role of Civil Legal Aid Within the Welfare State' (1994) 21 *Journal of Law and Society* 545.

Greatbatch, David and Robert Dingwall, 'Selective Facilitation: Some Preliminary Observations on a Strategy Used by Divorce Mediators' (1989) 23 *Law and Society Review* 613.

Greenberg, David, *The Construction of Homosexuality* (University of Chicago Press, 1988).

Grewal, David S and Jedediah Purdy, 'Law and Neo-Liberalsim' (2015) 77 *Law and Contemporary Problems* 1.

Griffin, James, 'Group Rights' in LH Meyer, SL Paulson, and TW Pogge (eds), *Rights, Culture, and the Law: Themes from the Legal and Political Philosophy of Joseph Raz* (Oxford University Press, 2003).

Grillo, Trina, 'The Mediation Alternative: Process Dangers for Women' (1991) *Yale Law Journal* 1545.

Guggenheim, Martin, *What's Wrong with Children's Rights* (Harvard University Press, 2005).

Gyorfi, Tamas, 'Between Common Law Constitutionalism and Procedural Democracy' (2013) 33 *Oxford Journal of Legal Studies* 317.

Harding, Maebh and Annika Newnham, *How Do County Courts Share the Care of Children between Parents?* (The Nuffield Foundation, 2015).

Hareven, Tamara K, 'Recent Research on the History of the Family' in M Drake (ed), *Time, Family and Community: Perspectives on Family and Community History* (Blackwell, 1994).

Harman, Elizabeth, 'Harming as Causing Harm' in MA Roberts and DT Wasserman (eds), *Harming Future Persons: Ethics, Genetics and the Non-identity Problem* (Singer, 2009) ch 7.

Hart, HLA, 'Definition and Theory in Jurisprudence' (1953), re-published as ch 1 in HLA Hart, *Essays in Jurisprudence and Philosophy* (Oxford University Press, 1983).

Hart, HLA, *Punishment and Responsibility* (Oxford University Press, 1968).

Hart, HLA, 'Are There Any Natural Rights?' in J Waldron (ed), *Theories of Rights* (Oxford University Press, 1984) ch 4.

Harvey, David, *A Brief History of Neoliberalism* (Oxford University Press, 2005).

Harwin, Judith, Mary Ryan, and Jo Tunnard, *The Family Drug and Alcohol Court (FDAC) Evaluation Project: Final Report* (Brunel University, 2011).

Haskey, John, 'Cohabitation in Great Britain: Past, Present and Future Trends—and Attitudes' (2001) 103 *Population Trends* 4.

Haskey, John and Jane Lewis, 'Living Apart Together in Britain: Context and Meaning' (2006) 2 *International Journal of Law in Context* 37.

Hendrick, Harry, *Child Welfare in England 1872–1989* (Routledge, 1994).

Herring, Jonathan and P-L Chau, 'Assigning Sex and Intersexuals' (2001) 31 *Family Law* 762.

Herring, Jonathan, Rebecca Probert, and Stephen Gilmore, *Great Debates in Family Law* (Palgrave Macmillan, 2012).

Herring, Jonathan, *Older People in Law and Society* (Oxford University Press, 2009).

Herring, Jonathan, *Caring and the Law* (Hart Publishing, 2013).

Herring, Jonathan, *Relational Autonomy and Family Law* (Springer, 2014).

Herring, Jonathan, 'Together Forever? The Rights and Responsibilities of Adult Children and Their Parents' in J Bridgeman, H Keating, and C Lind (eds), *Responsibility, Law and the Family* (Ashgate/Routledge, 2008).

Herring, Jonathan, 'Medical Decisions about Children' in J Eekelaar (ed), *Family Law in Britain and America in the New Century: Essays in Honor of Sanford N Katz* (Brill, 2016) ch 9.

Herring, Jonathan, 'Compassion, Ethics of Care and Legal Rights' (2017) 13 *International Journal of Law in Context* 158.

Hohfeld, Wesley N, *Fundamental Legal Conceptions as Applied in Judicial Reasoning* (Yale University Press, 1923).

Honoré, Tony, *The Quest for Security: Employees, Tenants, Wives* (Stevens, 1982).

Honoré, AM (Tony) 'Responsibility and Luck' (1988) 104 *Law Quarterly Review* 530.

Honoré, Tony, 'The Dependence of Morality on Law' (1993) 13 *Oxford Journal of Legal Studies* 1.

Hunt, Joan and Ceridwen Roberts, *Intervening in Litigated Contact: Ideas from Other Jurisdictions* (Family Policy Briefing 4, University of Oxford Department of Social Policy and Social Work, 2005).

Idriss, Mohammed M, '*Laïcité* and the Banning of the "Hijab" in France' (2005) 25 *Legal Studies* 260.

Ipsos Mori, *Online Survey of Individuals' Handling of Legal Issues in England and Wales 2015* (The Law Society and Legal Services Board, 2016).

Israel, Jonathan, *A Revolution of the Mind* (Princeton University Press, 2010).

Jackson, Emily, *Regulating Reproduction: Law, Technology and Autonomy* (Hart Publishing, 2001).

Jackson, Emily, 'Conception and the Irrelevance of the Welfare Principle' (2002) 65 *Modern Law Review* 176.

James, Adrian, 'Responsibility, Children and Childhood' in J Bridgeman, C Lind, and H Keating (eds), *Responsibility, Law and the Family* (Ashgate/ Routledge, 2008) ch 8.

Judt, Tony, *Ill Fares the Land* (Penguin Books, 2010).

Kaganas, Felicity and Alison Diduck, 'Changing Images of Post-Separation Children' (2004) 67 *Modern Law Review* 959.

Kaganas, Felicity, 'Justifying the LASPO Act: Authenticity, Necessity, Suitability, Responsibility and Autonomy' (2017) 39 *Journal of Social Welfare and Family Law* 1.

Kaspiew, Ray, Matthew Gray, Ruth Weston, Lawrie Moloney, Kelly Hand, and Lixia Qu and the Family Law Evaluation Team, *Evaluation of the 2006 Family Law Reforms* (Australian Institute of Family Studies, 2009).

Katz, Sanford N, 'Dual Systems of Adoption in the United States' in SN Katz, J Eekelaar, and M Maclean (eds), *Cross Currents: Family Law and Policy in the United States and England* (Oxford University Press, 2000).

Katz, Sanford N, *Family Law in America* (Oxford University Press, 2nd edn, 2015).

Kennett, Wendy, 'It's Arbitration, but Not as We Know It: Reflections on Family Law Dispute Resolution' (2016) 30 *International Journal of Law, Policy and the Family* 1.

Kiernan, Kathleen and K Smith, 'Unmarried Parenthood: New Insights from the Millenium Cohort Study' (2003) 114 *Population Trends* 23.

Kilkelly, Ursula, 'The Child's Right to Religious Freedom in International Law' in MA Fineman and K Worthington (eds), *What Is Right for Children?* (Ashgate, 2009) 243.

King, Michael and Christine Piper, *How the Law Thinks about Children* (Gower, 1990).

King, Michael, *A Better World for Children?* (Routledge, 1997).

King, Anthony and Ivor Crewe, *Blunders of Our Governments* (Oneworld, 2014).

Kocourek, Albert, *Jural Relations* (Bobbs Merrill, 1927).

Kukathas, Chandran, 'Are There Any Cultural Rights?' (1992) 20 *Political Theory* 105.

Kymlicka, Will, *Multicultural Citizenship* (Clarendon Press, 1995).

Kyritsis, Dimitrios, 'Constitutional Review in Representative Democracy' (2012) 32 *Oxford Journal of Legal Studies* 297.

Lader, Deborah, *Non-Resident Parental Contact 2007/8* (Office for National Statistics, 2008).

Laslett, Peter, *The World We Have Lost: Further Explored* (Methuen, 1983).

Law Centres Network, *Funding for Law Centres* (ICF International, 2014).

Law Commission, *Family Law: Illegitimacy* (Law Com No 118, 1982).

Law Commission, *Family Law: Review of Child Law: Custody* (Working Paper No 96, 1986).

Law Commission, *Review of Child Law: Guardianship and Custody* (Law Com No 172, 1988).

Law Commission, *Cohabitation: The Financial Consequences of Relationship Breakdown* (Law Com No 307, 2007).

Law Commission, *Matrimonial Property, Needs and Agreements* (Law Com No 343, February 2014).

Law Commission, *Getting Married: A Scoping Paper* (December 2015).

Laws, Sir John, 'Beyond Rights' (2003) 23 *Oxford Journal of Legal Studies* 265.

Leckey, Robert, 'Cohabitation, Law Reform, and the Litigants' (2017) 31 *International Journal of Law, Policy and the Family* 131.

Lefaucheur, Nadine, 'The French "Tradition" of Anonymous Birth: The Lines of Argument' (2004) 18 *International Journal of Law, Policy and the Family* 322.

Levin, Irene, 'Living Apart Together: A New Family Form' (2004) 52 *Current Sociology* 223.

Lewis, CS, *The Four Loves* (Fontana, 1960).

Lewis, Jane, *The End of Marriage? Individualism and Intimate Relations* (Edward Elgar, 2001).

Lind, Craig, 'Power and the Taking of Responsibility: Shifting the Legal Family from Marriage to Friendship' in C Lind, H Keating, and J Bridgeman (eds), *Taking Responsibility, Law and the Changing Family* (Ashgate/Routledge, 2010).

Lind, Craig, Heather Keating, and Jo Bridgeman (eds), *Taking Responsibility, Law and the Changing Family* (Ashgate/Routledge, 2010).

Lowe, Nigel, 'English Adoption Law: Past, Present and Future' in SN Katz, J Eekelaar, and M Maclean (eds), *Cross Currents: Family Law and Policy in the United States and England* (Oxford University Press, 2000).

Lundy, Laura, 'Family Values in the Classroom? Reconciling Parental Wishes and Children's Rights in State Schools' (2005) 19 *International Journal of Law, Policy and the Family* 346.

Lyon, Christina and Peter de Cruz, *Child Abuse* (Family Law, 1993).

MacCormick, Neil, 'Children's Rights: A Test Case for Theories of Rights' in N MacCormick (ed), *Legal Right and Social Democracy* (Clarendon Press, 1982) ch 8.

MacIntyre, Alasdair, *After Virtue* (Duckworth, 1981; 2nd edn, 1985).

MacIntyre, Alasdair, *Dependent Rational Animals: Why Human Beings Need Virtues* (Open Books, 1999).

Maclean, Mavis and John Eekelaar, 'Child Support: The British Solution' (1993) 7 *International Journal of Law and the Family* 205.

Maclean, Mavis and John Eekelaar, *The Parental Obligation: A Study of Parenthood across Households* (Hart Publishing, 1997).

Maclean, Mavis and John Eekelaar, 'The Significance of Marriage: Contrasts between White British and Ethnic Minority Groups in England' (2005) 27 *Law and Policy* 379.

Maclean, Mavis and John Eekelaar, *Family Law Advocacy: How Barristers Help the Victims of Family Failure* (Hart Publishing, 2009).

Maclean, Mavis and John Eekelaar, *Lawyers and Mediators: The Brave New World of Services for Separating Families* (Hart Publishing, 2016).

Maidment, Susan, *Child Custody and Divorce* (Croom Helm, 1984).

Malik, Maleiha, 'Family Law in Diverse Societies' in J Eekelaar and R George (eds), *Routledge Handbook of Family Law and Policy* (Routledge, 2014) ch 7.4.

Manea, Elham, *Women and Shari'a Law: The Impact of Legal Pluralism in the UK* (IB Tauris, 2016).

Mann, Michael, *The Sources of Social Power*, vol 1 (Cambridge University Press, 1986).

Marquand, David, *Decline of the Public* (Polity Press, 2004).

McEvoy, James, 'The Theory of Friendship in the Latin Middle Ages' in J Haseldine (ed), *Friendship in Medieval Europe* (Sutton Publishing, 1999) ch 1.

McCrudden, Christopher, 'Using Comparative Reasoning in Human Rights Adjudication: The Court of Justice of the EU and the European Court of Human Rights Compared' (2012–13) 15 *Cambridge Yearbook of European Legal Studies* 383.

McEwan, Ian, *The Children Act* (Jonathan Cape, 2014).

McClain, Linda C, 'Marriage Pluralism in the United States' in JA Nichols, *Marriage and Divorce in a Multicultural Context: Multi-tiered Marriage and the Boundaries of Civil Law and Religion* (Cambridge University Press, 2013).

McWhinnie, Alexina, *Adopted Children: How They Grow Up* (Routledge & Kegan Paul, 1967).

Meulders-Klein, Marie-Thérèse, *La Personne, La Famille & Le Droit* (Bruylant, 1999).

Miles, Joanna, F Wasoff, and E Mordaunt, 'Cohabitation: Lessons from North of the Border' (2011) 23 *Child and Family Law Quarterly* 302.

Miles, Joanna, 'England and Wales' in JM Scherpe (ed), *Marital Agreements and Private Autonomy in Comparative Perspective* (Hart Publishing, 2012) 89–121.

Miles, Joanna and Jens M Scherpe, 'The Legal Consequences of Dissolution: Property and Financial Support Between Spouses' in J Eekelaar and R George (eds), *Routledge Handbook of Family Law and Policy* (Routledge, 2014) ch 2.6.

Mill, John, *On Liberty* (1865).

Millham, Spencer, Roger Bullock, Kenneth Hosie, and Martin Haak, *Lost in Care: The Problems of Maintaining Links between Children in Care and Their Families* (Gower, 1986).

Ministry of Justice, *Court and Tribunal Fees: The Government Response to Consultation on Enhanced Fees for Divorce Proceedings, Possession Claims and General Applications in Civil Proceedings and Consultation on Further Fees Proposals* (August 2015).

Minow, Martha and Mary L Shanley, 'Relational Rights and Responsibilities: Revisioning the Family in Liberal Political Theory and Law' (1996) 11 *Hypatia* 4.

Mnookin, Robert, 'Child Custody Adjudication: Judicial Functions in the Face of Indeterminacy' (1975) 39 *Law and Contemporary Problems* 226.

Mnookin, Robert, 'Child Custody Revisited' (2014) 77 *Law and Contemporary Problems* 249.

Mody, Perveez, 'Forced Marriage: Rites and Rights' in J Miles, P Mody, and R Probert (eds), *Marriage Rites and Rights* (Hart Publishing, 2015) ch 9.

Montaigne, Michel, *Essays of Michel, Seigneur de Montaigne* (trs Charles Cotton, London, 1685).

Morag, Tamar, 'Child Participation in the Family Courts' (2012) 26 *International Journal of Law, Policy and the Family* 1.

Morgan, Richard I, 'The Introduction of Civil Legal Aid in England and Wales 1914–1949' (1994) 5 *Twentieth Century History* 38.

Morris, Colin, *The Papal Monarchy: The Western Church from 1050 to 1250* (Oxford University Press, 1989).

Myers, Fiona and Fran Wasoff, *Meeting in the Middle: A Study of Solicitors' and Mediators' Divorce Practice* (The Scottish Executive, Central Research Unit, 2011).

Nagel, Thomas, *Concealment and Exposure & Other Essays* (Oxford University Press, 2002).

Nichols, Joel A, 'Multi-tiered Marriage: Ideas and Influences from New York and Louisiana to the International Community' (2007) 40 *Vanderbilt Journal of Transnational Law* 135.

Noddings, Nel, *Caring: A Feminine Approach to Ethics and Moral Education* (UCLA Press, 1984)

Nussbaum, Martha, *Women and Human Development: The Capabilities Approach* (Cambridge University Press, 2000).

O'Donovan, Katherine, *Sexual Divisions in Law* (Weidenfeld & Nicolson, 1985).

O'Sullivan, Kathryn and Leyla Jackson, 'Muslim Marriage (Non) Recognition: Implications and Possible Solutions' (2017) 39 *Journal of Social Welfare and Family Law* 22.

Okin, Susan M, *Justice, Gender and the Family* (Basic Books, 1989).

Office for National Statistics, *2011 Census Analysis: What Does the 2011 Census Tell Us about Inter-Ethnic Relationships?* http://www.ons.gov.uk/peoplepopulationandcommunity/birthsdeathsandmarriages/marriagecohabitationandcivilpartnerships/articles/whatdoesthe2011censustellusaboutinterethnicrelationships/2014-07-03 (accessed 16 June 2017).

Office for National Statistics, *Ethnicity and National Identity in England and Wales 2011* (December 2012).

Packman, Jean, *Who Needs Care? Social Work Decisions about Children* (Blackwell, 1986).

Pahl, Ray, *On Friendship* (Polity Press, 2000).

Parizer-Krief, Karène, 'Gender Equality in Legislation on Medically Assisted Procreation in France' (2015) 29 *International Journal of Law, Policy and the Family* 205.

Parker, Stephen, 'Rights and Utility in Anglo-Australian Family Law' (1992) 55 *Modern Law Review* 311.

Parkinson, Patrick, 'Keeping On Contact: The Role of Family Relationship Centres in Australia' (2006) 18 *Child and Family Law Quarterly* 157.

Parton, Nigel, *The Politics of Child Abuse* (Macmillan, 1985).

Parton, Nigel, *Safeguarding Children: Early Intervention and Surveillance in Late Modern Society* (Palgrave Macmillan, 2006).

Parton, Nigel, 'Social Work, Child Protection and Politics: Some Critical and Constructive Reflections' (2014) 44 *British Journal of Social Work* 2042.

Paterson, Alan, 'Professionalism and the Legal Services Market' (1996) 3 *International Journal of the Legal Profession* 137.

Peacey, Victoria and Joan Hunt, *I'm Not Saying It Was Easy ... Contact Problems in Separated Families* (Gingerbread, 2009).

Pearce, Julia, Judith Masson, and Kay Bader, *Just Following Instructions? The Representation of Parents in Care Proceedings* (ESRC and University of Bristol, 2011).

Pedersen, Frederik, *Marriage Disputes in Medieval England* (Hambledon Press, 2000).

Peleg, Noam, 'Reconceptualising the Child's Right to Development: Children and the Capability Approach' (2013) 21 *International Journal of Children's Rights* 523.

Phoenix, Ann and Fatima Hussein, *Parenting and Ethnicity*, Review Paper for the Joseph Rowntree Foundation (2006).

Piketty, Thomas, *Capital in the Twenty-First Century* (The Belknap Press of Harvard University Press, 2014).

Picontó-Novales, Teresa, 'Parenting Issues After Separation in Spain and Southern Europe' in J Eekelaar and R George (eds), *Routledge Handbook of Family Law and Policy* (Routledge, 2014) ch 3.4.

Pierson, Christopher, *Beyond the Welfare State?* (Polity Press, 1998).

Pintens, Walter, 'The Impact of the International Commission on Civil Status (ICCS) on European Family Law' in JM Scherpe (ed), *European Family Law*, vol 1 (Edward Elgar, 2016) ch 4.

Pinto, Meital, 'What Are Offences to Feelings Really About? A New Regulative Principle' (2010) 30 *Oxford Journal of Legal Studies* 695.

Pollock, Frederick and Frederic W Maitland, *History of English Law Before the Time of Edward I*, vol 2 (Cambridge University Press, 1895).

Pollock, Linda, *Forgotten Children: Parent–Child Relations from 1500 to 1900* (Cambridge University Press, 1983).

Popper, Karl, *The Open Society and Its Enemies*, vols 1 and 2 (Routledge & Kegan Paul, 1945, 4th edn, 1962).

Poulter, Sebastian, 'Muslim Headscarves in School: Contrasting Legal Approaches in England and France' (1997) 17 *Oxford Journal of Legal Studies* 43.

Poulter, Sebastian, *Ethnicity, Law and Human Rights: The English Experience* (Oxford University Press, 1998).

Probert, Rebecca, 'Control over Marriage in England and Wales, 1753–1823' (2009) 27 *Law and History Review* 413.

Raz, Joseph, *The Morality of Freedom* (Clarendon Press, 1986).

Raz, Joseph, *Ethics in the Public Domain* (Oxford University Press, 1994).

Reece, Helen, 'The Paramountcy Principle: Consensus or Construct?' (1996) 49 *Current Legal Problems* 267.

Reece, Helen, *Divorcing Responsibly* (Hart Publishing, 2003).

Reece, Helen, 'From Parental Responsibility to Parenting Responsibly' in M Freeman (ed), *Law and Sociology: Current Legal Issues 2005*, vol 8 (Oxford University Press, 2006) ch 26.

Regan, Milton Jr, *Law and the Meaning of Marriage* (Oxford University Press, 1999).

Rhoades, Helen and Susan B Boyd, 'Reforming Custody Laws: A Comparative Study' (2004) 18 *International Journal of Law, Policy and the Family* 119.

Robinson, Jane, *In the Family Way: Illegitimacy between the Great War and the Swinging Sixties* (Viking, 2015).

Rogers, Alan, *The Child Cases: How America's Religious Exemption Laws Harm Children* (University of Massachusetts Press, 2014).

Rogerson, Carol, 'Child Support, Spousal Support and the Turn to Guidelines' in J Eekelaar and R George (eds), *Routledge Handbook of Family Law and Policy* (Routledge, 2014) ch 2.7.

Ronen, Ya'ir, 'Redefining the Child's Right to Identity' (2004) 18 *International Journal of Law, Policy and the Family* 147.

Ryrstedt, Eva, 'Mediation Regarding Children: Is the Result Always in the Best Interests of the Child—a View from Sweden' (2012) 26 *International Journal of Law, Policy and the Family* 220.

Sachs, Albie, 'Foreword: Unfamiliar Families—the Strange Alchemy of Life and Law' in C Lind, H Keating, and J Bridgeman (eds), *Taking Responsibility, Law and the Changing Family* (Ashgate/Routledge, 2010).

Sands, Philippe, *East West Street: On the Origins of Genocide and Crimes against Humanity* (Weidenfeld & Nicolson, 2016).

Scherpe, Jens M 'Marital Agreements and Private Autonomy in Comparative Perspective' in JM Scherpe (ed), *Marital Agreements and Private Autonomy in Comparative Perspective* (Hart Publishing, 2012).

Scherpe, Jens M, *The Present and Future of European Family Law* (Edward Elgar, 2016).

Schneider, Carl E, 'Rethinking Alimony: Marital Decisions and Moral Discourse' (1991) *Brigham Young University Law Review* 197.

Scott, Elizabeth S, 'Pluralism, Parental Preferences and Child Custody' (1992) 80 *California Law Review* 615.

Sen, Amartya, *Identity and Violence: The Illusion of Destiny* (Allen Lane, 2006).

Sen, Amartya, *The Idea of Justice* (The Belknap Press of Harvard University Press, 2009).

Seymour, John, *Children, Parents and the Courts: Legal Intervention in Family Life* (The Federation Press, 2016).

Sezgin, Yüksel, *Human Rights under State-enforced Religious Family Laws in Israel, Egypt and India* (Cambridge University Press, 2013).

Shabde, Neela and Alan Croft, 'Covert Video Surveillance: An Important Investigative Tool or a Breach of Trust?' (1999) 81 *Archives of Diseases in Childhood* 291.

Shachar, Ayelet, 'Privatizing Diversity: A Cautionary Tale from Religious Arbitration in Family Law' (2008) 9 *Theoretical Inquiries in Law* 573.

Shachar, Ayelet, 'State, Religion and the Family: New Dilemmas of Multicultural Accommodation' in R Ahdar and N Aroney (eds), *Shari'a in the West* (Oxford University Press, 2010).

Shaher, Shulamith, *Childhood in the Middle Ages* (Routledge, 1990).

Shah-Kazemi, Sonia, *Untying the Knot: Muslim Women, Divorce and the Shariah* (The Nuffield Foundation, 2001).

Sharpe, Alex, 'Transgender Marriage and the Legal Obligation to Disclose Gender' (2012) 75 *Modern Law Review* 33.

Sheehan, Michael, *Marriage, Family and Law in Medieval Europe* (Toronto University Press, 1996).

Shorter, Edward, *The Making of the Modern Family* (Collins, 1976).

Sigal, Amanda, Irwin Sandler, Sharlene Wolchik, and Sanford Braver, 'Do Parent Education Programs Promote Healthy Post-Divorce Parenting? Critical Distinctions and a Review of the Evidence' (2011) 49 *Family Court Review* 120.

Simpson, AW Brian, *Human Rights and the End of Empire: Britain and the Genesis of the European Convention* (Oxford University Press, 2000).

Singer, Anna, 'Parenting Issues after Separation: A Scandinavian Perspective' in J Eekelaar and R George (eds), *Routledge Handbook of Family Law and Policy* (Routledge, 2014) ch 5.

Singer, Peter, *How Are We To Live?* (Opus Books, 1993).

Skinner, Christine, 'Child Maintenance Reforms: Understanding Fathers' Expressive Agency and the Power of Reciprocity' (2013) 27 *International Journal of Law, Policy and the Family* 242.

Sloan, Brian, 'Conflicting Rights: English Adoption Law and the Implementation of the UN Convention on the Rights of the Child' (2013) 25 *Child and Family Law Quarterly* 40.

Sloan, Brian, 'Adoption Decisions in England: *re B (A Child) (Care Proceedings: Appeal)* and Beyond' (2015) 37 *Journal of Social Welfare and Family Law* 437.

Smart, Carol and Bren Neale, *Family Fragments?* (Polity Press, 1999).

Smart, Carol, 'Law and the Regulation of Family Secrets' (2010) 24 *International Journal of Law, Policy and the Family* 397.

Smith, Ian, 'European Divorce Laws, Divorce Rates, and Their Consequences' in AW Dnes and R Rowthorn (eds), *The Law and Economics of Marriage and Divorce* (Cambridge University Press, 2002) ch 12.

Solot, Dorian and Marshall Miller, 'Taking the Government Out of the Marriage Business: Families Would Benefit' in A Bernstein (ed), *Marriage Proposals: Questioning a Legal Status* (New York University Press, 2008).

Spaht, Katherine S, 'Solidifying the "No-Fault" Revolution: Postmodern Marriage as seen through the Lens of ALI's "Compensatory Payments"' in RF Wilson (ed), *Reconstructing the Family: Critical Reflections on the American Law Institute's Principles of the Law of Family Dissolution* (Cambridge University Press, 2006).

Steinbock, Bonnie, 'Wrongful Life and the Counterfactual Element of Harming' in MA Roberts and DT Wasserman (eds), *Harming Future Persons: Ethics, Genetics and the Non-identity Problem* (Singer, 2009) ch 8.

Stone, Lawrence, *The Family, Sex and Marriage in England 1500–1800* (Weidenfeld & Nicolson, 1977).

Storrow, Richard F, 'Parenthood by Pure Intention: Assisted Reproduction and the Functional Approach to Parentage' (2001–2) 53 *Hastings Law Journal* 597.

Strathern, Marilyn, *After Nature: English Kinship in the Late Twentieth Century* (Cambridge University Press, 1992).

Sutherland, Elaine, 'Unmarried Cohabitation' in J Eekelaar and R George (eds), *Routledge Handbook of Family Law and Policy* (Routledge, 2014) ch 1.5.

Tamir, Yael, 'Against Collective Rights' in LH Meyer, SL Paulson, and TW Pogge (eds), *Rights, Culture, and the Law: Themes from the Legal and Political Philosophy of Joseph Raz* (Oxford University Press, 2003).

Taylor, Charles, 'The Politics of Recognition' in A Gutman (ed), *Multiculturalism* (Princeton University Press, 1994).

Taylor, Rachel E, 'Responsibility for the Soul of the Child: The Role of the State and Parents in Determining Religious Upbringing and Education' (2015) 29 *International Journal of Law, Policy and the Family* 15.

Terminal, Laurence F, 'The Changing Concept of 'Family' and Challenges of Family Law in France' in JM Scherpe (ed), *European Family Law*, vol 2 (Edward Elgar, 2016) ch 3.

Teubner, Gunther, *Law as an Autopoietic System* (Blackwell, 1993).

Théry, Irène, *Le Démariage* (Editions Odile Jacob, 1993).

Thompson, Sharon, 'In Defence of the "Gold-Digger"' (2016) 6 *Oñati Socio-Legal Series*, available at SSRN: https://ssrn.com/abstract=2887022 (accessed 16 June 2017).

Treloar, Rachel, 'The Neoliberal Context of Family Law Reform in British Columbia, Canada: Implications for Access to (Family) Justice' in M

Maclean, J Eekelaar, and B Bastard (eds), *Delivering Family Justice in the 21st Century* (Hart Publishing, 2015) ch.1.

Trinder, Liz, Alan Firth, and Christopher Jenks, '"So Presumably Things Have Moved On Since Then?" The Management of Risk Allegations in Child Contact Dispute Resolution' (2009) 24 *International Journal of Law, Policy and the Family* 29.

Trinder, Liz, Rosemary Hunter, Emma Hitchings, Joanna Miles, Richard Moorhead, Leanne Smith, Mark Sefton, Victoria Hinchly, Kay Bader, and Julia Pearce, *Litigants in Person in Private Family Law Cases* (Ministry of Justice, 2014).

Triseliotis, John, *In Search of Origins: The Experiences of Adopted People* (Beacon Press, 1975).

Unger, Roberto, *The Critical Legal Studies Movement* (Harvard University Press, 1986).

Utting, William (chair), *People Like Us* (HM Stationery Office, 1997).

Vanderbeck, Robert M and Paul Johnson, 'The Promotion of British Values: Sexual Orientation, Equality, Religion and England's Schools' (2016) 30 *International Journal of Law, Policy and the Family* 292.

van Krieken, Robert, 'The "Best Interests of the Child" and Parental Separation: On the "Civilizing of Parents"' (2005) 68 *Modern Law Review* 25.

van Nijnatten, Carolus, 'In the Name of the Father: Changing the Law on Naming Children in the Netherlands' (1996) 10 *International Journal of Law, Policy and the Family* 221.

von Hayek, Friedrich, *The Road to Serfdom* (Routledge, 1944).

Waite, Linda and Maggie Gallagher, *The Case for Marriage* (Broadway Books, 2000).

Waldron, Jeremy, *Law and Disagreement* (Oxford University Press, 1999).

Waldron, Jeremy, *The Harm in Hate Speech* (Harvard University Press, 2012).

Wallbank, Julie, '"Bodies in the Shadows": Joint Birth Registration, Parental Responsibility and Social Class' (2009) 21 *Child and Family Law Quarterly* 267.

Wilmot-Smith, Frederick, 'Necessity or Ideology?' (2014) 36 *London Review of Books* 15.

Wilson, Graeme B, 'The Non-Resident Parental Role for Separated Fathers: A Review' (2006) 20 *International Journal of Law, Policy and the Family* 286.

Woodward, Hilary with Mark Sefton, *Pensions on Divorce: An Empirical Study* (Cardiff Law School, 2014).

Zee, Machteld, *Choosing Sharia? Multiculturalism, Islamic Fundamentalism and Sharia Councils* (Eleven Publishing, 2015).

Index